PAYBACK IN PANAMA

ALSO BY NOEL HYND

The Russian Trilogy

Conspiracy in Kiev
Midnight in Madrid
Countdown in Cairo

The Cuban Trilogy

Hostage in Havana
Murder in Miami
Payback in Panama

Available on Kindle

Flowers from Berlin
Revenge
The Sandler Inquiry

PAYBACK IN PANAMA

THE CUBAN TRILOGY: BOOK 3

NOEL HYND

ZONDERVAN®

ZONDERVAN.com/
AUTHORTRACKER
follow your favorite authors

ZONDERVAN

Payback in Panama

Copyright © 2013 by Noel Hynd

This title is also available as a Zondervan ebook. Visit www.zondervan.com/ebooks.

This title is also available in a Zondervan audio edition. Visit www.zondervan.fm.

Requests for information should be addressed to:

Zondervan, *Grand Rapids, Michigan 49530*

Library of Congress Cataloging-in-Publication Data

Hynd, Noel.
  Payback in Panama / by Noel Hynd.
    pages cm. -- (The Cuban trilogy : bk 3)
  ISBN 978-0-310-32455-3 (trade paper)
  I. Title.
  PS3558.Y54P39 2013
  813'.54--dc23
                          2013015110

All Scripture quotations, unless otherwise indicated, are taken from the Holy Bible, *New International Version®, NIV®.* Copyright © 1973, 1978, 1984, 2011 by Biblica, Inc.™ Used by permission. All rights reserved worldwide.

Any Internet addresses (websites, blogs, etc.) and telephone numbers in this book are offered as a resource. They are not intended in any way to be or imply an endorsement by Zondervan, nor does Zondervan vouch for the content of these sites and numbers for the life of this book.

Printed in the United States of America

13 14 15 16 17 18 19 20 /RRD/ 20 19 18 17 16 15 14 13 12 11 10 9 8 7 6 5 4 3 2 1

For years you swam around in a sea of
    meaninglessness,
searching for Love, hoping for hope. All that time I was
    pursuing you,
aching to embrace you in My compassionate arms.

JEREMIAH 31:3

(PARAPHRASED BY AUTHOR)

ONE

Someone shot a young Mexican man shortly before two a.m. on the tenth day of February 2009 in a seedy motel room in Jacksonville, Florida. Someone whacked him in the side of the head and then poured two gallons of gasoline on the body. Someone, it looked like a man from a surveillance camera mounted above the parking lot—slightly built, hoodie, dark jeans, quick deft movements—doused a newspaper in some gasoline, stood in the doorway to the room, a doorway that opened to an outside walkway and the parking lot, lit the newspaper, and threw it in.

The killer recoiled from the blaze as soon as it erupted but left the door open. A fire needs air. Then the killer fled to a car.

Good so far. Nothing unusual.

A few minutes later an alarm erupted at the Jacksonville Fire Department. The firefighters responded with two engines. The blaze had spread quickly, but there were only six other inhabitants of the motel, plus the owners, a Pakistani man and his wife. The fire department was only five blocks away and the roads were clear due to the hour of the night, so the firefighters had the blaze under control within a few minutes. Only when the fire was out and they found a charred body did the firemen realize that this particular call would have to be passed along to the Jacksonville Police Department as well.

Yet by this time the victim had been thoroughly cooked. Whoever he had been, wherever he had come from, and for whatever reason he had died, he was now unrecognizable.

The Homicide Division of the Jacksonville Police Department, Fourth District, was notified at three minutes after five a.m., and two officers of that unit, Sergeant John Langley and Detective Sharon Ruiz, arrived at ten minutes before six.

They came in the same car, parked near the fire engines, and walked toward the wet remains in the room. The dead man's charred limbs, from which rose a mixture of steam and smoke, were contorted at horrific angles. There was the repulsive odor of death in the air, much like the aftermath of a small plane crash.

"Oooh," Detective Ruiz said. "Nasty."

"Yeah," her partner said.

Langley was a good homicide cop when he cared to be, which was less and less as the years passed. In comparison, Sharon Ruiz, Langley's partner, was a quiet, thin family woman of thirty-six. She had been a cop for eight years and a homicide detective for five. She looked a little like a high school math teacher. With Langley, Ruiz completed an unlikely but effective team.

Langley looked down at the corpse.

"Drugs," he said. Ruiz nodded. They could tell without looking. A deal had gone bad in some way large or small, particularly for the guy on the motel floor. It happened all the time. They saw it all the time.

Ruiz nudged the dead man's left arm with the toe of her

shoe. She said nothing, but rolled her eyes to her partner. She looked to the doorway where a man with a forensics bag was arriving.

"Look what the cat dragged in," she said. "Here's our favorite ME."

The doctor from the medical examiner's office was named Kenneth Huong. Langley and Ruiz liked Huong a little less each time they saw him. He was in his thirties and Taiwan-trained. He was on the staff of one of the city hospitals that specialized in DOAs. Huong's job seemed easy to the two cops.

Ruiz added a thought. "Natural causes? Cigarettes, maybe?"

Huong didn't answer. He fumbled with his glasses, his bag, and his notebooks. His work with the proper forms elevated speed writing to an art form. He handed the completed form to the detectives so that they could start work with their forensics team and he could get out of there.

A uniformed cop entered the room.

"The motel owner's out there in pajamas and a raincoat. Name's Kahn. Says there's a surveillance video available from a position in the parking lot. He'll download it to a flash drive if you want it."

"We want it," Ruiz said.

"Yeah, we'll take it," Langley said.

The van from the morgue arrived with a body bag and a set of shovels. So did Captain Robert Mazari from the Jacksonville Second District police command, along with the department photographer. Mazari was a big, strapping man with gray hair and wide shoulders. He'd seen things go bump in the night in South Jacksonville for twenty-four years and was looking forward to retirement in another five months.

"Just tie a ribbon around him, wrap him up, and get him out of here," Mazari said.

So with little further discussion the charred remains of a human being were loaded onto the body wagon and removed.

There it was. A single, unidentifiable man murdered, his body mutilated beyond recognition. Off he went to the city morgue where, in the absence of his connection to any missing person's report, his case would diminish daily among the priorities of the homicide division. Three weeks later he was cremated, and the next day his urn was buried. It was all too typically the sort of case that drifts into the daily oblivion of the unsolved and forgotten among the big-city police forces of North America. Within four days, Langley and Ruiz had moved on to other work.

A year later, Langley's name arose in an investigation of a local gambling scandal. He retired. Sharon Ruiz drew another partner, a woman with whom she worked better. She moved to sex crime investigations and was much happier. Lieutenant Mazari retired and bought his own motel down south in Clearwater.

Had anyone cared to look deeply in the ashes, bones, and rubble, there were nonetheless certain physical clues and—just as important—certain deductions that might have been made. But no one ever bothered. And for a long time concerning the events in Room 108 at the Paradise Vista Hotel in Jacksonville, Florida, nothing else was known.

TWO

Early on a Friday afternoon in January 2013, Alexandra LaDuca sat in her office, still deeply immersed in an ongoing investigation known as Operation Párajo. Outside her forty-first-floor window, a cold five p.m. darkness had descended across lower Manhattan and all of New York City. A resolute snow had begun to fall and the workweek was nearing its conclusion.

It was oddly quiet and strangely serene in Alex's suite of offices. Due to the heavy snow alert, employees who lived in the suburbs would be allowed to leave at three p.m., before the roads became impacted, before train service became erratic. By two forty-five, the exodus from the office had already begun.

Alex LaDuca, now thirty-one years old, worked as a Senior Investigator and Administrator with a division of the US Treasury: the Financial Crimes Enforcement Network, or FinCEN. Her agency researched and investigated financial schemes and enforced laws against domestic and international financial crimes that targeted US citizens and corporations. Technically, Alex still remained a Special Agent of the FBI, but was now on permanent loan to FinCEN to combat international financial fraud. Unlike most of her peers at FinCEN, she actually went out into the field from time to time to experience, among other things, the exhilarating feeling of being shot at and—hopefully—missed.

During the previous spring, Alex had rallied those under her command at the Financial Crimes Enforcement Center in New York, a division of the United States Department of Justice. Alex and FinCEN had inflicted several devastating and punishing hits to the international drug-dealing and money-laundering operation headed by Yardena Dosi and her husband, Misha. Alex's work, and that of her surrogates across the United States and Central and South America, had left the Dosis' villainous Panama-based operation in disarray. But Señora Dosi and her husband had successfully fled before being arrested. They had traveled a circuitous route around Central and South America as well as Europe, evading arrest at every juncture, before settling down at a plush, well-guarded estate in northern Morocco.

There they lived, swore revenge, and, even more ominously, plotted it. Two attempts to assassinate Alex—a sniper firing at her through a high-rise window in New York and another gunman on a motorbike on a crowded Manhattan street—had failed. But it was no secret that others, known and unknown, were in the works. Three times was often the charm, or the curse, in this line of work. And everyone knew it.

The various attempts had driven Alex to live under the "protective cover and alias" of Susanna Ferrara in a well-protected private condominium in Chelsea on Manhattan's Twenty-First Street. It was nice to be armed with one's faith and a sense of righteousness, but some urban strategy was wise, too.

How long all of this would last was anyone's guess. It was common currency among those familiar with the operation that the lethal chess game—meticulous move, followed but meticulous move, suddenly augmented by bold, brazen attack—would end only when one of the two queens was down and out of the match. The scurrilous Dosi couple were frighteningly resilient, always ready to come back blazing with every weapon they had. So Alex would continue to live under her nom de guerre. King and Queen Dosi, lions of the international underworld, were a big battle in a major war.

The war was fought on many fronts, not just in back alleys, on cargo piers, and on beaches, but also in boardrooms, in luxury hotel suites, on accounting ledgers, and in various sunny places for shady people, places where offshore "banking secrecy jurisdictions" provided the ideal cover to shroud money and its various paths.

Earlier at FinCEN, the case had come across Alex's desk of the Russian arms dealer Viktor Anatolyevich Bout. Bout had been arrested in Thailand in 2008 before being extradited in 2010 to the United States. In November of 2011, he had been convicted by a jury and sentenced to twenty-five years in prison by a federal judge for conspiring to sell antiaircraft missiles to agents posing as foreign revolutionaries.

Court papers suggested the intent was to sell arms sales to Al-Qaeda and the Taliban for use against American soldiers and citizens. Most of Bout's transactions had used such "secrecy banking" locations. It was no coincidence that Bout—known as the Merchant of Death—had found a Bulgarian weapons supplier based on the offshore haven of Gibraltar. Nothing in the offshore havens happened by coincidence. The British Virgin Islands, a popular haven for secret transactions, were home to about thirty thousand citizens and half a million companies and bank accounts. In China, Alex knew from her old comrade in arms Peter Chang, it was said that a businessman was not a true success until he had his own subsidiary in the British Virgin Islands, where more assets belonging to Chinese nationals were held than in any other location except Hong Kong. And then there was Ugland House, a building in the tax haven of the Cayman Islands. More than twenty thousand corporations were listed there. There was more money on deposit in the Caymans than combined in all the banks in New York City.

The secrecy laws protected home-grown American crooks and con men, also. Bernie Madoff had worked in New York, but the funds that fed his Ponzi scheme were stashed in the sunshine of scores of exotic offshore locales. The accounts looked like independent hedge funds, but were conduits that funneled investor money back to Madoff. They furnished no information to the United States Treasury or regulatory authorities.

Similarly, another recent Ponzi figure, Robert Allen Stanford, inherited a legitimate and profitable insurance company in Texas. Planning for bigger things, however, he branched out into banking fraud, and he moved to Antigua. Taking advantage of secrecy laws and outright bribery, Stanford cheated investors out of seven billion dollars by selling phony certificates of deposit. Not only did the friendly government of Antigua fail to stop him, Alex noted as the Stanford case passed across her desk and through FinCEN, but the Antiguans decorated him with a knighthood. He used the knighthood to further impress his potential victims. A bit later, following his arrest in the United States, a federal judge rewarded him again, this time with a one-hundred-ten-year prison sentence for fraud. During trial, Houston-born Lord Stanford claimed amnesia due to the terrible stress of the trumped-up charges against him and the horrible things people were saying about him.

So it went, as Alex spent several tedious hours a day scouring leads and tips from leaked information from these off-shores. She meticulously read through a library of files on drug trafficking in Central America, all of which bore upon the involvement of the Dosi money-laundering operations. For these times, when concentration was at a premium as she searched for interplay between accounts and operations, she kept herself locked up in her office like a monk or a nun poring over ancient manuscripts in a convent, searching for inspiration.

The ground game itself was spreading: north of Panama, the home base of the departed Dosi family, smuggling operations were sprouting across countries like Guatemala and Honduras. Increasingly, those two Central American nations were on Alex's radar screen.

And yet, additionally, the previous November, Alex had opened a new line of investigation and attack against the Dosis. It was well known that they were behind several homicides, both in the United States and in at least seven other countries. Alex and her staff had pored through many of the cases attributed to them, looking to establish links, hoping to parlay good luck into a sealed indictment.

From time to time, even the meticulous Dosi couple had to emerge from hiding and travel to maintain their networks. It had been Alex's strategy to build a homicide case against them, wait for them to set foot in a country with extradition, and prevail upon the locals to make an arrest. So far, some cases were coming tantalizingly close to success. But there had been no payoff so far and as of that morning she and her assistants had pursued thirty-six separate leads.

Around four p.m., Rick McCarron, Alex's best CIA contact,

phoned Alex on a secure line. McCarron had a lead on a thirty-seventh. Maybe.

"I'm calling to find out how Párajo is going," Rick asked. "I had an inquiry from a foreign government. They have something that might help you but want something in return."

"How big is the 'something in return'?" Alex asked.

There was a pause. "Considerable," McCarron said. "But it can be handled out of some middle-range CIA assets. Inventory, you know."

She grimaced. "Inventory," she repeated. Inventory meant sale or exchange with other police units or intelligence service. It was a loathsome back alley commerce in crooks, defectors, and scam artists, usually small-time at this level, where even pretenses of official justice and morality were completely absent.

Alex was ill at ease with the practice, or at least had been when her tenure at FinCEN had begun. Now, having seen a few examples, she hadn't changed her position, but she knew it was one of the pieces of currency in which people in her position traded.

"I assume this is back channel."

"Totally. A 100 percent black operation which is about to turn a few shades darker."

"Am I familiar with the asset?" she asked.

"You are."

"I don't suppose you can share a name with me."

"No names yet," McCarron said. "I just wanted to see whether you were in a position to need a new ingredient in the Dosi case. If so, I'll tell my foreign contact he may have a buyer." McCarron paused. "This is not to sway you one way or another," he said, "but if you were inclined to say you're in the market, it would complete another arrangement for us. And there's a little frontier justice at the far end of this, also. A couple of ne'er-do well 'some-ones' are going to get exactly what they have coming to them."

"Making it a little easier for me, huh?" Alex asked. "The well-deserved payback thing."

"Maybe," McCarron said. "Payback is a good thing, don't you think? It balances the karma around the world."

"If you say so, Rick," she parried, thinking it through further. "I can always use another good lead," she said. "If it doesn't cost too much."

"That's what I wanted to hear," McCarron said. "I hear it's snowing in New York. True?"

She glanced out the window again and managed a slight smile. "You Agency guys have all the top info, don't you?" she said. "Even the weather."

"We like to think so," he said. "Have a good weekend. I'll be back to you next week."

Yet right now, at the end of this particular week, other matters currently encroached on Alex's precious time. Two in particular. One pleasant, one unpleasant.

Several weeks earlier, a Congressional committee had served a summons on Alex, formally requesting that she testify in public before an investigative committee in Washington. The subject: the sphere of influence of Russian and Russian-American orga-nized crime in the United States. On this subject, Alex was a working expert, having spent a good part of her early career at FinCEN on the track of one shining example of Ukrainian-Russian gangster culture: one Yuri Federov.

Comrade Federov was currently deceased, gone but hardly forgotten, and his posthumous shadow continued to loom large over Alex's life. Having buried the hatchet with her in the final weeks of life, and even having taken a self-styled and unreciprocated romantic interest in her, he had bequeathed her two million dollars. The money still sat where it had first arrived, at a branch of Credit Suisse on Park Avenue in New York City, split among various accounts, earning interest.

Then, after the Congressional nuisance, there was the other distraction, a much brighter personal path. There was a handsome new man in her life, and one whom many women would have killed for. His name was Eric Robertson—an actor a few years older than Alex, his success matched by his immense magnetism, talent, and charm. Eric had been in several notable and successful films and was currently in one of the biggest and most successful productions on Broadway, playing the role of Lt. Joe Cable in *South Pacific* at the Gershwin Theatre, one of the biggest and most prestigious theaters in the United States.

It was, Alex had concluded many times, a strange twist in God's plan for her: Robertson resided in the same New York brownstone in Chelsea where Alex lived under her "Susanna" alias. Fate, happenstance, or divine intervention—whatever one wanted to call these things—these twists in life's road had brought them together, caused them to meet and deeply enjoy each other's companionship, a relationship that had continued and flourished over the past few months. Where it would lead, like most other things in life, was anyone's guess.

A few minutes before five o'clock, Alex's phone rang again. Her assistant having left for the day, Alex picked up herself. A female voice was on the other end of the line.

"Alex LaDuca?" the caller asked.

"That's me," Alex answered. "Who's calling?"

"I have Joshua Silverman on the line for you. Please hold."

It took Alex less than a second to process the name and identify it. Joshua Silverman was the founding attorney of the firm Silverman, Ashkenazy and DeLauro. The firm was a hard-hitting New York power firm, well equipped to provide happy legal landings for unscrupulous people. They were well known for their heavy underworld connections. Alex's previous contacts had not been all that unpleasant, however. Joshua Silverman, the founder and principal partner, had been the American executor of Yuri Federov's will. It had been Silverman, a year earlier, who had placed in Alex's hands the cashier's check for two million dollars after taxes, a posthumous gift from the Federov estate.

The money still posed a moral dilemma in Alex's conscience. She had left it in an account at the New York Branch of Credit Suisse, the bank that had issued the draft, and had barely touched it since, even though she thought about the money and its implications every day. There was still an air of surrealism to it, that and the fact that she had quietly and unexpectedly become a wealthy woman. Yet the money mingled with a taint that she still found a little odious and couldn't quite explain, not even to herself.

Her first contact with Silverman having not been so awful, Alex was willing to take a chance on a second, though she was immediately on guard.

Silverman came cheerfully on the line. "Hello, Alex," he said in his normal silky tone. "I may still call you 'Alex,' I hope?"

"That's my name. That's fine," she said.

"How has life been treating you?" he asked.

"Unfairly," she said, "but that's how it treats everyone. So I march forward and don't complain. What about you?" she asked.

"I'm doing well," he said. "I don't even think I'm under any federal or state indictment at the time, unless you know something I don't. I'm a lucky man."

"I'm glad you admit it, Joshua," she said.

"You should have been an attorney, Alex," he said. "I would have hired you. I like the way you can toss the bull back and forth."

"It's something I learn as a government employee," she joked. "You're in the big money end of things. I'm just a poor federal employee."

"Not as poor as many of them, if memory serves," he said.

"Touché," she said. "So tell me. What's on your mind today, Joshua?" Alex asked. "Here we are late on a snowy Friday. Somehow I don't think this is a social call. What is it that can't wait till Monday?"

"Well, partially it *is* a social call," he said. "I have a young woman coming in from out of town a few days from now. A professional contact as well as a personal one. She has expressed an interest in meeting you. I offered to make a call and see if you'd be willing."

"Who is she?" Alex asked, her nerves sharpening instinctively.

"Her name is Lena Smirnova. You've never met."

"A Russian name, obviously."

"Obviously."

"When you say she's coming in from out of town, does that mean Brighton Beach, Grand Rapids, or Minsk?"

"Does it matter?"

"It might. Call me curious," Alex said. "I'd like to know what this is about before I agree to meet."

"She lives in Canada," Silverman said.

"So do several million other people," Alex said.

"Here's a verbal snapshot, Alex. Lena is in her twenties. Professional person. Wealthy. Blond. Very good-looking." He paused. "You know how those Slavs are such attractive people."

"So she's sitting in your office right now, isn't she?" Alex asked. "And you're buttering her up as you make a call for her."

"Close. She's on the other line. And yes, I am."

"So why should I agree to meet?" Alex asked. "I have a lot going on, and I have some personal security issues to deal with which makes moving around the city a bit tricky from time to time." She paused. "Since there's no such thing as coincidence, I'm assuming this somehow plays back to Yuri Federov."

"Yes, it does."

A pause and she asked, "Does it have anything to do with the two million dollars?"

"No. That's a done deal. Not an issue. Ms. Smirnova wishes to meet with you. She also has something to discuss with you. I think you may find it interesting."

"And she had a relationship with Federov?"

"Oh yes."

"Are you acting as her attorney or just a go-between?" Alex asked.

"Let's say both," he said. "I'm willing to be there, too," he said. "To make the introduction if you're more comfortable that way."

Alex thought about it.

"How does it relate to Yuri Federov?" Alex pressed.

There was a long pause, as if Lena was actually patched in from the other line and monitoring the call.

"It's on the up-and-up, Alex," the attorney said. "There's nothing negative here. I represent some dubious people from time to time but I don't put people in harm's way. As I personal aside, I'd advise you to take the meeting."

"Why?"

He paused again, then, "Lena is Yuri Federov's daughter, Alex. Is that enough?" The impact of Silverman's words came from left field, whacking Alex by surprise. "Now will you meet?" Silverman asked.

A moment's pause. "Okay. Time and place?" Alex asked.

"Ms. Smirnova suggested Wednesday night of next week. She'll only be in town for a few days."

Alex glanced at her calendar. Her office time was booked up and she didn't like bringing strangers into the FinCEN suites.

"Wednesday, no can do," she said. "What about Thursday?"

A pause, then, "That will work."

"It will need to be a clean open place," she said.

"She would have it no other way," Silverman said. "In fact, she suggests Peacock Alley at the Waldorf Astoria. She's never been there and is curious. She knows you met her father there on one occasion."

"And how does she know that? I never knew Federov to communicate with his daughter. Did she find out about my involvement with him after his death?"

"Ask her that question yourself."

"Thursday at seven thirty," Alex said. "I'll be there."

"So will she."

Alex put the phone down and stared at it. She considered in disbelief the strange, unpredictable direction the call had taken. She thought about it.

Federov's daughter? Who could have seen that coming? And what in the world could she want? Nothing good, Alex guessed. The apple never fell far from the tree.

The prospect of a meeting didn't scare her. But it disturbed her. It also shattered her final bit of concentration for the week. She started to shut down the computers on her desk.

"Face it. I am so out of here," she muttered to herself. Well, why not? She was entitled to her last bit of sanity as much as anyone.

She glanced at her watch. Time to go home. She went to see her boss to inform him of the Lena Smirnova development. She found his office empty. He had gone home at four, feeling unusually tired, his assistant said. Okay, she would bring him up to speed on Monday. Nothing would change over the weekend.

She was out her office door and down to the street within another fifteen minutes. Wearing her weapon as always—a Glock-12—under a winter coat, she altered her route walking home. A simple daily precaution.

She enjoyed the feeling of the snow against her hair and face, the bustle of lower Manhattan in a snowstorm that gathered intensity. She grabbed a slice of pizza at a nearby storefront that was still open and spoke Italian to the counterman who recognized her as a regular customer. She munched it on her way to her usual downtown gym, which remained open despite the snow.

She had just enough time for an hourlong workout: moderate weights, running a half mile of laps, and a swim. On her mind was not Operation Párajo but her rendezvous with Eric a few hours hence for a late supper after his Friday evening performance, if she still had energy and stamina after another bruising week. If not, she would definitely join him after the Saturday night performance.

It was good to keep her body fit, her senses alert, and her mind positive. And at least tonight, with no mandatory appearance in the office on the weekend, she could stay out later.

Overall, despite everything, she felt good and at one with the universe. Happiness and an overall sense of well-being were rare commodities, highly elusive from time to time. She wished the feeling could last forever, but deep down she knew it couldn't.

THREE

Sometimes, in this private and most protected part of her life, Alex felt as if she was living the dream of another woman. Or millions of other women.

Saturday night. She stood backstage in the wings of the Gershwin Theatre on Broadway and watched the curtain come down on the final scene of *South Pacific*. Onstage, the older Frenchman Emil de Becque returned from an operation against the enemy. He watched US Navy Ensign Nellie Forbush singing "Dites-moi" with his two children. He basked in her newfound acceptance and joined them at their table. The romance between the navy nurse and the older Frenchman, who had mixed-race children from a previous marriage, shocking to some at the time, had formed the moral core of the story.

Alex had watched this final scene from this spot more times than she could count, all in the last year. It still moved her and gave her chills. And it still filled her with disbelief, not just the scene itself, which she found beautiful, but that she stood in the wings with one of the principals of the show. Who, she wondered to herself, ever could have predicted that she would be standing here?

The orchestra hit its final bars and the curtain descended.

Alex was then again deafened by the applause that thundered from the nearly two thousand seats of the packed house, the former Uris Theater.

Beside her stood the actor Eric Robertson, still in the wardrobe of the character he played in the production, Lt. Joe Cable. Eric wore the outfit of a young Marine lieutenant in World War Two, a soldier who had fallen about twenty-five minutes before the show ended. Eric gave her hand a squeeze. He had completed two performances that day, including the matinee. She could tell he was tired, but he remained clear-eyed and on an adrenaline high.

The curtain calls began. Dozens of actors trouped onto the stage as applause swelled: the soldiers and nurses who formed the chorus fell into their proper positions, and then the supporting actors boldly went onstage for their calls.

Eric was the third lead, after the actors who played Nellie Forbush and Emil de Becque. They, too, were accomplished performers, stars of movies and shows.

Eric's moment came. "Uh-oh," he said mischievously. "Dirty job, this singing and acting and pandering for applause. But somebody's got to do it. Might as well be me, don't you think? Gotta go work, honey. Don't go away."

"Where would I go?" she laughed.

"I don't know. It's New York after dark. There are options, most of them unsavory."

He released her, gave her a wink, and broke into an energetic jog toward the stage, a ten-thousand-kilowatt smile and his hands raised to acknowledge a tumultuous standing reception from the audience. Eric and the two principals were the three major stars who carried the show. But there were tremendous contributions from all quarters, including the orchestra and the great talent of James Michener, Richard Rodgers, and Oscar Hammerstein.

And yet, while Eric may have been the third lead, it was his magnetism, his star power, that gave the show its pizzazz and its public image. Nothing against the other leads, who were also at the top of their profession, but Eric was the singular cast member who "put the fannies in the seats," to use the producer's term, although the producer normally conveyed the idea more colorfully. His was the handsome image on the posters in the train stations and airports, in Times Square and on the web.

Alex stepped as near to the stage as her spot in the wings would allow. The techies who ran the production gave her nods and smiles. They knew her, though they didn't know what she did for a living. She always said hello. Her own blue-collar upbringing taught her to always be respectful of the nuts-and-bolts hardworking people who held any operation together, whether it was a Broadway production, Operation Párajo, or a family store.

Eric held the audience's emotional embrace for several seconds and took two deep and dramatic bows. From her oblique angle in the wings, Alex could see that there was a standing ovation for the entire cast, not unusual. It happened almost every evening. She never grew tired of marveling at it, or at least she hadn't yet.

And yet, it was still odd—odd in a strange and wonderful way—to know Eric and to be part of his life and to have him as part of hers. In her mind, however, there couldn't help but remain a bizarre disconnection. Here he was, a famous actor, known to millions, a man whom audiences adored, and yet behind the public persona was a shockingly decent, intelligent, and down-to-earth man.

After several seconds, Eric turned sideways and raised his arm to welcome the stars, the actors who respectively played Nellie Forbush and Emil de Becque. There were seven curtain calls before the audience allowed the cast to leave. With such receptions each night, the production remained one of the hottest tickets on Broadway.

The pace of the show, however, was exhausting. Eight performances a week. What Eric did was so different from what Alex did that she first had difficulty comprehending it and then never ceased to marvel at it. How did he pull it off so brilliantly every night, week after week?

She had never known any actors before, much less fallen for one of this magnitude. It was fascinating to know him on a personal level and yet watch him work. She was pleased to be able to share this part of it and wished it would last . . . well, as long as it could.

Pumped up, flush, sweating, Eric walked briskly offstage as the applause finally died and the audience started home. He came to her, a man in perpetual motion. "Got time for some late supper?" he asked. "A bunch of us are going to Sardi's."

"Sure," she said. "Of course."

He took her by the hand and gently pulled her along. "Come on. Chase after me worshipfully like everyone else," he said. "Otherwise I get all gushy and insecure and turn to hard drugs."

"Oh, stop it," she laughed.

"Never," he said. "Admit it. I'm the most obnoxious person you know." He nudged her.

"Hardly!" she said. "Just the opposite."

"Ha! Tell that to the producers. Let me get clean quickly. I'll be ready in twenty minutes."

"I'll be here," she said.

FOUR

For Alex, watching Eric from the wings was often not the easiest thing. She would sometimes see him before he went on, or when he was offstage during the production. At those times, he was Eric. Her friend. Her romantic interest. The man in her life. So what that he was all dressed up as a World War Two US Marine and playing a role? Theater was fantasy, right? Make-believe. A willing suspension of disbelief between actors and audience.

But then when he stepped back onstage, he morphed quickly into someone else, or, more accurately, someone who was part Eric and partly someone else. In the story, he falls in love with a young Tonkinese girl named Liat, the daughter of a character named Bloody Mary. He holds her, he embraces and kisses her. At first, Alex was fine with this. Then, the more she personally fell for Eric, the more the scenes bothered her for reasons that she couldn't immediately explain. But then she realized that when she watched these scenes, she saw Eric more than she saw the character Joe Cable. That was her romantic interest out there holding another woman—an insanely pretty one at that!—singing the devastating romantic ballad "Younger Than Springtime" to her as she nestled into his strong arms, those arms that held *her* back in the real world that Eric inhabited for the other twenty-one hours of the day.

Yes, she finally admitted to herself that from time to time she was jealous. It was not made any easier by the fact that there had recently been a cast change and Liat was now played by an adorable twenty-two-year-old girl named Priscilla Kim, a Korean-American beauty who had just graduated from Harvard the previous May.

Priscilla—devastatingly gorgeous in a thin low-cut sarong—had no lines, but was a magnet for the audience whenever she was onstage. When Priscilla snuggled into Eric's arms, it made Alex genuinely uncomfortable. It was known backstage that Priscilla's predecessor had been difficult, as well as not the sharpest knife in the drawer. She had been cast as a favor to the show's director. Eric had privately complained about her; her movements onstage had been awkward and sometimes she undercut some of his scenes. So Eric had been delighted when the producers replaced her with Priscilla. Now the pendulum swung in the other direction: Eric couldn't stop talking about what an asset "the new girl" was to the show, how much he enjoyed working with her.

Alex never volunteered an opinion. But frankly she had heard enough. It was hard enough for Alex to feel her heart thaw out and feel the enormous pleasure of falling in love again, let alone suddenly encountering even a remotely possible threat.

Then there was the scene in which Eric dies. For Alex, who had lost her fiancé several months earlier when he had been killed in the service of his country, it was too close to home.

Some nights she had to turn away from it. She couldn't watch.

In the end, though, she deeply admired Eric's work and his

professionalism. He would put everything he had into every moment of every performance; every night was a triumph, every night saw standing ovations at the end of the show. Every night Eric would take a final step forward toward the audience for the final curtain call, he and the actors who played Emil and Nellie. Then they would crouch forward sometimes on the edge of the stage and shake hands with members of the audience who crowded forward for a close look, a touch, a picture. Meanwhile close to two thousand people would be applauding.

Then Eric would come offstage as if he did nothing more special for a living than carpentry. The adulation never swelled his head, never changed him that Alex could see. He remained well-grounded, even-keeled, and pleasant.

"I want to ask you something," Alex said to Eric later that night at Sardi's. They sat at a round table for ten, cast members and friends, beneath a wall of caricatures and portraits that were distinctly Sardi's. Eric, who had showered and shaved after the performance, sat in a crisp white shirt and dark slacks. He had a heavy parka to protect him against the winter night. But right now it hung over the back of his chair and his arm was draped across Alex's shoulders.

"Ask me anything," he said.

Across the table sat Priscilla with a studious young Asian-American guy who may or may not have been her brother. Eric gave them both a smile and a small playful wave of the hand as he glanced to them.

"How do you do it?" Alex asked.

"Do what? Calculus?" he asked.

"No," she said. "How do you show up in the South Seas in 1944, meet a beautiful girl, fall deeply in love, sing three beautiful love songs to her, ditch her, and then die all in the space of two and a half hours onstage, then step out of it and return to the real world?"

"It's a miracle," he shrugged.

"Come on," she answered.

"It's called 'acting,' Alex, my dear," he said with a wink. "That's what I do for a living. It beats honest work, Lord knows."

"That's not a full and complete answer," Alex said. "I can't imagine being able to do that. So how is it done?"

"You really want to know?"

"Yes."

He smiled and shrugged, almost dismissively. "The trick," he said, "is trying to make it look easy and convincing. It's a creative bluff; I'm betting that I can convince the audience that they're really watching a story from seventy-five years ago in a world that doesn't exist anymore. It's a tremendous physical and intellectual effort. It's training and concentration and being ready for work every day. It's as easy and simple as that."

"I could never do what you do," she said with admiration.

"I could never do what *you* do," he answered. "So we're even." He leaned to her and kissed her on the forehead. "So there, Miss Nosy."

Alex glanced across the table at Priscilla. Then she looked back to Eric.

"How do you keep from being swept away with your co-star?" she asked.

"What do you mean?"

"That bodacious little armful that you cuddle and kiss onstage all night."

"Aha! Now I see where this is going."

"Okay, reassure me," Alex said.

"It's not 'all night.' It's two or three scenes. And the two love stories in *South Pacific* are the framework of the larger story as well as the emotional crux. If the love stories don't work artistically, the performance flops."

"Keep talking," Alex said.

"It's a stage performance. One hundred percent."

"Getting better."

"You believe that good things, blessings for example, come in threes, okay? Three wise men. Father, Son, and Holy Spirit?"

"Good so far," Alex said.

"Okay then, to allay your worst fears, here we go. First," he explained in a low voice so no one else at the table or in Sardi's could hear, "Priscilla is not my costar. Emil de Goofball and Nellie Flatbush are the costars with Lieutenant Cable Guy," he said, "as are the magnificent Rodgers and Hammerstein. Second, Priscilla has a boyfriend. If you'd been here yesterday, you would have met him. Third, what transpires onstage is fantasy and disappears like *Brigadoon* and *Camelot* as soon as the houselights fade out. That's fantasy land over there," he said, nodding toward the direction of the Gershwin Theatre, "and this is real life here. In real life, to paraphrase Nellie's song, I'm already in love with a wonderful girl and she's right here right next to me right now. How's that?"

"You have a silver tongue."

"I'm told," he said in mock conceit, "that I have a more-than-okay singing voice, also."

"That would be accurate," Alex said.

"Some would say an 'admirable' singing voice."

"Let's leave it at 'more-than-okay,'" Alex said.

"Well, gosh, thanks!" he laughed. "You're worse than the critics on the ten o'clock TV."

He embraced her and she laughed deeply once again, enjoying life anew. And so it went during some of the happiest weeks of Alex's life.

FIVE

Antonin Debray always felt at home in his native Paris. He lived in a modest three-story home on the rue Jaclycot near the popular Flea Market at the Porte de Clignancourt. His only affectation of wealth was the silver BMW that normally was parked on the curb somewhere on his block.

Debray was known in the neighborhood and respected as a quiet, generous man. Had anyone asked what he did for a living, the answer to be heard in his neighborhood was that Monsieur Debray was a "courtieur," a broker, a merchant of commodities. Those commodities were said to be precious metals. He had, it was said, a vast network of business associations in South America and from there, following frequent visits, he "brokered" his wares on European and Middle Eastern markets. Like most truths, this one was misleading. What he actually brokered was assassinations.

On a gray misty night in Paris, toward eleven p.m., he stepped out of a taxi at the curb before his home. He had dined that evening at Julien, one of his favorite spots, the historic brasserie on the rue du Faubourg Saint Denis. Content, and stuffed with a fine meal, he paid the driver and tipped generously. He had a new girlfriend and was looking forward to a month's vacation halfway around the world in Fiji. But first there was impending business and for that he would soon be traveling, not to Fiji, but to the North of Africa to call upon his clients. One good job like the one he had been contacted about, and many vacations would follow.

He huddled against the heavy mist in the air as he walked from the taxi. He unlocked the outer doorway to his home and walked through a small corridor that led through a pleasant garden. He scanned the surroundings as he always did, ever alert for a sign of danger. He saw none.

He used a key to unlock his door and stepped into his home.

He reached for the light switch in his entrance foyer.

The wooden baton came from his left side and hit him in the left shin. It hit the bone with a crack. At the same time, from the darkness within his home a squad of men emerged. They hit him hard, rocked him, and took him quickly to the hardwood floor.

Debray fought fiercely, not knowing if these men were police or robbers or something worse. He threw his powerful elbows and fists at his assailants, nailed a few of them, but was no match. There were at least six of them, he calculated quickly, and they were professionals. They knew what they were doing.

Debray managed to get a hand to the gun he carried under his coat. He moved the gun toward one of his assailants but two strong arms twisted his wrist backward so hard that the gun flew from it. From there, two men forced his hands behind his back and manacled them. Two others leaned on his legs and shackled them.

Debray counted five intruders now. Then there was a sixth, a man who was sturdy, smaller, and older. He was standing back, his arms folded, watching.

The intruder with the police club pushed it behind Debray's neck and pinned him to the floor. Debray continued to curse at them.

The older man stepped forward, positioning himself so that his shiny shoes were just in front of Debray's head where it was pinned.

"You have something to say to us, Antonin?" the leader of the squad said, stooping down to get a better look at his catch.

Debray continued to sputter and curse until, in an inspired move, the leader moved the toe of his shoe a few inches closer and brought it down on Debray's tongue, pinning it to the floor. The fact that the shoe was of the finest, softest Italian leather didn't make the moment any more enjoyable.

"There now," the leader said in French. "Silence is much better, isn't it, Antonin?" He grinned. "Wiser, no? After all, it is time for me to speak and you to listen."

His eyes alive with rage, Debray looked up at the man. He had never seen him before and never wished to see him again.

"Alejandra LaDuca," he said. "You've received lucrative overtures, have you not? She is marked for assassination and you are to arrange it. Our good friend Señora Dosi has contacted you about this. I am correct, yes?"

Debray growled in response. He was still breathing hard, wondering who had betrayed him.

"Well, that is exactly the mission we are here to discuss," said the leader. "Entendu, we have unorthodox methods. But we are here to see you along the next part of your path. Isn't that thoughtful of us?"

The shoe slipped back and Debray had his tongue back. But he didn't have long to use it. A needle slid into the muscles in his left arm, and a section of sticky gray tape came across his mouth. These assailants were brutes, he thought to himself. But he didn't have much time to think, either, because within a few seconds he lost consciousness.

SIX

By eight thirty Monday morning, Alex had downloaded and printed nearly a hundred pages of files sent by Rick McCarron late the previous afternoon. She bound them into a Top Security folder and sat down at her desk to read. There were several documents within one far-reaching file.

It was:

FBI Document US.HON-2012-9Ja-13b

Subject: Honduras/ Organized Crime/ Drug Trafficking/ Cartels/ Honduras

Initial report date: July 29, 2009

Amended: (9 times, most recently) January 12, 2013

Source: Federal Bureau of Investigation, Washington DC

Status: Highly Classified; AA-1

Author: SA Frank Gonzalez, FBI, Miami, FL, Southeastern District/CenAm

Most of the file dated from the last five years. Names came and went. Alex tried to keep track of the important ones in a notebook that she freshly dedicated to this inquiry. There were interviews, reports from agents in the field, photographs, surveillance recordings of questionable legality, and more cross references than any one sane person could possibly keep straight.

And yet the document held her like a magnet. From her own memory, from her own knowledge of the Dosi operation, she sensed a devious interplay between the rise of the Dosi influence in Central America and the financial underpinnings of some of the drug cartels that plundered the region.

It was a gut feeling more than anything. It was not something she could yet prove. She asked herself if her anxieties and desire to put the Dosi operation into oblivion were getting the best of her, whether she was being the worst type of investigator —seeing a conclusion or a result and working it backward to fit her own theory.

She tried to put that notion on the shelf to be examined later. Meanwhile, she trawled hungrily through page after printed page, looking for the strongest meat contained therein.

Cocaine traffickers have used Central America as a stopover point since at least the 1970s . . .

the file declared upfront,

. . . but since 2009, the aggressive crackdowns on criminal organizations in Mexico and Colombia, coupled with intensified efforts to limit smuggling across the Caribbean, have increasingly brought the powerful syndicates of Colombia and

Mexico, along with their brothers-in-arms, the Panamanian money launderers, to the so-called northern triangle of Central America: El Salvador, Guatemala, and Honduras.

Urban areas and coastal towns, particularly in Honduras, had experienced explosive increases in drug-related crime. Prisons in Tegucigalpa and San Pedro Sula, the two largest cities of Honduras, were beyond packed . . .

The cartels have spread so quickly and insidiously throughout the region . . .

wrote Special Agent Frank Gonzales, the principal FBI author of the report,

. . . that five of Central America's seven countries are now on the United States' list of 20 "major illicit drug transit or major illicit drug producing countries." Guatemala, Honduras, and Nicaragua were added in 2010. The Mexican cartels out-muscled the Colombians in recent years, succeeding by recruiting local gangs and militias, financed by partners in Panama who send money around the world with keystrokes into and out of offshore tax havens. The locals help expand shipment. Meanwhile, local consumption—and collateral crime and violence—is paid for with drugs. An expansion of extortion and kidnapping networks rounds out the complete enterprise.

All of this is at great cost to local society. In Honduras, the already high murder rate has climbed rapidly and is much higher than Mexico's, 76.5 per 100,000 people. It is the worst in Central America. The hospital morgue in San Pedro Sula alone saw 622 victims of violent death in 2011.

Part of the explanation for the soaring homicide toll in Honduras was political, the report explained. There had been an army coup in 2010 that ousted the leftist president Manuel Zelaya. The recriminations were still being played out via assassinations of political activists and overly nosy journalists. But most of the murders were purely criminal and linked to the phenomenon known as "Maras," youth gangs that form a chain of drugs, extortion, and violence stretching from Los Angeles to Panama City. But the gangs didn't just deal drugs. Their members provided customers to the cartels as well as smuggling supply lines.

Alex scanned over examples of how Honduran society was wrenched apart by the advent of the drug cartels and how corruption seemed to be everywhere. She read of a case in San Pedro Sula, Honduras, where a woman of forty wept over the coffin of her daughter, a twenty-year-old mother of two who was killed with two shots to the head. The reason for the attack was unclear, but the Maras operated in the region and made people pay what is known as Impuesto de Guerra, or War Tax. Anyone refusing or failing to pay is executed.

The overwhelmed system in San Pedro Sula was symbolic of the larger lack of resources to deal with the drug-related problems in Central America. Along the Mosquito Coast in eastern Honduras, speedboats with contraband flagrantly plied the shipping lanes. The fishermen from Puerto Cortes and Ceiba said their radios had been crackling for years with lucrative requests for food or offers of a few thousand dollars to carry drugs ashore. The well-financed Mexican and Colombian cartels underwrote the offers.

Alex scanned several items. Among them:

—Mauricio Milanes, who occupied a newly created position as Honduran drug czar, said the Mexican cartels were buying any legitimate business to hide their product. "They buy everything—the farms, the means of production, the transport," Milanes said. "It's all to move their product: cocaine. Without immediate help, the region will degenerate into another Mexico."

—In Honduras, as with other countries in Central America, the largest seizures have come only with American assistance. In June of 2012, after an American radar picked up a plane near the Honduran coast, Drug Enforcement Administration helicopters with night-vision gear pinpointed where the plane landed. A ton of cocaine was seized, only because police and American agents happened to be training nearby. But even these victories could be isolated and ephemeral. The single-engine plane that had been seized and stored at a military base in San Pedro Sula was stolen. Five armed men somehow slipped past guards, broke into the hangar, and flew the plane away.

No sooner had she digested these accounts, however, than she came across a conflicting opinion on what was going on in Honduras and what the root causes were. She noted that the name of Frank Gonzalez was attached to the previous reports. Now someone named Raoul from the State Department rang in with his two cents' worth.

The previous reports on the homicide rates in Honduras are very misleading. The agent suggests that the high murder homicide rate is caused by the growing drug trade. This is absolutely NOT true. The agent has misinterpreted data and reports. Official Honduran sources surveyed by an independent Honduran organization state that homicides related to drug trade and gangs have been no more than 5 percent in the last three years. That is, as far as the cause of death is being reported to and/or investigated by the local police. Also, the agent compares Mexico with Honduras, which is also misleading. In Mexico a drug cartel war is going on. Honduras has been Los Zetas territory for fifteen years.

[Editor's note; DOJ-Doc. 45a-12-18-12: Los Zetas is a powerful organized crime syndicate in Mexico, identified by the DOJ as "the most dangerous cartel in North or Central America. Its origins date back to 1999, when several dozen commandos of the Mexican Army's elite anti-narcotics forces deserted their ranks and decided to work instead as the armed wing of the Gulf Cartel, a powerful drug trafficking organization. Due to their military background, Los Zetas is well armed, technologically advanced, highly organized, and equipped." In February 2010, Los Zetas broke away from its former employer and formed its own criminal organization.]

Honduras is mostly a transit country. There is no drug cartel war going on in Honduras, only transit and ancillary crime as to be expected. It is not in Los Zetas' interest or pattern of doing business to jeopardize its own existence with arbitrary murders. When Los Zetas people kill, they murder to protect their business. They always leave a clear signature, which include beheadings, torture, and indiscriminate slaughter, to show that they prefer brutality over bribery. They kill to intimidate competitors or associates, police officers, prosecutors, or judges. Yet killings attributed to Los Zetas in Honduras are relatively rare. It is common knowledge that Los Zetas has been cooperating with the Honduran army in weapon deals.

Yes, I am Catracho. Originally from Honduras. Things are difficult there due to the drugs, the unemployment, and many generations of exploitations from American companies and government. But it is ironic that Honduras is being used as a bridge for drugs, which our agents and government deplore, but most of the product comes here to the United States which is where so many people consume drugs. I think the US should join and help us with this drug war which is ruining your society too. I am entitled to an opinion due to the fact that I live in the country that you so despicably call the most violent country in the world.

Wondering what she had gotten into this time, Alex skimmed through a spirited argument between Special Agent Gonzalez and the indignant detractor Raoul who challenged or attempted to re-spin everything the agent had said.

Alex put Raoul's remarks in the back of her mind and continued with the rest of the document. Gonzalez wrote of a police operation against mahogany timber smuggling on the Mosquito Coast, a remote section of coastal Honduras between Ceiba and Puerto Lempira. A close connection had been documented for years between timber smuggling and drug trafficking in Honduras, the agent wrote.

Then in May of 2012, the wheels flew off the wagon with an incident that sparked angry protests over an American presence and prompted human rights groups and at least one US congressman to question US involvement in these operations.

According to US officials, at about three a.m. on May 11, US helicopters carrying Honduran police officers and DEA agents swooped toward a boat loaded with cocaine in the Patuca River. As the helicopters approached, people who were loading the boat fled, but a second boat approached and began to fire, prompting the Honduran officers to return fire. But survivors and local residents claim that the agents fired at the wrong boat, killing and wounding innocent people who were returning home from a daily trip.

When I heard last week about the fatal shooting of four people, including two pregnant women, by a joint Honduran-US anti-drug raid in the Mosquito Coast of Honduras, I was only surprised that it hasn't happened more often. Anyone who has visited the Mosquito Coast in recent years knows that the remote northeast shore has become a favorite route of transport of cocaine from Colombia and Venezuela to the United States. The area is smaller than the state of Connecticut. It is one of the most isolated places in Central America. Its stretches of uninhabited rainforests are accessible only by plane or boat. Historically, it has never been policed. It is a jungle in more ways than one, with vast ungoverned areas and little institutional presence. This last aspect is probably behind the US decision to establish three new military bases in northeastern Honduras to increase logistic support to its Honduran counterparts in the fight against drug trafficking in the region, for that purpose . . .

Its indigenous inhabitants are among the poorest in Honduras. Few houses have electricity, running water, or sanitation. Miskitos and other indigenous people have traditionally lived as hunters, subsistence farmers, and fishermen, but their survival is threatened by the encroachment on their land by illegal loggers, cattle ranchers, slash-and-burn farmers, and now narco-traffickers.

"A friend of mine had his house burned down for speaking out against narco-traffickers and was forced to leave our town for good. Honest farmers in the region are being forced by narco-traffickers to sell their lands for nothing," the then Honduran head of anti-drug-trafficking operations, retired general Julián Arístides González, told me over a meeting at his Tegucigalpa office. González was murdered by cartel gunmen in 2009, a day after voicing concerns over the alarming rise of landing strips in Honduras.

Alex sighed.

"When you see a high volume of drug trafficking, like in Honduras, it means that there is widespread police corruption," Arístides González said. "Maybe this is something to keep in mind for the US when supporting security forces abroad with dubious human rights records, as is the case of Honduras, according to human rights groups."

"Beautiful," sighed Alex as she signed off on the final page. It was eleven thirty a.m. Fighting off an understandable wave of depression and empathy for the people of the Mosquito Coast, she closed the document, resealed it, and locked it in her office safe. She dug into another document from Gonzales, which took her entire lunch hour.

This job was knocking the stuffing out of her and she knew it. She sighed. Eric had made the same point the last time they talked. This job was beating her up, emotionally and psychologically, the same as it had beaten up her boss for a quarter century. For the first time, she wondered how much longer she would last here.

SEVEN

At one point during the afternoon, Alex sought to pursue a point about tracking the Dosis in Europe. She phoned her partner in crime intervention, Gian Antonio Rizzo in Rome.

No answer, no response. Not unusual. It was also after eight p.m. in Rome, and she knew her friend had better things to do with his evenings—both personally and professionally—than to hang around an office. He was still sharing his life with his brilliant but goofy girlfriend, Mimi, for example, which was a good enough reason as any for a man to split from his office each day at a reasonable hour. Alex had word that he would be passing through New York, however, and she always wished to meet with him, compare notes, and exchange ideas, some noble, some nefarious.

In the middle of the preparations, Alex's secure cell phone rang.

On her caller ID, she recognized the Miami area code and number of Rick McCarron. She had almost forgotten what Rick had in progress. The reappearance of McCarron pushed Rizzo out of her mind.

"Hello, Rick. Talk to me," she said, answering. "I'm suffering through all these Central American documents you sent me. What have you got? Maybe something more uplifting?"

"Well, I have some interesting stuff," he said. "Still trying to pin the tail on Dosi the Donkey here, so I'm looking in every direction on your behalf."

"I'm grateful. Amuse me with what you have."

"The other shoe is about to drop," Rick said. "The 'inventory' swap that I mentioned last week? I'm ready to tell you a little more. Seems as if I have an excited customer somewhere on an island south of here."

"Cuba?" she asked.

"Bahamas."

"Banking?" Alex asked.

"Offshore banking and drug running to keep the bank accounts healthy. No wonder this should bounce onto your desk," he said.

"Too true. You can talk more?"

"I can give you the overall framework of what's going on," he said. "Then it's on you to tell me if you want to pull the trigger on this. I'll tell you ahead of time that the 'inventory' is going to be in for some rough times if they get swapped out."

"I believe you said that they may have brought their misfortune upon themselves."

"Absolutely. In spades," McCarron said.

"Then I'm listening, Rick," she said.

"Okay, let's go back to when you were working that murder in Miami a few months ago. The defector who was murdered? Mejías."

"Of course."

"During that case I had you run a covert IRS inquiry on an American couple. Penny and Jonas Frederickson. A couple of aging yuppie ne'er-do-wells who got themselves in some hot water in the Bahamas. Frederickson and his wife, or one or the other of them, were accused of a murder there. They walked. Got out of the country scot free."

Without much trouble, Alex pulled it out of her short-term memory. The case was repulsive in all aspects, with plenty of abuse and people to dislike on all sides. The Fredericksons were poster people for Ugly Americanism, the kind who give their otherwise noble nation a lousy reputation and even bring cringes from their own countrymen.

Jonas was the heir to a mining-equipment fortune in eastern Ohio and Penny had married into it. Together, they crashed around the world in all their venal charm, drinking, fighting, offending people, and inciting trouble, serious trouble wherever possible.

Recently, and famously, they had moored a big obnoxious yacht on the outer reaches of Freeport harbor. One night, according to the legal case brought against them a year earlier in the Bahamas, a boat-taxi driver named Lonnie Sharp disappeared after having last been seen giving the Fredericksons a ride back to their yacht at one a.m. one morning. His boat taxi was found adrift the next morning. And the body of the unfortunate Mr. Sharp turned up on a beach a few high tides later with a bullet hole in his head. The bullet hole had had many characteristics, but self-infliction was not one of them.

The Fredericksons were charged with first-degree murder. A conviction would have carried a mandatory death sentence by hanging in the Bahamas. The Fredericksons were well known for getting into violent squabbles over small grievances and were equally known for pulling guns on people. They were also known as being virulent racists and they were white and the victim was black. Wealthy trash was what they were to Alex, from what she remembered of the case. Trash came in all of God's wonderful colors, as did dignity.

Nonetheless, the Fredericksons went out and bought the best legal help they could get and, according to rumor, spread some cash around the ever-malleable jurisprudence system in Nassau. Result: they managed an acquittal from a judicial panel. The verdict was read in a closed courtroom, and the Fredericksons took a police escort car to a waiting aircraft to get them back to the United States before the furious locals could lynch them. Sharp had had many friends himself, some in the local police forces; there was plenty of angry talk about unofficial payback after the Fredericksons bolted the islands by private aircraft.

"I remember it," Alex said. "And I thought you traded off those scumbags already. You're still sitting on their IRS information, aren't you? Their location and all. They were in New Jersey, weren't they?"

"I was ready to deal them away in November," McCarron said. "That arrangement never happened. Lucky for you. They may be more valuable than ever. See, the thing is, the Fredericksons have been involved in so much dirty stuff that their name comes up from many directions. But here's what I have right now. Follow closely—this has several moving parts."

"Go ahead," Alex said.

"The Bahamian government has a prisoner, an American, age twenty-two. For the purposes of this call, or until you actually meet the prisoner, if you do, I'm going to refer to the prisoner as 'Suarez.' Suarez claims to have some heavy incrimination on Yardena Dosi. Major stuff."

"Where did the Bahamians get Suarez?" Alex asked.

"Nassau. Suarez got busted in one of the banks trying to cash a forged check for twenty-five grand. It was drawn on a Dosi account. It's obvious Suarez had inside knowledge of the account and where the money was hidden."

"Okay," Alex said. "Good so far."

"The Bahamians could put Suarez in prison for ten years. But why would they want to do that? They'd have to clothe and feed a convict and pay for the jail space. It makes much more sense that they want to deal the asset somewhere. They came to us first, figuring there was a Dosi connection and knowing there'd be interest."

"Nice of them," Alex said sarcastically.

"They're corrupt cutthroats, too," McCarron said. "Same as everyone else we deal with. But that's how we do business, right?"

"Right," Alex said, not convinced but not wishing to take issue, either.

"Suarez has been around. The prisoner is a person of interest to the national police of Honduras, also," McCarron said.

"Smuggling?"

"Exactly. The new cocaine routes across Central America to the east coast of the United States. The individual has been involved in that. No secret about it."

"None," Alex said. "As usual, I've been dealing with the financial underpinnings of it."

"So here's how this is going to go down," McCarron said. "I've got an American soldier who's one of our top go-to guys in Central America. He's a US Army officer with some pretty good juice. Lieutenant colonel. No name right now, but you'll meet him. He's in Honduras on an anti-narcotics operation. If we do this deal, he's going to fly from Tegucigalpa to Nassau, pick up Suarez, and take the prisoner to Honduras."

"So the prisoner is a witness? Against Señora Dosi?"

"The prisoner is a former participant in Dosi enterprises. Middle level, but with a lot of inside knowledge. One who can be turned."

"Then why take Suarez to Honduras? If the prisoner is in Honduras, what good does that do me?" Alex asked. "Extradition would be difficult and could take years, although I get the idea you're planning to bypass it some way. But if you do that, Suarez is going to lawyer up in court here and claim illegal arrest and detainment. So why would Suarez even cooperate?"

"Because the Hondurans want this person, also. Both the government and the underworld. No place to go. The colonel will take Suarez to an army base in Hondo, not that we have any official army bases there. The Bahamians picked up the detainee's passport also. The colonel is safekeeping it."

"So it's an agency setup, the military base?" Alex said. "One of your operations?"

"You could assume that if you wish."

"Is there anything legal about this?"

McCarron thought about it. "I suppose there are a few aspects that have arguable legality," he said.

Alex sighed. Little by little, her job, her goals, led her to larger and larger moral compromises. Situation Ethics 101. Or maybe she was a graduate student by now.

"I don't want to build a case and watch it implode from a shaky legal start."

"Not even with what might happen to the Fredericksons afterwards?"

"They're not my problem," she said. "Why should I care?"

"Good, because Suarez is going to have to make a deal," McCarron said. "It might as well be with you." He paused. "Here's the thing. The prisoner is going to be scared to death that our people are just going to do a catch-question-and-release and then open the door and send the individual out into the general population without a passport. Suarez's butt is between a rock and more hard places than you can count. If Suarez is released in Honduras, the local government's going to slap Suarez in prison or the contrabandistas are going to cut Suarez's throat. Even if Suarez manages to get a passport and get back to the US, there's an American arrest warrant out."

"For what?"

"It's a murder warrant. One in which Suarez can sit in a courtroom and implicate a Dosi or two."

Alex whistled low. "Wow. This person has made some bad career choices, I'd say."

"You'd say right. Do you know what's going on in Honduras these days? New drug routes? Cocaine traffic?"

"Honduras and Guatemala get mentioned increasingly in the reports I see. I know the Dosi network has been trying to reorganize from the initial Párajo hit. I'm sure they have an increasing presence there."

"That's the word we're getting, too," McCarron said. "Check your secure email in fifteen minutes. I'll send you a couple of additional reports that I saw earlier today, plus some background."

"Thanks. I think."

"And so how do you feel about Suarez? Are we playing ball on this? You'd need to travel down to Honduras, have a look, have a talk, and get the feel of the situation. Then you let me know if you want to take possession. If not, Suarez gets peddled to the Honduran army for six bushels of bananas and a case of coconut milk. In either case, I'm ready to trade the

Fredericksons to the Bahamians for Suarez unless you give me a reason not to."

"I don't have a reason not to," Alex said.

"Then I'm getting Suarez and I'll decide what to do with the asset later."

"That's okay with me," she said.

"Want to run it past your boss?"

A moment, then, "No," Alex said. "I'll go out on a limb. Andy's been out of the office and I'm guessing you'd like an answer right now."

"I would, yes. Sooner the better."

"So I'll say yes and keep him in the loop. All right? Make your trade."

"And you can go down to Honduras to take a look at the asset?"

"I'll go," Alex said.

"Good," McCarron said. "That's the right way to go, if you don't mind my opinion. I'll send you the background on the situation on the ground in Honduras. It ain't pretty, you know."

"I'd be surprised if it were," Alex said. "By the way, this Frank Gonzales whose reports I've been reading. Is he credible?"

"Usually. Why?"

"He's got a pretty dark view of things."

"He's a pretty dark guy," McCarron said. "He's sort of a mongoose the FBI uses to go after the cobras out there. Recruited as a young thug. Now he's a middle-aged thug."

"Still on the job?"

"Technically, yes. But I don't think he's on assignment. Want to talk to him in person? He's in New York."

"Sure, if you can set it up. Why not?"

"I'll see what I can do. But he's a loose cannon, I'll warn you."

"He won't be the first I've met."

"Or the last," McCarron said. There was a pause. "'Gonzo' is bad news, Alex," he warned. "The guy's got his private demons. He's on administrative leave right now."

"Talking with an agent whose feet have been on the ground in a location gives me a better sense of things," she said. "So can you set something up?"

"If you insist," McCarron said.

"I insist."

In the late afternoon, Alex met for the first time in person with the attorney who would accompany her to the Congressional hearings. She was a sharp legal lady named Sarah Fedderman. She was in her late thirties, a New Yorker by birth and accent. She had worked as a junior counsel for two US congressmen, one a Democrat, one a Republican. The sessions with the attorney were lengthy and tedious. At one point, Alex broke through the legal-ese and inquired point blank:

"Why are they after me?" she asked. "Or am I just being paranoid?"

"It's good to be paranoid," Sarah answered. "That way you won't be ambushed. I don't know if they're after you in particular, but let's assume they are. Then we'll be prepared."

"I get it," Alex said.

Sarah looked pensive for a moment, tapped a finger thoughtfully, then her gaze settled in on Alex. "I was going to ask you this eventually, but I might as well ask you now. Did you ever sleep with Mr. Federov?"

"*Excuse* me?"

"Sorry. I need to ask. And I need to know."

"No!" Alex answered, insulted. "How stupid would that have been?"

"Very," Sarah Fedderman answered. "But let's face it, sometimes otherwise bright people get carried away in a foolish moment. I see it all the time in my line of work. And it's the type of thing the people on the Congressional committee will be snooping for."

"They don't have better things to worry about?"

"It's the conflict of interests, Alex, not a libido watch."

"You heard my answer," Alex said firmly. "It's a categorical no!"

"Never accepted a personal gratuity while he was alive, never spent the night with him, went clubbing, anything like that?"

"I went to a night club with him in Kiev. I was assigned to keep watch on him, ply him for information. That's all."

"Okay. All right," Sarah said. "I just need to be ready for anything."

"Now you are."

"Now we both are," Alex said, still simmering.

They continued into Monday evening. At a few minutes after six, there was a light rap on the open door to Alex's office. Alex looked up as her assistant, Stacey, poked her head in. "The boss wants to see you," Stacey said.

"He's here today?" Alex asked, surprised.

"He came in at four p.m.," Stacey said.

"Does it have to be right now, or can it be 'right now' in five minutes?" Alex asked.

"Five minutes might work," Stacey said.

"No problem," Attorney Fedderman said. "We're good for today."

Alex logged off her two secured computers as her counsel departed. On a third computer screen, one she used for personal administration, she did a quick scan of her emails.

One in particular caught her attention. She finally had contact from her most dependable European law enforcement contact, Gian Antonio Rizzo, who worked out of Rome. Rizzo was pleased to announce that he would be in New York within the next two weeks and would coordinate his arrival with Alex's schedule.

She shot an email back to him, good natured and amusingly cynical. They often commiserated about what a horrible world they were up against. Rizzo had come very close several months earlier to capturing the Dosis in Rome. But somehow they had been tipped, and evacuated their hotel less than an hour before police arrived.

"Well," as Rizzo commented philosophically, "why do only once what you can do over and over until it works. Right?"

Aside from that, the world seemed calm. So did the personal one when she checked her personal email. Maybe suspiciously calm, she thought. She stood and walked down the hall to her boss's office. Just before she arrived, she took a moment to gather herself. When one stepped into a boss's office, one never knew what was in the offing.

EIGHT

A ndy De Salvo's door was open. Alex stepped into his office.

"Aha!" Andrew De Salvo said, looking up. "Come in, close the door, and take a seat. We have things to talk about, things for you to see."

She closed the door before answering.

"Trouble?" she asked.

He shrugged. There was a mischievous glint in his eye. "More trouble for you than for me," he answered. "But there's nothing unusual about that."

"I can't wait to hear about it," Alex said. She found the closest chair, a utilitarian but comfortable leather throne a few feet from the front of De Salvo's desk.

"Ready?" he asked.

She waited.

"I just resigned," he said.

"What!?"

"Resigned. As in, quit. Finito. Terminado. Outta here. I'm leaving this job."

She sat dumbstruck before him. After several seconds, she managed to sputter, "Andy, I don't know what to say. What's going on?"

De Salvo laughed. "Oh, go easy," he said. "Not the worst

thing. And I'm not leaving right away. Here's the deal. In six months, lucky number six, I'll be sixty-six years old. All those menacing sixes! I can take a hint. The people in the Department of Justice would be pushing me to retire by that time, anyway. Never mind whether a man or woman can still do the job or not, they'd be looking to shove me out the door or walk a plank out the window. So, as it happens, this June also marks my twenty-fifth year with FinCEN and, believe me, the time has long since come. Enough is enough. My kids are through college and my heart not only is not in this job the way it used to be, but it's not in as good a shape as it used to be."

"Is there a problem? Health?"

"A few heart problems, Alex. But that's strictly between us, as is this entire conversation. I have some great doctors. So it is what it is."

"I'm sorry," she said. "Of course, I won't mention anything."

"Ah, look, health-wise? I'll be fine," he said with a dismissive wave of the hand. "The doctors saw some little blips on my EKG and we talked it out, and it was just the impetus I needed. Call it a blessing in disguise. Time to move on."

"So when would this take effect?" Alex asked.

"August first. And know what? Now I can't wait. I figure I've still got a good decade of living in front of me. Medical science and all. God bless it. There might be a pacemaker in my future, but if there is, so what? In any case, I'm going to enjoy my time. My wife, Helen, and I. Think of us as the latter-day Sonny and Cher, Westchester County. Don't you think that's a good idea?"

"Acting like Sonny and Cher?"

"No. Retiring while I can still enjoy it."

"Definitely," she said. "Or at least I think so."

"Good! Glad you agree. So. Here's the good stuff. I've been waiting for the right moment to show you something," he said, opening a drawer. "And again, right now, even this is just between us. Can you keep another secret? Only tell ten of your best friends?"

"I can keep as many secrets as you tell me," Alex said.

"Look at this," he said. "We bought ourselves a retirement place."

He pulled from the drawer an extensive series of five-by-seven photographs. He handed Alex the pictures and fell silent as she filed through them one by one.

In the pictures, her boss and his wife, rested and smiling, seemed to be on vacation. They were standing in front of a small building, immaculately maintained, dark wood, surrounded by flowers and fauna that looked tropical.

"Very pretty. Impressive. Looks like Hawaii," she said.

"It certainly does. And it's not."

Alex flicked through the next few pictures, which showed a small but modern European town. It was sunny and pleasant, a bit exotic. Leisure hung in the air so heavily that Alex could almost cut it with a knife. She felt a surge of envy.

"It's Hawaii on one-third of the price," De Salvo said.

Alex riffled through the collection of photos until she found one that showed storefronts and street signs. It took a brief moment, but she pegged the language, and hence the location, right away.

Alex spoke five languages and was familiar with several more, including this one. "That's Portuguese," she said. "Brazil?"

"Nope."

"Portugal?" she said. "You bought a place in Portugal?"

"Yes, ma'am," he said proudly. "The Algarve. Southern tip of Portugal, on the Mediterranean."

"Wow. That's kind of out of the blue, isn't it?" she asked. "Lovely pictures, by the way," she added, handing them back.

"I want to get away from the rat race for a couple of years before settling into my dotage here in the US. Or maybe I'll never come back. Who knows? Helen and I, we wanted to do something together that we'd never done before and do it together while we still had health and time."

"I get it," Alex said. "Life is short."

"Life is short," he agreed. "And mercifully, so is the time before I retire and get out of here. Only a few months."

"Wow," Alex said again.

De Salvo took a final affectionate glance at his handful of photographs.

"Six rooms, a half mile from some great beaches, less than two miles from some fabulous golf courses. I can't wait to shank a Titleist into the Mediterranean."

"I know the area," Alex said. "The Algarve. The year I studied in France I went down there with some friends. We were partying on twenty dollars a day. It was a hoot."

"Parties till sunrise on the beach, I assume," he said in a mock avuncular tone. "Wayward young people, barely clad, living a sybaritic existence under the sun."

"Sort of," Alex laughed. But not really. It had been much tamer than that: a Christian writing workshop held annually at an old Roman Catholic monastery. But it had been great fun in any case, and her boss was entitled to his fantasies.

"Anyway, Helen and I are going to sell the place in Mamaroneck. We're going to become beachcombers as we welcome our old age and infirmities. My wife will maintain middle-class respectability, but I will set myself up as an aging eccentric, unshaven, mildly withdrawn, discursive old goat, wandering the beaches at dawn and dusk, shamelessly ogling bikinis worn by girls a fraction of my age, as I bumble along the beaches of Portimão talking to myself."

"Sounds like a solid plan," Alex said.

"It is," he said, folding away the pictures. "Better yet, it's *my* plan. And it beats talking to myself in this office, Alex. See, I've paid a big price in this job," he said with an edge. "I don't know what I bought, but I paid." He paused. "I hope we can wrap the Dosi case before I go. I'd like to see a nail in that coffin."

"I hope so, too," she said.

"Think we can?"

"I'm doing my best. The whole team is."

"I know. I know," he said. "Hey, look. Here's the pitch: Under normal circumstances, you'd be in line for my job. Do you want it?"

"Are you kidding?"

"Does that mean yes or no?"

"Neither. It's my way of expressing shock. I never thought about it because I thought you'd be here for a few more years."

"Well, look, you'll need to think about it. But I'll be blunt. Even if you do want it, I don't think they'll give it to you. First, it's more administrative than what you do now. You're still too valuable in the field. But the big thing is age and experience. You've had a ton of experience wrapped into the years you've been here, but they—the powers that be in the Department of Justice—would be looking for someone who has put in ten or twelve years at least. And probably someone with ten or fifteen more years than you who'll give them a decade if he or she lives that long and if the world doesn't blow up. Does that bother you?"

"Which? The world blowing up?"

"No. Being passed over for my job, even though you'd be welcome to apply. It has to go through the Justice Department. The attorney general has to sign off on it, too."

Taken aback completely, Alex fumbled for a response. "Look, I really don't know what to say," she said. "This isn't something I've thought about. You're springing this on me. There are evenings when I'd just like to be an ordinary person. You know, kicking back in jeans with friends."

"I know. You can't let the job destroy you. No job is worth that. I've stayed at the party too long. I'll be happy to set foot in the Portuguese sunshine and not look back."

"I get it," she said. "So, well then. I'll think about it."

"That's all I'm asking."

"And day to day," Alex asid, "I assume nothing here changes. Until you leave."

"Actually, one thing does," he said. "That's one of the reasons I asked you to come in."

She waited.

"You know those moments, those situations," De Salvo asked, "where you said to yourself, 'I need to ask my boss,' and then you'd trundle in here and run something past me, see if it's okay, see if you have a green light to proceed in a certain way?"

"Yes?" she said.

"Don't bother anymore." He paused. "What can they do to me, right?"

He glanced out his window and looked at the steady snowfall. "Why don't you go home?" he asked. "I'm going to."

"Sure," she said. De Salvo looked at her with a mischievous smile. "What?" she asked.

"Got something good on tap for a snowy evening in Manhattan tonight?"

"What's that mean?"

"Don't be coy. The actor. Your boyfriend."

"Eric?"

"Yes, Eric. How many boyfriends do you have?"

"Just the one."

"Ah, enjoy," he said. "Live your life. You grow old faster than you think."

She smiled and stood. "Thanks, Andy," she said. "I'll remember that."

"You better," he said.

In an unusual moment and gesture, he stood and came around the desk. He faced her for an awkward moment. Then he wrapped his arms around her in an embrace.

"I worry about you, Alex. Honestly, I shouldn't but I do. I sometimes get the worst feelings, the worst premonitions. So be careful," he said.

"About . . . ?"

"The Dosis," he said. "They're the scum of the earth. They'll come from any direction and they'll strike at anything to hurt you. That includes Eric."

"He has a bodyguard."

"How many?"

"One."

"And who knows how many hired killers the Dosi woman has? Or how many she can hire? Don't for a second think she's fallen into a long-term stalemate with you. The war's not over. There's not even an armistice."

"I know. I'm careful. I've thought about it. We've discussed it, Eric and I."

"Don't ever stop thinking about it. Not while that woman is still alive and free. Let it be," he said, moving his hand from a file to the pictures, "let it be like I do, thinking incessantly about Portugal and retirement. Hold on to the future so tightly that it can't get away."

"I will," she said.

"Promise?"

"Yes."

"I know what you're going to do, Alex," De Salvo said. "That actor fellow is smitten with you. He's going to marry you and sweep you away."

"Andy, come on. That would be a long way off, somewhere between Fantasy Land and Never-Never Land. I'm not even thinking about that right now."

"But if you were . . . ?"

She folded her arms. "Andy . . . ?"

"Okay, okay," he said, dismissing it. He hugged her, released her, and stepped back. "Sorry, Alex," he said. "That was over the line. I'm getting maudlin in my old age. Forgive me."

"Don't worry about it," Alex said. "We'll wrap up the big case and give you the send-off of your life in August. I promise. Is that okay?"

"That's good," he said quietly. "That's good."

He seemed awkward and embarrassed at his own show of emotion. But she had almost collapsed with him into the same mood.

"Oh. Hey. There is one other thing. That two million bucks that your gangster friend Federov left you," he said. "Is that still pretty much intact?"

"I never touched it," she said. "I give some of the interest to charities and I moved it to various other accounts. Don't want it all sitting in the same place. But I never spent it if that's what you're asking."

He nodded. "Smart lady," he said.

"You never got any further feedback from the Justice Department on it, did you?" she asked.

"That's what I wanted to mention. For some reason, someone took another look at that in the last week. We're lucky we did all the right stuff at the time," he said. "Reported the gift. Kept you away from any cases where there could even be the appearance of conflict of interest. Let them take their own look at the situation. Nobody objected, nobody said squat. So I even had a private conversation with an Assistant AG this afternoon on the subject and he was happy with your good fortune. So you've covered your backside on this, Alex. Just be ultra, ultra careful that if it ever comes into play in any remotely contiguous case that you're assigned to, let me know and you'll need to be reassigned."

"Obviously," Alex said. "I'd do that in an instant."

"Of course you would. We both know that." He shook his head. "Frankly, I'm happy for you, too. Maybe I'm old and cynical, but this job as a career isn't worth two million dollars. If you had to resign to keep the dough, you should do it. What the heck do you think they're going to give you at the end of twenty years here, a subscription to the monthly FBI bulletin and a gold Timex?"

"Andy, you've done a lot of good over the years. Don't fool yourself."

"I'm feeling old and worn out these days, Alex. I'm playing out the schedule with no hope of going into the postseason, which is fine with me. I want some personal postseason, know what I mean? Maybe when I get to Portugal my perspective will change."

"I hope it does."

"So follow your conscience and your heart. And don't give your youth away. You'll land on your feet."

"Thanks," she said.

"Don't ever forget that," Andy said. "See you tomorrow."

NINE

The drill was simple. Like most evenings, Alex went to the "pink room," as it was called in the Gershwin, a plush private lounge situated backstage for family and friends to wait for cast members. There Alex would rendezvous with Maurice, Eric's chauffeur and bodyguard, while Eric did a quick cleanup in his dressing room and changed from wardrobe to street clothes. Each night, stars could leave the theater via an elevator that went down to an underground parking garage. Their drivers could then take one of five garage exits to avoid paparazzi and tourists. This was by design to afford unpredictability of exits and privacy. Or the stars could leave the "old-fashioned way," via the stage door that led to Shubert Alley, Fiftieth Street and Fifty-First Streets, where limousines could wait for them.

On most nights, Eric let Alex descend with Maurice to a limousine with tinted windows and climb into the back. Eric would then brave the autograph seekers on Shubert Alley who thrust copies of *Playbill* at him as he moved along. His security at that point was negligible. But his only concerns were the occasional rowdy and overenthusiastic fans who pushed and shoved. He considered himself, despite star-power good looks and extensive fame, just an ordinary guy whom God had blessed. He always wanted to give back. And, from a professional point of view, he felt pressing the flesh, signing souvenirs, letting the public take pictures was an investment.

"Those people who come and see the shows, see my movies, are the only reason I get to be in those shows or movies. Without them," he said with his usual mock conceit, "I'm just another incredibly handsome dumb kid from the Midwest."

On this night, Eric spent twenty to thirty minutes getting washed and changed and another fifteen walking the gauntlet of his fans. He hated to disappoint them. But by eleven fifteen, he had slid into his limo with Alex. The vehicle had waited on Fifty-First Street. Maurice pulled away from the curb.

"Where to, Mr. Robertson?" Maurice asked.

Eric looked at Alex, sitting in the backseat, his hand on hers. "I don't know. Ideas?" he asked her.

"Why not Sardi's?" she asked. "It's right here."

"Ah, not tonight."

"I like Sardi's," she protested. "It's fun with you."

"We all like Sardi's. On Halloween even Vincent Sardi's ghost comes back and buses the tables. But not tonight, okay? I want to talk."

"Okay. Then where?"

"Oh, wait a minute. I know," he said. "A place named Il Trovatore. Down in the Village. I know the owner. He's open till midnight. He'll set up a private table if we call ahead."

Alex grinned.

"Why the pretty smile? You dreaming of crooks you're going to put away tomorrow?"

"No such luck," she said. She paused. "I'm smiling because I love being here with you. And I also know Il Trovatore. It's on

Fourth Street near Seventh Avenue. I've been there. I didn't know you knew the owner."

Eric signaled Maurice to proceed. The vehicle moved smoothly through an armada of taxis and limos on Fifty-First Street, then turned downtown on Seventh Avenue and eased into a flow of moderate traffic.

"Been there when? With whom?" Eric asked.

"Don't even ask."

"Aha! Do tell," Eric said, teasing. "Now I'm jealous. Previous boyfriend?"

"Hardly. A mobster that I involuntarily had to dine with."

"Oh, well, that's a great story," he said with a pout.

"I shouldn't have told you," she said. "Office secrets."

He waited. Over the last months, as their relationship solidified, she had been in the habit of trusting him with office shoptalk. He had trusted her as well. Neither had ever betrayed a confidence. She shook her head with mock stubbornness at his silence, trying to keep a straight face.

He continued to watch her and wait. "No dinner for you unless you squeal," he said as he hugged her. "I'll lock you in the trunk of this road locomotive until you talk!"

"Threatening a federal law enforcement official, huh?"

He paused thoughtfully. "I suppose I was."

She laughed and playfully slapped his arm. She leaned to him and whispered, "Paul Guarneri," in his ear. "Believe me, business only. I got stuck into going to dinner with him a few times, mostly to pry him for information."

There was a moment before he recognized the name. "Ah! Your Cuban 'date,' if I recall?" he said, remembering. "Your overly amorous wise guy."

"If you can call him that. 'Date' isn't quite right either but I'll let it slide."

"Well, I need to distinguish him from that Ukrainian hoodlum you used to hang with before I started to lure you back into civilized society."

"I did not 'hang with' Yuri Federov," she said with mock indignation.

"Sure. You have lots of sleazy friends," he countered. "You're as bad as a producer or an agent. They're always hanging out with crooks, too."

"Guarneri was part of an assignment. Same as Federov. As you know!"

"As I know," he said. He put an arm around her.

"Do I detect a trace of jealousy?" she teased.

"There would be more than a trace," he said, "if I didn't know better. I'm just envious of anyone who knew you before I did. Why didn't they steal you away? That's what I can't figure."

"They both tried."

"And?"

"I was waiting for you to make a move."

"Ah! That explains it," he said. "But we didn't know each other yet."

"I was still waiting for you."

He pulled her to him and kissed her. In the front seat, Maurice made himself busy by phoning ahead to Il Trovatore. Alex could hear him getting the owner on the phone and arranging a table.

It remained a heady time of Alex's life, these days and evenings at this point in this year. She had almost despaired of finding a new man with whom she could share so much. Even though her professional schedule was packed and highly stressed, she managed to find time almost every evening to spend with Eric. It was a time when she survived five nights a week on six hours of sleep, adrenaline, and caffeine. It was not uncommon on nights like this to not roll home until one a.m. and then be up at seven fifteen and at her desk shortly after eight thirty in the morning. Fortunately, she could crash and sleep in on weekend mornings. And fortunately, the excitement pumped her. She knew she could survive this way for maybe a few years if she had to, long enough to see where it would lead her, and see what part of God's plan for her this was.

Maurice spoke from the front seat. "They'll have a table for you when you arrive, Mr. Robertson," he said.

"Great," Eric answered. "Thank you, Maurice."

A few moments went by in silence as the limousine passed Thirty-Fourth Street and then Twenty-Eighth. A string of consecutive green lights made a quiet lower Seventh Avenue seem like Oz, brightly lit, a few places still open, a moderate amount of traffic and pedestrians. Alex liked the city like this. They passed within a few blocks of where they lived, but kept going. A few snow flurries persisted into the winter night.

Eric turned to her. She looked at him and saw something uneasy in his eyes. He had turned more serious.

"What?" she asked.

"There's something I need to tell you," he said.

"Go ahead."

"It hasn't been announced yet and won't be for another week," he said. He paused for a moment and then continued. "And this just became definite today, so it's why I didn't say anything yet. I'm leaving *South Pacific* in June."

She was stunned. "Early June or late June?" she finally said.

"June eighth."

She was silent. "Okay," she said. "That's a few months away. So? Time off?"

"Well, not exactly," he said. "There's a film I want to do, a major part I've been offered. Most of the filming is in Europe. Alex, I'm leaving New York."

TEN

Il Trovatore was a small but intimate Tuscan restaurant on a corner in Greenwich Village. The owner had been kind enough to set a private candlelit table in a side room, and then pulled shut the sliding door. The restaurant was situated in an old brownstone and the owner had restored two fireplaces. One was in the room where they dined. A pair of logs crackled. Alex and Eric had all the privacy they needed.

A bottle of bold Chianti was open and two glasses were in progress. Alex sipped from a nearly full glass. Eric, unwinding, loved two or three glasses after a show, not that he hadn't earned them, and not that he couldn't hold them. He was already midway through his second. They glanced at menus. Eric made his selection quickly: often he stuck to broiled fish of some sort to watch his weight. Alex spotted a small salad that sounded good. When she had put down her menu and looked back to him, he continued.

"The movie is based on a novel titled *Flowers from Berlin*," he began. "It's a World War Two spy story, set in 1939. Mostly Washington and New York, but the script calls for six weeks of filming in England and Germany. Action, adventure, espionage. Not like anything I've ever done before."

She took a moment to let all of this sink in. Then she asked, "When would production start?"

"July twenty-third of this year. I'd need to be in Ireland in early July."

"*Ireland?*"

"Well, you know how film locations work," he said. "We'll do some exteriors in Washington, New York, Berlin, and London. But we'll be shooting Ireland for England, and Hungary for Germany. Cheaper, obviously. The interiors we'll do either in Vancouver or Los Angeles. Postproduction would be in Los Angeles, also."

"How long is the shoot?"

"Eight weeks," he said. "That's if everything goes smoothly. Usually, it doesn't. So figure maybe ten weeks."

"Wow," she said with no emotion.

"This is a big film for me, Alex," he said. "I have the starring role."

"Yes. I can follow that." She paused. "Who else is in it?" she asked. "Major people?"

He named his prospective female costar, an English actress who had already won an Oscar. She was a sultry brunette, sexy and very A-list. She was also, to anyone with two eyes, drop-dead gorgeous. Alex felt a pang of incipient jealousy.

"Wasn't she just in the news for something?" Alex asked.

Eric hesitated. "Her husband turned out to be a serial womanizer," Eric said. "She just got a divorce. It's been all over the tabloids. I feel sorry for her."

"Don't feel too sorry," she said impetuously. The words were out of her mouth before she could stop them. She knew how bad she sounded. Eric looked at her oddly, as if he was completely baffled by her reactions.

Fortunately, the waiter eased into the small private room. They gave their orders and the waiter disappeared again.

Alex took a long sip of her wine. She had to draw a breath to calm down. Somehow she felt ambushed by this conversation, this turn of events. Within her were emotions that she suddenly recognized but hadn't known existed.

"Well, all that's great," she said, trying to recover. "Just great." She was trying to cover her inner feelings. What was meant to sound cordial sounded sarcastic and she knew it.

"Alex, what's wrong?" he asked.

A long pause. Then, "Isn't it obvious?" she answered. She couldn't believe how obtuse he could be, unless he was doing it intentionally. Was this, she wondered, how people like this broke off relationships? "What about us?" she asked.

"What do you mean?"

"What are you telling me tonight? You're leaving New York? You're easing out of our relationship? What are you saying?"

His eyes went wide. "No, no! Not at all! None of those things," he insisted. "Why would you even think that?"

"Well, I don't know. Maybe because you're telling me you're going to be off in Europe and California or Canada for ten weeks where, let's face it, women throw themselves at you. And it's not supposed to bother me?"

"It shouldn't. I'm not interested in anyone else or one-night flings."

The waiter arrived and rearranged the table with different utensils that would work best for their order. They made pleasantries with the server and were about to resume their conversation when a busboy arrived with a tray. The waiter officiously served them dinner and then departed, closing the sliding door again.

"This is what I do, Alex," Eric resumed. "I may be highly paid and it might look glamorous and I admit it's a lot preferable to what ninety-nine point nine percent of the people in the world do, but there's a downside. I have to keep moving and be away sometimes for long stretches." He sipped some wine. "It's not an easy decision for me, Alex," he said. "You're a big part of my life. I want you to continue to be. It won't be easy being away without you."

"Then don't go," she said, almost without thinking. "There will be other roles."

"No. Not like this one. This role is huge."

A grudging pause. "I get it," she said.

"There's nothing to 'get,' Alex. It's not going to change anything between us."

"Being three thousand miles away for six to ten weeks isn't going to change anything? Be realistic, Eric."

"And you need to be realistic, too. I can't change how my business works. This show in New York—I love *South Pacific* and I love being in this city. But this has been a luxury for me to be here for ten months. I can't wait to do it again, to get back to Broadway. Maybe in a straight drama or a comedy. But this is a huge studio production. The movie money rules the world of acting. I'm sorry. I thought you understood that."

She let his words sink in. "All right. Well, I do now," she said. "I'm just a little surprised that you didn't tell me earlier."

"This all happened within the last two days. I knew I was up for the role, but I'm always up for roles. I thought one of the younger action stars was going to get the call. He would have, but had a conflict. I think I was third on the list. So when it was offered, I accepted. My agent came over tonight before curtain with a deal memo and I initialed it. Sometimes things take forever. Sometimes they take two heartbeats. I could have told you sooner, but, so help me, the agreement is only five hours old, and aside from the producers of *South Pacific*, no one knows. My sister and parents don't even know."

"Okay, okay," she said, picking at her salad. "Sorry I seemed a little on edge."

He laughed. "You didn't. And even if you did, you didn't, okay?"

"Okay," she said. "Look," she continued, "if I get clingy sometimes, I'm sorry. I don't mean to do it. Relationships are tough for me. I've seen the best turn into dust in half a heartbeat." She paused. "I may have some authority in the office, but deep down I'm vulnerable. Know what I mean?"

"I know," he said. He looked her squarely in the eye. "Alex, trust me: If I didn't think our relationship could survive this, I wouldn't go. But I think it will." He paused. "And there's something else," he added. "As long as we're getting everything out and on the table."

"Uh-oh. What?"

"I want you to join me for part of the shoot," he said.

She looked up. "In Europe?"

"Well, yes. There are daily flights from New York, you know. Ever been to the fair city of Dublin?"

"Once when I was a student."

"Then it's time for you to visit again."

"Eric, I have a job here."

"And when did you take your last vacation?" he asked. "Spain a couple of years ago, if I remember. You must have some time coming."

"I haven't even thought about it," she said. "With Párajo going on there is no such thing as vacation. Time accrues but it's impossible—"

"Is it, Alex? Is it impossible to consider joining me for a little bit? No job is worth killing yourself over."

"I'm not killing myself."

"Perhaps someone else is doing it for you."

"Doing what? My job?"

"No. Killing you."

"Not funny, Eric."

"It wasn't meant to be."

They had rarely squabbled. They almost always saw eye to eye on everything. But, "What does that mean?" she asked.

"It means I care about you and what happens to you. I worry," he said. "You know what? I worry a lot. You're the one who should have the bodyguard, not me."

"Eric, I appreciate your concern."

"Ukraine. Venezuela. Then you were shot at and hit in Paris—an amulet saved you, or a coin or something, I forget. And you got a shoulder wound in Washington. You know what they say. Things happen in threes. Father, Son, and Holy Spirit. Three strikes and you're out. Purity, body, and flavor. Curly, Larry, and Mo. Huey, Dewey, and—"

"Oh, stop it." Her anger dissipated into a grudging smile.

With one of his usual brilliant touches, Eric had taken a serious subject and deflated its seriousness. It was one of the things that she so loved about him.

"Crosby, Stills, and Nash," he said, trying to conclude. She was laughing now. He reached across the table and took her hand.

"Earth, Wind, and Fire," she said. "Bacon, lettuce, and tomato."

"Groucho, Chico, and Harpo," he said. "Always think in terms of actors."

"I do," she said. "I think in terms of my favorite actor. And we both know who that is." Her voice caught for a moment. "I'll miss you horribly," she said.

"Okay, Alex, look. Listen to me," he said, switching back to seriousness and holding her hand. "Look me in the eye and listen. Please?"

She did. He was rarely more handsome and forceful than when he turned boldly serious like this.

"Alex, I say all these things to you only because I care about you so deeply. But I'll be blunt: I wish you were in another line of work. Okay, I finally said it. If someone walked in here right now and aimed a gun at you, I have no doubt that I'd jump up, get in the way, and take the bullet for you. But I don't want to live a life where something like that could ever happen."

She was quiet.

"It's not as dangerous as that, Eric," she said, trying to dismiss it.

"Yes, it is, Alex," he said. "Sometimes I pray that you give this job up. You're lying to yourself if you don't think it's as dangerous as it is."

"Eric, it's—"

"And this latest operation thing is threatening to change your personality," he said, in a tone of objection but without following the matter any further. "You're also the only person I know who's been shot twice," he said. "How long do you stay at the roulette table until your number comes up?"

"Eric, this is what I do."

"But do you have to? Are you going to change the world? Are you going to save it?"

"Probably not."

"Then there are other options," he said. "Alejandra LaDuca doesn't have to be in the line of fire every day of her life."

"I hear you," she said. "There's not anything I can do about it tonight or tomorrow, but I hear you. All right?"

"All right," he said. He went back to his meal. They ate in silence for what seemed like several minutes but was actually only one.

Then, "Sorry," he said. "I didn't mean to lay a heavy topic on you. Two, in fact: me leaving New York and all the stuff about your job. I didn't mean for us to have this conversation now. You're smart, you're beautiful. You're young, you're talented. But this job of yours. Man! If I were your husband, I don't think I could handle it."

She stared at him.

"Sorry," he said.

"That's all right. There's never anything wrong with honesty," she said.

"Párajo," he said after a moment. "Can't you hand it off to someone else?"

"I don't want to."

"Why? Because it's personal now between you and that . . . that monstrous woman hanging out in Mauritania? Or Monrovia?"

"Morocco," she corrected. "And maybe it is personal."

"Maybe? Of course it is."

She searched for a snappy response and realized that she didn't have one.

"Promise me you'll come see me when I'm filming. I have no desire to be with anyone but you. It's you I want to spend the time with. Promise me that if there's any way you can get away—two weeks, three weeks, leave of absence—you'll do it."

"Eric . . ."

"Promise me."

"If I can, I will," she said.

"That's better," he said. He came around the table and kissed her. At that same moment, the waiter slid back the sliding door, stepped in to see how things were going, began to speak, and saw that things were going commendably. He quickly pivoted, closed the door, and left.

Eric and Alex laughed.

"Let me get to the other side of Operation Párajo," she said. "Let me see if the operation can be wrapped up or at least the central part. There are a few new leads in the works, nothing I can tell you about. Then we'll see where we are, you and I. Okay?"

"That's all I ask," he said. "I realize it's quite a lot. But it's all I ask."

ELEVEN

The next morning Alex returned to the usual daily grind, made worse this week by the time needed to review with her legal counsel any material that might come up in the upcoming Congressional inquiry. Sarah Fedderman, the lawyer, was scheduled to teleconference with Alex that afternoon. But now the meeting with Lena was also on Alex's mind. She looked for Andy De Salvo first thing in the morning, but he wasn't in yet. Another doctor's appointment. He would be there after lunch, his secretary told Alex.

Alex went back to her office and made a move on her own. Trying to maximize her odds of survival, she put in a call to FinCEN security and arranged for an armed federal marshal—male if possible—to be present with her on Thursday evening. The marshal would take up a position in the hotel lobby and maintain surveillance on Alex, her guest, and the room. There was no point going over there alone and making herself so vulnerable. There was something about the meeting that she already found unsettling.

What, she wondered, was the subtext for the meeting? Where, if anywhere, was the hidden agenda?

She thought further about her meeting with Lena Smirnova,

Federov's daughter, on Thursday. Some of the federal marshals who provided security were great. The others were a bunch of semi-senile old goats who couldn't be depended on to be there on time. One never knew who would show up, or not show up. Hardly in a mood to relax her caution, Alex phoned her old acquaintance Sam Deal. What would be so wrong with double coverage on Thursday?

Sam was one of her most useful friends, if not the slipperiest. The lamentable but ever so valuable Sam Deal was retired, or so he alleged. In a previous lifetime, however, he had been the moving spirit of the "Nightingales," an old CIA black bag and dirty tricks team for Central and South America. Sam was a glorious sort. Not only did he know where the bodies were buried, but he knew where the shovels were stashed, and whose palm prints were upon them.

Deal was currently enjoying his "retirement" as the head of security of one of the best-known and most highly respected New York jewelry stores on Fifth Avenue. Sam didn't know everything but he had opinions of everything and, despite being nearly seventy years old, still had contacts almost everywhere.

"Sam, honey," Alex intoned. "I'm calling to flirt."

"Sounds good," Sam said.

"You still carrying a gun twenty-four/seven, I hope. Didn't lose your permit or anything?"

"Same as you, Alex. It's like that little green plastic card. I don't leave home without it."

"Good. Want to watch my back on Thursday night in Peacock Alley? I'll buy you dinner sometime later in the month."

"Why not that night?" Sam asked.

"I have a boyfriend. He's an actor."

"Unemployed, huh?"

"No, actually, he's doing well. He's on Broadway."

"Have I heard of him?"

"I'd be surprised if you hadn't."

"You're on, LaDuca. I want a name."

"Between us?"

"Yes, ma'am."

"Eric Robertson."

"Holy smoke! Yeah?"

"Yeah."

"Why are you even working?"

"Sam," she sighed, "we're going out, that's all. We're not married or anything. No ring, no future talk, just having fun."

"I like it," Sam said anyway.

"Well, keep it to yourself," she said.

"I've seen him in the store here a couple of times, your Mr. Big Shot friend."

"Well, you don't know anything from me or anyone else, okay?"

"Okay, LaDuca," Sam said. "Now what's the burr under your saddle?"

"Waldorf. Two Thursday evenings from now. Watch my back, please? I'd like that."

"How do you know either of us will be alive in two weeks, Alex?" Sam asked.

"Don't joke about stuff like that, Sam."

"Okay, okay. You got it, sweetie. God willing. I'll see you there. I like it a lot, Alex," he said. "A lot. Not just the dinner, but watching your back. Take that any way you want."

"I'll take it as polite, flirtatious, fantasy-ridden, lecherous, and harmless all in the same breath," she said. "And right now, after a beast of a day, I can use it. So, thanks, you old letch."

"You know me too well," Sam laughed. "See you on Thursday."

Alex sat quietly for a moment, pondering the conversation with Sam. Then the phone rang again and Sarah Fedderman her attorney was on the line,

"What's up, Sarah?" Alex asked.

"You just got a reprieve," Fedderman said.

"What's that mean?"

"The day you're going to be called has been rescheduled. In fact, the whole hearing is being pushed back a few days. We have some extra time to prepare."

"I'd just as soon testify and get it over with."

"We don't get to choose the dates, obviously. And sometimes there are reasons for these delays," she said. "Sometimes the committee is on to some new line of questioning, something new they want to look into before calling witnesses. Doesn't mean it's about you, of course. Could be, but probably isn't. Might be, might not be. Who knows? It's a guessing game. All we can do is be ready."

"A guessing game," Alex repeated. It was, increasingly, more than that. It was a pain and a distraction, a grenade in her work schedule. She and her attorney conferenced for ninety minutes. Then they adjourned for the day. They scheduled a final tune-up for the following Monday.

If the committee was going to give Alex a reprieve, she was going to take it. After all, there was always the chance they might lose interest altogether and never call her.

She could dream, at least.

Then, glancing at her watch, after breaking to get a cup of

coffee, she returned to the miseries of Central America, as set forth in a classified file in front of her.

Andy, her boss, never turned up for the entire workday. The FinCEN offices continued on autopilot once again. Increasingly, Alex prayed for Andy's health. She was getting a bad feeling about it, despite the cheerful façade he seemed to maintain.

Alex never saw Eric that day, either, although she did check in with him by phone three times. He was having dinner with his agent that night. Alex had been invited to join them but couldn't break away from the legal hound or the office till eight thirty. Then she picked up dinner on the fly, spent an hour at the gym, and collapsed into bed by ten thirty.

Too many days, she thought to herself as she drifted off to sleep, were resembling each other.

TWELVE

The gated community of Vista Del Lago, two miles north of Tucson, Arizona, was the final address and destination for about a thousand residents, most of whom had moved there from other parts of the United States. It was comfortable and secure—usually—a place in the sun in the sunny Southwest. Never mind that the "Lago" was man-made and that the fish that had originally inhabited the lake for recreational purposes had all died from a bacterial infection. A few of the sharper souls, usually grown children visiting, saw that as a metaphor but kept their mouths shut, much like the deceased fish should have.

The new couple had introduced themselves as David and Sarah Lee Davenport. David was in his late fifties and Sarah Lee appeared to be about a decade younger. They had purchased one of the prime condos in the complex about six months earlier, one of the big three-bedroom ones that overlooked the golf course. Both of them played. They said they had had a sailboat in Florida but had sold it. David produced pictures. There was something funny about them to the other residents—funny, not as in amusing. Anything but. Funny as in there was just something about them that didn't add up.

Their money added up, however. They spent it as if it were going out of style. David said that his family had been in the mining business back east. Anthracite coal in Pennsylvania, he said, although he was hazy on the specifics beyond that. He hated the miners' unions with a passion, didn't care much for black people or Catholics, didn't like the federal government or any government. David was a sorehead, a major one. At Vista Del Lago, he made several new acquaintances, but no friends.

At least he had a golfing partner: his wife. Sarah Lee Davenport was actually better than her husband. She was a big, broad woman, an inch taller than David, and could hit a golf ball farther by thirty yards. David had been a wrestler in college, reputedly at a private place back east.

The Davenports didn't endear themselves to the community of mostly retired Americans who lived within the walls of Vista Del Lago. David was habitually cranky, as if suffering from an unseen malady or disease, or maybe even some bad recent memories. His wife was worse, most frequently described by the other ladies at the community with a one-word, two-syllable adjective that rhymed with "twitchy." But, again, most people in the community were older people, most of them white, and everyone took it as common knowledge that when people grew older, they either became mellower or their character flaws became more accentuated. The Davenports fell into the latter category.

The first serious issue was the flap over golf balls and extra lights.

The Davenports' condo was split level. It was built onto a hillside that overlooked the golf course, though the entranceway was at ground level off one of the roadways. Every once in a while, a duffer shanked a shot and it hit David's roof or balcony. This wasn't all that unusual. People who live around golf courses tend to get used to such things, but David always made something akin to a federal case out of the incident. He would emerge from his condo in a fury, carrying a nine iron. He would find the offending ball and chase down the suspected sportsman whom he felt was culpable. That, or he'd tee it up and whack it back toward the course, laden with verbal obscenities.

Then there were the lights. David seemed obsessed with security around his unit, even though the larger community was gated with a guardhouse and there were plenty of security cameras. So David installed extra lights on the side of his unit, lights that would illuminate the contiguous area surrounding his unit as if it were the landing field of a major airport.

Neighbors complained. The lights were a violation of condo rules. They blazed all night. The Davenports were asked to remove them. They refused. The condo board took the case to a local court where the condo board prevailed. Grudgingly, David went and found a ladder, made a noisy production, and removed the lights from the exterior of his unit. Then he repositioned them indoors within his unit, one in the living room, one in the bedroom, and aimed them out the windows at the same area.

The unit had no legal recourse on this wrinkle. The lights remained. Neighbors purchased heavy curtains.

Sarah Lee Davenport, David's charming bride, didn't lag far behind in the obnoxiousness factor. Shortly after arrival she quickly made herself unpopular in most of the lounges. She was abrupt, argumentative, would violate the prohibitions against smoking within the buildings, and was given to testy, patronizing arguments with the condo's staff, most of whom were Latino.

She would yell orders at them in her poor Spanish. She was mean and condescending, and made contemptuous, racist remarks about them behind their backs. No one complained, but many residents were ill at ease with the behavior. "David and I lived south of the border," Sarah Lee once explained to another resident. "You have to know how to deal with these people."

"Where did you live?" the neighbor asked.

"All over," she said after a pause. She never elaborated.

In turn, the Davenports' neighbors and acquaintances made contemptuous and unkind remarks about them, too, behind their backs. Rooms were known to fall silent when they entered. Golfing foursomes went out of their way to exclude them, or as one golfer said, "To include them out."

"Everybody doesn't like someone," said Mrs. Hawkins one day after the Davenports had thrown yet another ugly, spiteful tantrum in a common area, then stalked away, "but nobody dislikes Sarah Lee and her husband."

The line traveled around the community as if Vista Del Lago were a high school and this line was the latest who's-going-out-with-whom rumor. The line was repeated everywhere with great mirth.

At last, the Davenports had given their neighbors something to laugh about.

THIRTEEN

A lex's old friend Gian Antonio Rizzo had worked with her on a dicey operation or two in the past and had been a mentor as well as a spiritual advisor, spiritual in the sense of high spirits rather than of the theological sort. Nonetheless, Rizzo, a devout Roman Catholic, was a man who knew the world, how it functioned—or at least how it was dysfunctional. He was formerly of the Roman city police as well as the CIA bureau in Rome. He exuded both charm and brash opinions.

Rizzo arrived in New York and was staying at a midtown hotel, one of the best ones, naturally, so Alex took the occasion to grab the subway uptown immediately after work. They met at a hip Mexican restaurant on Lexington Avenue in the '50s and spoke Italian.

"I need the brush-up on my Spanish," Rizzo said, "if I'm going to South America."

"But you're going to Brazil," Alex retorted.

"And Portuguese, the mongrel language they speak in Brazil, is beyond me, Alex dear," he said. "Far beyond me. Ever heard it? It sounds like a drunken Spaniard trying to speak French. So Spanish is my back-up tongue."

"Fair enough," said Alex over guacamole.

Rizzo was traveling alone this time. His dear Mimi, his

current young squeeze, had gone ahead of him to Brazil where she had a developing business in cell phone apps that carried agricultural reports. Rizzo began by touting the brains and beauty of his Mimi, how he missed her, and how he was so anxious to connect with her in another ten days. Then he started to sniff around what Alex was doing. Alex brought him up-to-date on the romantic interest in her life, how falling in love again made her secure and insecure at the same time. They laughed and joked about the things love does to otherwise sane men and women.

"My boss is retiring to the Algarve in Portugal," Alex said eventually, bringing the discussion back toward her office. "Andy says hello, by the way, and says I can tell you that."

"Ah, well, send my good wishes for his retirement," Rizzo said with raised eyebrows. "Armação de Pêra has some of the world's finest unspoiled beaches. Soft sand, beautiful cliffs. Mimi and I spent a week there last year. I believe I took a thousand pictures. May I also say, do tell your boss, that there is a tiny seafood restaurant called Al Tasca that is heaven on earth in the summer. Pleasant staff, wood-beamed interior, master chef, and tables spilling out into the late summer daylight. Their spicy grilled prawns are the best. Highly romantic," he said with a sigh.

"Andy's been married for forty years to the same woman, Gian Antonio."

"Well! Then he owes her a trip there for dinner. Better, after he moves, Mimi and I will take him and his wife there. Please tell him that."

"I will. He'll be amused."

"Now what's going on with this miserable Párajo project?" Rizzo asked next, with a squint and an inquisitive turn of his head. "Amuse me with the evil progress."

Alex brought him up-to-date, finding herself describing in summary a stalemated situation in which each side was waiting for the other's next significant move.

"Alex, my dear," Rizzo finally said. "Listen to me. In a game of chess, we do not need to attempt to capture the king with every move. One piles up smaller victories with other pieces until the king is defenseless. A knight here. A bishop there. A rook falls and the pawns go down. I do not know if I'm overstating or understating your war with the Dosis as a chess game, but it is a war and it needs a strategy. You agree?"

"I do," Alex said.

"Well then," he continued, "you also must learn to think outside the rules. How many times have I compared you to the noble character in *Braveheart*? Did you see that movie? Mel Gibson, before he darkened himself with his professions of anti-Semitism."

"I saw it," she said.

"Did you see the ending?"

"It's not like I walked out with fifteen minutes to go."

"So you recall how it turned out for the heroic and principled warrior?"

"I remember."

"Alex, you need to start thinking outside the box on your Dosi adversaries," he said. "Here's the thing. If the leaders, Signor and Signora Dosi, go down, their organization goes down. Right now, you have dealt them several blows. But you have not put them out of business. They will remain in business because they will stay beyond your grasp, rarely if ever showing their faces outside of countries that do not maintain extradition with the United States. It will be a game of tiger's paw. You will make attempts to bag them by the rules and you will be unsuccessful. Why? Because they will not be foolish enough to put themselves at a point of risk, the point where you want them to be. Meanwhile, they will break every law to eventually have you murdered. That's how they are, how they think. And they only have to be successful once and you are dead. I would not want that."

She was silent. Her eyes moved away then came back. "Gian Antonio," she said. "You're leading this conversation somewhere. Where?" she asked.

"Let's take an example," he said. "Do you know of a French singer and songwriter named Jean-Jacques Goldman?" he said.

"Of course. I remember from when I summered there as a university student. Very popular, very cerebral."

"For the last twenty years, Jean-Jacques Goldman has been the most successful French-language songwriter and singer, performing his own songs or offering them to the big stars: Céline Dion and Johnny Hallyday, to name two. I regret, he is little known outside French-speaking boundaries. Still, the French album he wrote for Céline Dion in 1995 is the French bestseller album of all times: more than six million copies in the world, including close to four million copies in France!"

"So?"

"I want to tell you about his late brother," Rizzo said. "Pierre Goldman. Pierre was born near the end of World War Two, the son of parents who were active in the French Resistance. When he grew, Pierre obtained his baccalaureate and pursued courses at the Sorbonne. In 1963, he joined the Union of Communist Students. In 1966, he refused his compulsory military service and traveled instead to Cuba, where he heard Fidel Castro. He remained in Havana for the memorial after Che Guevara's death.

From there, he traveled on to Venezuela and spent a year there in guerrilla activities: attacked an army arms depot, later robbed the Royal Bank of Canada in Puerto La Cruz, Venezuela, and returned to Paris and committed several robberies of small businesses, including one in 1969 on the Boulevard Richard-Lenoir near Place de la Bastille in Paris, in which two pharmacists were killed. He eventually drew a life sentence for his various undertakings. During his time in prison, he studied philosophy and Spanish. Like too many other smart people with too much time on their hands, he also wrote a book. The book was about his favorite subjects: himself and leftist revolution. As happens in America, he drew many intellectuals and celebrities to his case. He won a new trial, was acquitted, and was freed in October. This was in 1976, I believe. Upon his release, the little rodent that he was, he promptly returned to his left-wing agitations. A public menace. A criminal with no boundaries, no walls, no redeeming social value."

"So?" Alex asked. "Your point is?"

"Here is where it gets interesting and has what, to some, would seem to be a happy ending. In September of 1979, he was assassinated at point-blank range in Paris by three gunmen who appeared to be Spanish. The gunmen escaped and have not been found. There are various theories. The most serious one points to the criminal underworld of Marseilles. It is said they did the job on behalf of the Grupos Antiterroristas de Liberación, a death squad set up by Spanish officials to fight the Basque separatists, the ETA, in the 1980s. Goldman was helping ETA get weapons and planned to create an organization to fight the GAL, it was said. In April 2006, *Libération*, a communist publication, published an interview with a former French police officer named Lucien Aimé-Blanc. Aimé-Blanc stated that one of his informants had admitted, a few years later, having killed Goldman along with some other right-wing gunmen from the Marseilles underworld on behalf of the GAL. Well, that settled the Pierre Goldman problem, didn't it? Once and for all."

There was an awkward silence before Alex spoke. Finally, "So why are you telling me this, Gian Antonio?" she asked.

"How many times that you know of has the Dosi woman made an attempt on your life?"

"Twice that I know of," Alex said.

"And we wonder how many times that we don't know of," he said next. "Do you think she is somewhere in her Moroccan hideaway watching reruns of *The Six Million Dollar Man* in French or Arabic? I think not. I suspect, and I have heard rumors to this effect, she is embarked on yet another attempt."

"I'm not surprised," Alex said.

"I think you should get her first," Rizzo said bluntly.

"Well, that's what we're trying to do."

"No. I mean, I think you should kill her before she kills you."

There was a beat as Rizzo's suggestion sank in. Alex was horrified. "You're asking me to sanction her murder? Are you kidding me?"

"Why would I jest? Yes. That's what I'm suggesting. That is what I am urging, Alex. Put things in motion."

Her horror grew. "I can't do that! That's not the way we work. Even if I wanted to, I couldn't just order—"

"There are ways," Rizzo said softly, interrupting. "Maybe this is more common to European police agencies than American ones. But—"

"No!" Alex said.

Rizzo rolled his eyes in frustration. "Do you know, the murder of Goldman was first attributed to an organization known as *Honeur de la Police*, the Honor of the Police. He was an enemy to his own nation, he even said so himself! He killed people and probably plotted to kill more. The individual I mentioned, Lucien Aimé-Blanc, was a former French police officer in charge of the Narcotics Department. Why shouldn't these people have defended themselves with the very weapons that were being used by the criminals?"

But by now, Alex had frozen herself out of the discussion, knowing fully that any such attempt on Yardena Dosi's life was contrary to the law, morality, and her own sense of justice.

But Rizzo wasn't finished.

"You don't like my suggestion," he said.

"Not in the slightest," she answered.

"Well, if the Dosi woman burst into this room right now," he said in the noisy restaurant, "and drew a pistol and aimed it at you, would we not draw our own weapons and try to fire first?"

"It's not analogous, Gian Antonio," Alex said.

"Why not?"

"Because she's not in this room aiming a weapon at us. There remain other ways of dealing with her."

"Ah. But then you agree that it would be a last resort? In the end, when all else has failed, get her before she gets you."

"We're not there yet," Alex answered.

"Maybe we are," Rizzo said. "And you're just too decent and God-fearing. You just haven't admitted it yet."

At that time, two plates of quesadillas arrived. Alex was going to continue the discussion, but Rizzo changed the subject.

FOURTEEN

Six thirty in the evening. New York. Greenwich Village.

Carter Wilson walked eastward through Greenwich Village toward Astor Place. At age twenty-eight, trim with deep mocha skin and casually disheveled black hair, he had settled now in New York since legally emigrating from the West Indies. He made a good living on whatever brushes, an easel, canvas, oil paints, and imagination could bring to an aspiring artist, and made an even better living at what he referred to as "carpentry." By day he would paint and display in a section of Washington Square that was open to artists. In a good week, he might sell a painting or two to a tourist who would inevitably try to barter down the price. On most days, particularly in the spring or summer when the Square was alive with tourists, he could do quick sketches and portraits for twenty to fifty dollars. It was a comfortable way to make a living and an excellent way to cover what he really did. Whenever someone had a complicated problem, particularly from his old country, they would travel to Borough Park in Brooklyn and "visit the carpenter."

He dropped off his artist's supplies with a friend who lived on Second Street, stayed there for about an hour, split a sandwich, and refreshed himself. Then he walked to Astor Place, entered the subway, took a downtown local, and connected to Brooklyn. His one-bedroom apartment was in a six-story brick building, well maintained and comfortable. There was no elevator. He climbed the stairs two flights. He pushed a key into the lock on the door of his apartment—

Immediately he knew that something was not quite the way he left it. The door. The double lock on the door had been fully turned that morning when he left. Now it was singly locked. One turn of the key had opened the door. Not two.

There were only two explanations. Burglars. Or someone needed some carpentry work. He hoped it was the second.

"Michael?" he said aloud as he walked in.

It was always this way. He never quite knew when the connection would appear, the agent who arranged the jobs for the people back home.

"Who did you expect?" a voice said from the open kitchen area. The unannounced visitor sipped a can of beer from the refrigerator. "Santa Claus?"

Carter grinned and closed the door. "What's happening, man?" he asked.

"Got some work for you," Michael said. Like Carter, Michael spoke in the lilting intonations of the old country, a place he too had left far behind, but a place to which he still maintained some important links. "Like to travel? Out of town?" Michael asked.

Carter shrugged. "If the price is right."

"The price is very right, my friend," Michael said. "Safe to talk here?"

Carter booted up his sound system and accessed some Cee Lo Green. "The neighbors hate this," he said. "They come and bang on the door. They pound on the walls. I ignore them." He laughed. He grabbed a beer for himself and settled in on the sofa.

Michael settled on a chair across from the sofa, a coffee table between them. A calico cat emerged from somewhere, looked at the guest with disapproval, yawned, and walked sullenly to the adjoining room. "Two for one. You travel. You fix two pieces of furniture. You come home."

"Travel where?"

Under Cee Lo's boom and bawl, Michael named a place three-quarters of the way across the United States. He had photographs and information. He described the job in great detail. He also provided a throwaway cell phone with a hundred dollars of call credits on it—this way, Carter could communicate with him and whoever back home had ordered the repair.

Carter listened carefully, studied the information that had been prepared for him, and looked at the pictures. The latter had been taken very recently with a long-range surveillance camera. He nodded frequently and asked a few questions. It was an interesting job, fixing this situation.

"You want it?" Michael finally asked.

"What's the money?" Carter asked.

Michael found another envelope, this one inside his shirt. He pulled it out and dropped it on the table. It landed with a thud.

"Half now, half later, brother," he said.

Carter glanced down at the envelope. Then he reached for it and opened it. It was filled with well-worn United States currency. Hundreds. Fifties. Twenties. Carter did a quick count. There was ten thousand dollars in the envelope.

"These people must be in bad need of fixing."

"Very bad," Michael said. "You're in?"

"I'm in."

"Enjoy your travels," Michael said. "When it's confirmed the job is done, I'll be back with the other half."

The two men embraced. Michael disappeared into the night. Carter went out for an excellent dinner, pleased at his unexpected payday and his overall good fortune.

FIFTEEN

Rick McCarron brokered the meeting between Alex and Frank Gonzales.

They met at a bar in Brooklyn Heights, half past four on a cold, wet afternoon when Alex also had to be back in the office by six. Frank was a stocky man with a weathered look to him, a tired face that suggested that he had just returned from an uncomfortable voyage, which, Alex knew, he had, metaphorically at least.

Frank wore a New York Jets windbreaker and sat at a corner table facing the door, which was where Alex found him. He appeared as if he had been there for several hours, accompanied by a bottle of Jameson and a shot glass. As he spoke, as they initiated a conversation, Gonzales found it difficult to form a paragraph without a profanity in it. Alex didn't react and simply went with it. Then again, sometimes he shut off while she was speaking and scanned the room around him, keeping a watchful eye out for enemies, real and imagined.

Alex thought back to what Rick McCarron had told her about Frank: that his father had been mixed up with drug barons in Colombia and gangsters in Honduras, and that Gonzales had started out his adult life at sixteen in much the same profession. Someone had shot his father from an ambush when Frank was seventeen, and he'd become an emancipated minor. He would have been on his way to prison at eighteen, but a talent scout from the DEA had spotted him and offered him a job as a turncoat, ratting out some of his higher-ups.

He had been turning and ratting ever since, subsidized by the United States taxpayers even if they didn't know it. If Frank was in the gray area of the law, it was definitely dark gray, probably more than fifty shades of it. McCarron had made excuses for him and actually liked the man: he was an *hispanohablante*, he knew the Honduran underworld, and his information was good. What more could the CIA have asked?

"So?" Frank said to Alex after less than two minutes of small talk. He was nursing one straight-up shot after another. "What's on your mind, Alex?" His air was midway between affability and irritability. "I don't know why a pretty girl wants to get messed up in a sewer like Central American drug transit, but that's on you, not me."

"I read several of your reports," Alex said. "Impressive stuff."

He sniffed. "Sure. Yeah," he said. "Thanks."

"You don't think so?" she said.

He shrugged. "Not so much, no," he said. "What I wrote up was just looking out the car window, just seeing what was going down on the streets of San Pedro Sula. What else did you want to know about it? I put everything I knew in the documents."

"It's not so much that I want to know more," Alex said. "I'm trying to get a greater sense of what's happening in Honduras. A feel more than facts."

"Feel, huh?" Gonzales snorted. "That's a good one." He briefly gnawed his left thumbnail.

"Feel," she affirmed.

"San Pedro Sula, huh?" he retorted. "You going to go there?"

"Maybe."

"What for?"

"Things." It was her turn to shrug. "Don't be coy, Frank. You know what I'm working on. Operation Párajo. Trying to shut down the Dosi operations."

"Oh yeah, *that*," he said. "Well, listen, I'll give you your San Pedro Sula in a nutshell. You're talking about the most murder-ridden city of the most homicide-addled country in the world. How's that for one step out of the starting gate? Know what I used to do there, know where I used to hang?"

"Why don't you tell me?"

"I used to go see the murder families. The families of slain sons and husbands, wives and sisters and girlfriends. They'd meet every two weeks in a concrete slum building next to the Iglesia de Nuestra Señora de Guadalupe, a Roman Catholic church. Plastic chairs, wooden benches, cigarettes, little statues. Lots of prayer and torment. These people, they dreaded birthdays, anniversaries, and Christmas. They knew who the killers were who had ripped apart their families, who'd killed their loved ones, and they knew that the gunmen would never be arrested and that the local authorities weren't going to do diddly squat. The group, my group, had sixteen families when it started five years ago. Two weeks ago, last time I communicated, there were two hundred. Every one of them had someone in a case that remains officially unsolved. They lean forward, they whisper, they'll give you a name. They'll say, Hey man, you're American, you're powerful, you have the juice here; can't you whack the suspected killers? I'd like to but I have to tell them I can't." He paused and sipped some water. His eyes were red and angry. "The other name that surfaces, if you hang in the church, in tones real hushed-like, is 'Maras.' You know that one, right?"

"Yes. It's the street name for the local gang. It's the real power and force in San Pedro Sula."

"You done your homework. Good girl. You speak Spanish?"

"I'm fluent."

He tested her. She passed with high honors.

"You *are* good," he said. "Where'd you learn to talk Spanish so good?"

"On my mother's knee. She was Mexican."

"Ah. I shoulda known. Impressive. You got a boyfriend?"

"Yes, I do."

"He a cop also?"

"No."

"What's he do?"

With a pause, she said, "He's an actor."

"Ha! Meaning he waits tables, huh?"

"Oh, he works fairly often," she said.

"Yeah, right. Where else you going in Hondo?" he asked. "San Peedy, okay. Gonna get out in the countryside," he taunted, "let the trafficantes take a few potshots at you?"

"Mosquito Coast, maybe."

"You're loaded for bear, huh?"

"I'm trying to take down a kingpin," she said. "We both know that."

"And she does, too, right?" Frank asked. "Doña Yardena de los homicidos?"

"Correct," Alex said.

"Okay, go on out there to the Mosquito Coast, if you want a firsthand look," Frank said. "Maybe you'll see why the Dosi woman will probably outlast you. She won't come to the US so you have to play your game in her ballpark. That's a losing proposition. Go take a look in the harbors. Get the view the tourists don't see. The cartel speedboats are parked in the wharfs of the river towns in broad daylight. The merchants and traffickers live in big cement houses. They tower over the wooden structures of the typical Miskito home. The wise guys go out for walks through town, show off the hookers they've flown in from Miami, and don't even conceal their semiautomatic weapons. You're talking 'narcotierras.' Narco-land. A wholly owned subsidiary of international organized crime. The cocaine flights in, clandestine airstrips, clandestine landings in official airports, they're not even secret. The locals will tell you about the bales of cocaine that sometimes washed ashore; some villagers collect them to resell them to drug traffickers. Some villagers in the region are so involved in the narco trade that drug addiction has also become a problem. Go to the fishing towns. Take a look at some of the Miskito lobster divers. They juice themselves on cocaine and pot to dull the pain of decompression sickness. Know what? I don't blame them."

Frank followed his rant with another shot of whiskey.

"May I ask you a question about one of the reports?"

"Ask me anything you like. If I don't like the question, I won't answer it."

"You mentioned a DEA operation in May of 2012 that blew up. Some civilians got killed."

"Yeah. I remember it. I was there for that."

"What happened?"

"Read the report."

"No, what *really* happened?"

"My opinion? The Americans completely misread the situation, as usual. The army people, the CIA, the DEA, and the people like yourself who pull strings from an office in a skyscraper."

"How?"

"Look," he said. "The US drug people seem to think that everyone in the Mosquito Coast is involved in drug trafficking. That ain't so. I spent some time there. I lived in villages. You do that and you'll meet a lot of humble and honest people. They operate hostels for the tourists, work as guides or forest agents, prepare food, farm, build canoes, and fish. You'd be moved by their spine in forging a living in a tough, hardscrabble place like this. They work hard despite the long odds, the clear lack of government interest, and the vengeance of the drug lords. I was in Brus Laguna one time during a visit by President Manuel Zelaya. The trip was a fake photo op, nothing more. It was so short that leaders of fifty thousand indigenous people who live in the region didn't even have a chance to roll a tortilla with him. Zelaya scooted off in a private plane after posing for photographers sent from the capital papers."

"So you didn't like Zelaya. Get in line. What's your point?"

"My point is that the innocent people are caught in between. You got a triangle: the cartelistas, the Hondo government, the Americans. To my mind, it's hopeless. It's like that narco war that's been going on in Colombia for fifty years. No winners, just victims. Look, the raid in 2012 that left a bunch of local people dead? The Americans claimed no innocent villagers would be in the river in the middle of the night, near where helicopters had landed. The Hondo government parroted what the Americans said. That just showed you how little they knew. In that area the lagoons and rivers are the roads and highways. Residents use boats and dugout canoes to go from village to village. Helicopters and planes are too expensive, donkeys are too slow. Forget about cars and buses. There aren't any. Most of the inhabitants earn less than two dollars a day. So people travel on the water during the night, because covering the distance between one village and another can take up to a day."

Frank lit a cigarette and sipped more whiskey. Alex waited.

"Hey, I remember coming back by boat from a long trip in the jungle and arriving at the lagoon in Brus Laguna close to midnight," he continued. "The light of the moon showed my Miskito guides the way back. I remember thinking how peaceful and beautiful the Mosquito Coast was. How warm and welcoming the air of the lagoon was. It was a godly place, almost spiritual. Then along came mankind to ruin it. The Americans come out of the sky with choppers and automatic weapons. They should leave it alone, you know that?"

Alex shrugged. "Just let the coke lords have their way?"

But Frank was finally starting to feel his liquor and an aura of belligerence overtook him. "Who do you think buys their junk, Alex? Get real. It's smuggled into the US because white suburbanites want to use it. If there wasn't a market here, they wouldn't smuggle it in."

"I understand your point. But I draw the conclusions differently."

"Sure you do. You sit in an office. If you really do go to Hondo instead of blowing smoke about it, you might see things differently. It's like that botched raid in 2012. The explanations provided so far by the Honduran and US officials just show their lack of understanding of the realities of life in the Mosquito Coast. Even if US agents didn't open fire, they provided the equipment and support to the Honduran security forces to do so. There is blood enough to go on almost all the hands involved here: Honduran, American, mine, yours. If a hopeless situation exists in this world, this may be it."

"As I said, I'm trying to bring down a drug kingpin. The world will be a better place without her."

"And you don't stand a chance!" Frank snapped, suddenly very indignant and angry. "She'll be dancing on your grave before you even make her break a sweat. Can't you see that?"

"Again, we draw different conclusions."

"Aw, what are you even bothering for, lady?" Frank said, now furious. "I'd toss in the towel on this one, if I were you," he said. "Call your Dosi operation a stalemate. Or call it a victory. Or a loss. Call it anything you want. I'd just walk away while you still can from it, if I were you."

"You're not me."

"Nope. But I'm like you. More than you think. There was a time when no one could talk any sense into me, either. Wish I'd have listened. You take a good look at me here, lady. What you see is yourself, just a few years down the road."

She drew a breath. "So how do you think—?" she began.

But he gulped down the end of his whiskey. When he finished the bottle, he finished the meeting also. "Don't even ask!" he said. "There aren't any answers. And what do you care, anyway? You sit at a desk and draw a salary and it's the dumb humps like me who go out in the field who take all the risks. Want to know a secret? I hate all of you."

He wiped the last drops of whiskey off his lips and stood. "Go reread the reports," he snarled. "Everything's there. I got nothing more to say."

Frank's closing statement, as Alex would remember it, was remarkable in its prescience. He dropped money on the table, rose unsteadily, and traipsed to the door. He shouldered through the door with belligerence. Through glass panels on the door, Alex could see him stop outside in the cold and start a cigarette. Then she heard the sounds of a reception committee.

There was a rapid-fire burst of loud popping sounds. Alex recognized them immediately as gunfire: serious caliber, maybe nine millimeter, so fast that she took them to be automatic weapons and probably more than one.

She saw the frame of Gonzales's body as it hit the barroom door hard, and she saw the woodwork and windows ripped with holes from stray shots. She heard shouts on the street and she heard the sound of traffic. She saw Gonzales in silhouette as he slumped against the outside of the door.

She drew her pistol and ran to the door. She edged it open and went through, her weapon in one hand, her FBI ID in the other. Gonzales was at her feet, still moving. Whoever had whacked him was long gone.

Gonzales had been hit at least four times. Alex bunched his jacket and staunched the flow of blood. His heartbeat persisted. A cabdriver appeared from somewhere with a cell phone and called 911. The rain fell harder, cold, wet, and nasty, but Alex was on her knees and stayed with it. An EMT team was there within two minutes. The techies were swift and efficient. They put Gonzales on life support and plugged his holes as best they could.

Alex rode with him in the back of the ambulance. They arrived at Kings County Hospital twelve minutes later, and Gonzales was in the Emergency Trauma Unit within fifteen. Police arrived and debriefed Alex. She spent the evening at the hospital and didn't phone Eric till after his performance. Midnight arrived and Gonzales remained on life support, his words still echoing in Alex's mind:

"There was a time when no one could talk any sense into me, either. Wish I'd have listened. You take a good look at me here, lady. What you see is yourself, just a few years down the road."

SIXTEEN

The man in the white tropical suit sat in the corner of a well-shaded and well-guarded café in Rabat, Morocco. He nursed an iced espresso. A steely-eyed woman sat across from him.

"To your health," the man said. He sipped. They spoke in English.

"To yours as well, Monsieur Debray," Yardena Dosi said.

"And to the resurrection of your empire," the visitor added. "Which will, of course, be inevitable once the 'obstacle' is removed."

The visitor was in good spirits and looked none the worse for his tussle at the Debray residence in Paris. These things happened in the visitor's line of work. Sometimes frequently.

"So tell me what you have in mind, Monsieur Debray," she said. "This is the first time we've worked together. I know you by reputation. I know you can arrange to get things done. So talk to me."

"It's very simple," said the European. "I am Antonin Debray. I am the best broker of assassinations in the world. You need to have this meddlesome American policewoman murdered and I can arrange it. For a price, of course."

"What are we talking about in price?"

"Two million dollars. Plus expenses. Well worth your investment to get your empire back."

Señora Dosi kept him in her gaze. Around the room, the visitor counted at least six of her local guns.

"Keep talking," she said.

"I can set things up. I can get this job done for you. But you have two problems that I can see from the beginning."

"And those are?"

"First, Miss LaDuca would be impossible to successfully murder in the United States. Her death would be attainable, but escape would be impossible. And I have no good network within America anymore. Security since September eleventh has taken its toll, unfortunately for people like myself."

"I have an organization within the United States," she said.

"And it is filled with informers, stool pigeons, amateurs, and traitors. I wouldn't touch it with a stick."

Señora Dosi fumed.

"With me, nothing will go wrong," he said.

"And what's the second problem, Mr. Debray?"

"Since the target cannot be reached in the United States, she will have to be drawn out of the United States. For that, a trap must be baited." He paused. "And you must be the bait."

Now the señora looked fit to explode. "Excuse me?" she said.

"Only if the LaDuca woman is on her way to meet you will we know exactly where she is for the few seconds of vulnerability that we need to effect a kill. It's that simple."

"I have extradition problems in most parts of the world," Mrs. Dosi answered.

"And you have millions of dollars stashed all over the world as well. You grease the proper palms in the proper countries and your local police agencies will stand down, and governments will look the other way. I daresay you know how it works better than I do."

Dosi stared across the table at the European, not knowing entirely what to make of him. "You're bold, aren't you?"

"I need to be. How many guns do you have in this café, for example? Six? Ten? Most men wouldn't have walked in here. Plus I see your husband lurking in the front. I'm bold because I need you and you need me. Brazil, Guatemala, Uruguay, Venezuela, Paraguay, and Panama," he said.

"What are you talking about?"

"That's where my organization is most effective. That's where I have people. Match one of those countries with a settlement of your extradition problems and that's where the hit can take place. You'll need to travel there to draw out your victim. I see no other way to accomplish this."

"Two million dollars is much too high," she said.

"You employed a man named Velez in New York many months ago," the visitor continued, "and for your efforts you received nothing. Instead of being free to move around the world, you are captives in a half-baked Arab state."

"You seem to know a lot about me, Monsieur Debray." "Of course I do. You were making inquiries, about me. Don't you think the word would get back to me? As soon as I heard of your inquiries, I investigated why you might be asking. We both work for money, so there's very little mystery of our objectives. We are, in fact, a lot alike. However, if your empire has fallen so hard that you now must be cheap about what you are attempting, you will have the same results as you had with Velez in New York. That's your choice. Thank you for your time."

He half rose.

"Stay seated," Señora Dosi said softly. "We will meet your price."

The visitor sat. "Excellent," he said. "And the venue? Would you like more time to consider that?"

She thought for a full minute.

"No," she said. "The South American countries are too far away and difficult for easy entrance and exit. Guatemala is wild and unpredictable. But I still have friends in Panama, despite everything. I would think Panama would be the venue."

"Then as soon as I receive your payment, things will start to fall into place. Do we have a deal?"

"We do."

She extended her hand. They shook. Moments later, the visitor was in a car driven back to the airport by a Dosi gunman. There, under the watchful eye of his chauffeur, he caught the four p.m. Air France flight back to Paris, from whence he had arrived that morning.

SEVENTEEN

The activities lounge at Vista Del Mar was empty, other than the three women and one man who sat around the card table, deeply engrossed in both cards and conversation. Outside, the Arizona sun pounded anyone foolish enough to be out. Inside, in the lounge and in all the other buildings in the community, the air-conditioning churned.

"Witness protection," Ethel Rahilly said in low, subdued tones. "They're in the witness protection program. *That's* what's wrong with them."

The "them" in her sentence meant David and Sarah Lee Davenport. She sat around a bridge table with three friends. One could think not much different from this conclusion, Ethel said, almost whispering, after what she had seen this morning. Why, two gentlemen from the FBI had come to the door, inquiring.

"Whose door?" asked Goldie Klein from across the table.

"Mine. Then theirs," Ethel said, recounting.

It hadn't been the FBI's finest hour, as she described it. A pair of agents, big white guys who looked like alums from big Midwestern colleges, came to her door. "Nice young men," Ethel said. "They knocked. They showed their badges. Oh, I got a good look. FBI. Phoenix office. But they thought *I* was Sarah Lee Davenport. Imagine. Ha! Glad I'm not."

"Why did they think that?"

"Wrong address," Ethel said. "They drove all the way out here from Phoenix, then came to the wrong door. The Davenports live two doors down."

Her neighbor, the jowly ex–New Yorker Irving Klein, snorted and played a ten of clubs. "That's where your tax money goes," he said. "To people who can't follow directions."

"I wouldn't hold it against them so much, the FBI boys," Ethel said. "The doors aren't marked that well here. Easy to mistake one for the other."

"Did you send them to the right door?" Goldie asked.

"I did, yes," she said. "Two doors down. But I didn't close my door all the way. I stood and watched. You should have seen what happened. David, that's the man, came to the door and the next thing you know there's a tremendous argument, all this yelling and shouting. The FBI boys are trying to be calm and David is in a rage that they even showed up. They took a few steps back, delivered some sort of message, it looked like, or instructions. Then he threw a cup of coffee at them."

"*Who* threw *what*?" Irv Klein asked.

"David threw a cup of coffee at one of the FBI agents," Ethel answered. "Can you imagine that? No respect for anyone."

"Did it hit him?" Irv asked.

"Looked like he blocked it with his arm," she said. "But it was all over his sleeve. I watched him use a handkerchief to clean up. Then they were yelling at each other in obscenities. I won't repeat." She shook her head. "F-bombs. Disgraceful!"

"If they drove all the way out here, I wish they'd have shot him," Irv Klein said.

"They can't shoot him over a cup of coffee," Ethel Rahilly said.

"They can shoot you over anything these days," he said. "This administration will shoot anyone. That's what it's coming to."

"They let anybody buy into this community now. Not like it used to be when you could screen out the bad apples."

"Gin," said the third lady at the table, Mrs. Hazel Morrissey, laying down her cards.

The others stared at the suite laid down. They folded their cards.

"So what do you think—?" Irv Klein began to ask, sounding as if he was returning the topic to the FBI visit.

But Ethel Rahilly held up an index finger to her lips and threw an obvious glance toward the window that looked onto the walkway that led to the lounge. There was Sarah Lee Davenport approaching. A moment later, Sarah Lee entered the room, which had already fallen icily silent.

"Let's total up the points," Irv Klein said, returning to the cards.

EIGHTEEN

On Thursday morning, Alex was interviewed in her office about what she had seen when Frank Gonzales was shot. New York City detectives interviewed her as did representatives of the FBI. She was obliged to discuss parts of the Dosi case with each, which she did not wish to do. Again, her job seemed to be strangling her, leading her to uncomfortable places, and ratcheting up its suggestion of mortality.

Meanwhile, Gonzales remained in critical condition at a Brooklyn hospital in an area where NYPD cops stood guard. He had no immediate relatives to call.

In the evening, trying to retain her focus on the Dosis, Alex left work at six thirty. There was a secure government Escalade waiting to meet her in the building's garage, part of extra security that had been put on Alex since the incident in Brooklyn. The driver was armed, the vehicle bulletproof. It merged easily into the rush-hour traffic on Duane Street and made its way uptown, taking an indirect route on local streets. The driver was a plainclothes security man named Fred who had driven Alex before. They chatted cordially. Alex munched a PowerBar from her purse, a sorry excuse for a real dinner, and watched the city roll by. As was increasingly common at such times, she longed to "have a life," as her friend Laura Chapman would have termed it, to be able to be an anonymous woman in a good job but one not physically threatened at all hours.

She phoned Eric, who was backstage, preparing for his evening performance. They made plans to have a late dinner on Saturday and maybe spend some time together on Sunday. His showtimes had moved to five p.m., which gave them most of a day to spend together.

They arrived at the Waldorf at six twelve. Fred eased the car into the secure area of the garage under the hotel. As visiting diplomats from all over the world stayed at the hotel, the security was always tight.

Fred jumped out first, scanned the area for potential danger, saw none, and opened the backseat door for Alex. She stepped out. "My guess is that I'll be about an hour," she said.

"I'll be here," Fred answered.

Alex walked briskly to the entrance to the hotel. She spotted some Israeli security and American security, most likely from the United Nations. She exchanged a glance and a smile with some of the agents, a tacit professional courtesy, though guarded and wary. She proceeded to the lobby by elevator.

In another five minutes, she seated herself in the plush bar known as Peacock Alley. As was her habit, she picked a small table for two that gave her a good view of the lobby in front of her as well as the bar and restaurant that were behind her.

She looked around. She found the federal marshal easily. He was a dark-haired man of about forty. She recognized him. He was parked in front of a drink and a laptop, his attention split between the two. There was a long bar running toward the restaurant to her left, lit by mirrors, flattering lighting, and a prodigious collection of working bottles.

A row of plush bar chairs ran along the counter. Alex scanned the bar. She found Sam Deal easily, standing with his back to her about thirty feet away. Sam was watching her through the reflection in the mirror behind the bar. He lifted a drink—it looked as if Sam had a bourbon on the rocks going—and gave her a quick little salute that would have been picked up only by the two of them. She had told Sam about the marshal and had told the marshal about Sam. She guessed that they had made contact with each other. They probably even knew each other.

A waiter appeared. Alex ordered a sparkling water. She glanced to the lobby, looking for Lena Smirnova and appreciating the ironic echo of having met her father in this same place, at this very table in fact, if she recalled properly. Alex had a good mind for such details. The waiter reappeared swiftly with her drink.

He served. She sipped. No Lena. Not yet.

Alex watched the lobby as guests checked in at the reception area. Other guests reclined, relaxed, and chatted in the embroidered armchairs scattered generously around the lobby. There was an arcade of luxury shops, jewelers, clothiers, electronics, and cell phone companies. Two airline offices. The stores bracketed the distinctive gold clock tower in the center of the lobby.

Behind her, the bar was busy with wealthy New Yorkers and tourists, largely foreign, meeting for a drink after business, as a prelude to theater or to dinner. Still in a dark suit, she blended in nicely.

The waiter returned with a small dish of nuts and pretzels.

Alex, hungry, grabbed a few and munched, then scanned the lobby again. Bingo. A tall, blond woman in a trendy suit and a flowing leather coat was striding toward her. She was astonishingly pretty, drop-dead gorgeous in fact, with blond hair falling to her shoulders, a short black dress beneath an open flowing coat of soft brown leather.

She turned heads as she moved and she knew it. She could have passed for a Kournikova or Sharapova or one of the other world-class Russian tennis vixens. But no. She was a Federov: the face, the eyes, and the arrogant self-assurance. The swagger. Alex could tell instantly. She could feel it across the room.

She came to Alex's table and hovered for a moment. She stood about five-eleven in low heels. "Lena?" Alex asked.

"I'm Lena," she said. "You're Alex." She said it as a statement, not a question.

"I am," Alex said. "Please join me."

Like a tigress, Lena slid into the other chair at the table. Predictably, Sam turned sideways at the bar to watch, eyes widening. She slid out of her coat and let it fall onto the back of her chair. She was svelte in the stylish black dress: Alex guessed it was Vera Wang and brand new. Alex also guessed two grand for the dress, another five for the coat, another ten large worth of metal on the wrists and fingers, plus maybe five hundred for a pair of Jimmy Choo's. At such times, Alex hated the way her own mind worked. She had spent so much time on financial crimes that she was too familiar with the swag gained by them.

"I picked you out without much problem," Lena said pleasantly to Alex. "My father described you once."

"Oh? In person?"

"In a letter I received. After his death."

"Ah. I see," Alex said.

The waiter reappeared. "My father also mentioned a specialty drink here," she said. She turned to the waiter, looked up, and turned the full heat of her cornflower blue eyes upon him. "The 'Peacock'? Is that it?"

Alex was already assessing and assimilating. Lena had just a tick of a foreign accent to her English, with a few inflections of Canada as well. The thought bounced back into Alex's head that if Lena was the Federov daughter that she had once known about, she was most likely the daughter of the wife whom Federov had been in the habit of thrashing back in the 1990s, a woman who had fled to Canada, most likely with US government help as they sought to compile a case on the gangster.

"The 'Peacock' is one of our special vodka drinks," the waiter explained. "Cranberry-infused Russian vodka and apricot brandy with a sour made here at our bar."

"Sounds like fun," Lena said.

"It's very popular with our guests," the waiter said, with understatement.

"Go for it," Alex said. "The vodka is top of the line Sputnik stuff. You'll circle the earth on your way home."

Lena laughed. "You'll join me?" she asked.

"Not tonight, thank you. I'm on my best behavior these days."

"You don't mind if I do?"

"Why would I?"

"Then one Peacock," Lena said to the waiter. "No, actually, make it a double. May we do that?"

He didn't flinch. "Certainly, madam," he answered. He nodded and disappeared.

Sure, Alex was thinking with amusement, for the prices

they charge here, they'll bring you anything legal you ask for. Just be prepared to pay.

Lena turned back to Alex. "Ну что? Давайте говорить по-русски," she said, asking if they could switch to Russian.

Without missing a beat, "Я не против," Alex answered, agreeing.

Lena began with backstory. She had indeed been born in the United States and then moved to Toronto. Her mother had been the last of Yuri Federov's long-suffering estranged wives. Her mother had remarried another Russian in Canada, an émigré who was an upright businessman who owned some interests in the jewelry business, mostly on the importing end. Lena didn't explain much, other than that her mother had sought anonymity, her new father had been a good, loving parent, and she had taken her adoptive father's name. Lena's Russian was solid and fluent. There was a little tick in it, much like her English, an émigré accent. Alex wondered whether Lena was one of those international types she had encountered from time to time, who spoke no language perfectly, but several languages charmingly, and had something interesting to say in all of them.

Her drink arrived. It was tall and impressive. She fell silent, other than to thank the waiter in English. Then she resumed in Russian.

"Toward the end of his life," Lena said, "he reached out to me. I think he was seeking forgiveness. Or perhaps just peace of mind. Or solace of some sort. I don't know. I do know that my mother wanted no part of him. Always suspicious. Always afraid."

"Why shouldn't she have been?" Alex asked. "He was brutal

to her. He tyrannized her. If you don't mind my saying so, he was venal, vile, and despicable."

"Oh yes," she said, sipping. "This I know."

"How did he 'reach out'?" Alex asked.

"Yuri Federov had contacts in almost every important city. Toronto was no different. Anywhere there was a Russian mafia, he had his enemies but he had his friends. My father made a lot of trouble for a lot of people, but he also enriched a lot of people. So some emissaries came to see us. First my mother. Then me directly. I was finishing university at the time. University of Toronto. He let us know he knew where we were and wished to help us in any way he could."

"No threats? Nothing forcible?"

"Not at all."

"When was this?" Alex asked.

"In the final four months of his life, as it turned out," she said. She paused and took a longer sip of her drink. Alex liked it when her sources liberally consumed vodka. *In vodka veritas*. The alcohol didn't add to their eloquence but it enhanced their loquaciousness. "I also think he stalked me. Or had me stalked. Maybe had a picture taken. Or several. It was creepy, but I knew I was being followed, watched. But as soon as I caught on and started to avoid certain places, it stopped." Another pause, then, "The next thing I knew it was several weeks later. I heard he had died."

"How did you hear?" Alex asked.

"My mother received a certified letter from attorneys in Switzerland. There was a question of whether they had ever been legally divorced."

Alex laughed. "That's a fine mess. It reflects on your parents' marriage."

"My mother divorced him in absentia in Canada," Lena said. "Many years ago."

"Good career move," Alex said.

Lena ambushed Alex with her next sentence. Smiling, "I hear he wanted to marry you," she said. "And he left you some money."

Alex sighed. "It's a desire that I in no way shared with him," she said. "And, yes. He left me a generous sum. I didn't ask for it, by the way. It came as a surprise. A shock."

"Same with what I was left," Lena said. "He was a changed man in his final years. You had something to do with it, I think."

"I wouldn't know. I couldn't speculate," Alex said.

"But did you think he had changed?"

"Honestly?"

"I like honesty."

"I think he was starting to come to grips with the evil he had done in his lifetime. I think he had begun to understand, or maybe suspect, the presence of a higher authority. God perhaps. We discussed it a lot. He was always the skeptic. But to give the benefit of the doubt, I think he may have been concerned with heaven and hell or whatever he thought might follow, if anything. He couldn't undo what he had done, but maybe he tried to make amends. I don't know."

"That's interesting. Thank you," she said.

"Is that what you think?" Alex asked.

"Yes. It's very close to what I feel," she said.

About a third of Lena's titanic hit of booze was already gone. And she didn't seem to be affected by it yet at all. Ah, the Russian DNA, Alex marveled.

Lena's face took a different cast. She appeared as if she were about to propose a question on a touchier topic.

"Let me ask, also, since you're very pretty," she began, proving Alex correct. "I've been wondering. Were you ever his mistress, even for a short time?"

"No. Never."

"You never slept with him?" she asked, surprised. "Not even once?"

"No."

"You're sure?"

"I'd remember it if I had, Lena," Alex said with some annoyance. "And it's none of your business, anyway."

Lena finished her drink. "I didn't think so. But I wondered," she said with no apology. "He spoke so glowingly of you."

"'Spoke'?"

"*Wrote*, actually, I mean again," she said, continuing in Russian. "In his final weeks," Lena said, "I think he was in a hospice in Switzerland. He wrote me a long letter, asking for forgiveness, asking for understanding." Alex was silent. "That's how I knew about you," she said. "He wrote to me, mentioned you by name, said she had met someone wonderful in the latter stages of his life, someone who had showed him aspects of life that he never knew existed, talked to him about culture that he had always made fun of . . ." The waiter came by and glanced at Lena's empty glass. She gave him a nod and held up two fingers. He smiled and picked up the glass to get her another double round. "He also made a short recording. Put it on a computer disk. Said pretty much the same things, covered the same ground. Asked my mother to forgive him for his brutality. Tell me, did he believe in God and heaven and hell? Did he ever say anything?"

"We touched on it, as I said. I told him God would judge

him, which was all that was important. That's what I believe," Alex said. "I never thought he believed it."

"Don't be too sure," Lena said. "I showed the disk to my mother. I shared the letter with her. She was shocked in a way that she had never been shocked by him before. She said he was a changed man."

"He was a dying man," Alex said. "And, as I said, it's not for us to judge now that he's gone."

"I burned the letter. Would you wish to see the disk? I never thought of that."

"No. Not really."

"Good. I already destroyed it," she said as the waiter delivered another Peacock. "I'd had enough. I didn't want to replay the whole thing all my life. Better to move to the future."

"Probably wise of you," Alex said.

"I think so," Lena said. A long sip on her second drink and the glass was down by a third. She shifted in her chair to get more comfortable. A bare knee with perfectly tanned, smooth skin emerged at table level, then folded itself away again. She gave a prim tug to her skirt, trying to cover more leg. The tug failed. She gave up. Her blue eyes worked the room, then came back and crashed into Alex's.

"He left me eight and a half million dollars, US," Lena said. "He left my mother another twelve million. After taxes." Alex opened her mouth to speak but Lena kept going. "I know: he left you two million. That's fine. That's good. Thoughtful of him, you know? How dirty is the money?"

"What do you think?" Alex answered. "Your father was a hoodlum. A year of expiation at the end doesn't erase the previous half century. The money is what it is. Filthy."

"Have you kept yours?"

"So far."

"Would you advise my mother and me to keep ours?"

"Why not? You suffered for it. You can't give it back to his victims."

"That's what my mother said, too."

"Is that what you came here to talk to me about?" Alex asked.

"Only partially," she said. "That was the first thing, asking you about the money. There were three reasons. The second was, I wanted to meet you. Eye to eye. In person. I wanted to see the woman who had made such a profound effect on my evil father."

"Well, now you have," Alex said noncommittally.

"Can we be friends?" she asked.

"There's no reason why we can't be," Alex said. "I don't hold grudges, and even if I did, I have nothing against you."

"Thank you," Lena said. She finished her drink. "That means a lot to me. More than you might imagine. "You see, if my father was not getting sex from you, he must have seen something even more elevated in you, something that captivated and fascinated him. I think that is wonderful."

Lena offered her hand to Alex. Alex accepted it with a polite but tentative squeeze.

"What was the third thing?" Alex asked.

Lena reached into her purse and pulled out an alligator wallet. From it, she pulled a fifty and a twenty. Before Alex could offer to split the tab, Lena dropped it on the table.

"I did some research on you. Both formal and through contacts. I can see you're a principled person, but you've made a lot of enemies. Probably some very bad ones."

"You could say that," Alex said.

"Since my father died, his old adversaries have laid off me. They know I had nothing to do with him and have no desire to continue his business. So why would anyone hurt me? But some of his friends, people who owed him and liked him, have come forward. They've made themselves known to me. It's as if they liked my father but know he didn't treat me or my mother well. So they're available. I have ways of contacting them if you ever need a favor, help, something unofficial or official; I feel I owe you something huge. And they feel they owe me. See how it works?"

"I appreciate it," Alex said. "What type of favor?"

"Anything. Anytime. Any place."

"What type of favor?" Alex repeated.

"Oh, I don't know," she added facetiously. Maybe. "Suppose you need someone to disappear. And you want to do it back channel, hey?"

Alex stared at her and thought she was kidding, making a conscious imitation of her father. Then, when the thought had sunk in, "That's not the way I do things."

Lena laughed. "Perhaps not. But someday I would want to do you a favor. Maybe of another type."

"Maybe of another type," Alex said, now anxious to end this.

But Lena wasn't letting things finish. Not just yet. "My father said you were a highly educated woman. Wise and knowledge-able, particularly as to languages, literature, and history."

"Your father always flattered me," Alex said. She felt like glancing at her watch, but didn't.

"So this is my final question to you, Alex LaDuca," Lena said. "During the Second World War, even after hostilities were aflame, do you think that Franklin Roosevelt maybe had the telephone number of someone who knew the telephone number of someone who knew the telephone number of someone who knew Adolf Hitler?"

Sorting through Lena's hypothesis, Alex got the point. "Probably," she answered.

"Well then, seeing that you have your own war going, I read in the papers about you and Operation Párajo. I saw clips of your press conference. You and Mrs. Dosi. And I hear some things from my own sources. People I know, you know?"

"I don't doubt you have a few good connections, Lena," Alex said.

"Ah, yes. Of course I do. But now, don't you think I might know someone who might know the numbers that would contact Señora Yardena Dosi?"

"Okay. What's that got to do with anything, Lena?"

"Perhaps your adversary wishes to communicate with you. Perhaps she too has had a change of heart, like my father."

"I'd be shocked."

"The same way you were shocked with my father?" Lena asked.

"Point taken," Alex said. "But what I'd like from my adversary is surrender and an arrest," Alex shot back. A pause as Alex processed the idea. Then, "Are you here to sound me out on that?" she added in a whisper.

"I'm here to try to return a favor. I like you. I admire you."

"So you *are* sounding me out."

"Maybe. Are you saying that you would never negotiate a deal?"

"That's correct!"

"But you negotiated one with my father."

Stymied, Alex answered, "I was merely the conduit. It was 'negotiated' by the people I worked for."

Lena laughed. "The Eichmann rationale. Just 'following orders'? You?" she asked, a bit of a student of history herself.

"Don't compare me to a Nazi, Lena," Alex said.

"But if there were desire for negotiation from the other side, that would be something to relay to those you work for?" she asked.

Growing more irritated, Alex sighed. "I concede, it *might* be of interest," she said. "So if you wish to pursue it, feel free. It doesn't mean I'd be inclined to do a deal, far from it. But if you want to look into that route, go for it. I'll report whatever you come back to me with."

"Very fine," Lena said.

"I'm not holding my breath," Alex said.

"The world is strange," Lena said. "Remember, I came here to do you a favor."

"I'll remember."

Then Lena flashed some more leg, along with a radiant smile. She slid her arms into her coat and rose to go.

Lena pulled a business card from a coat pocket and handed it to Alex, who accepted it. The card bore only Lena's name and a Canadian phone number. "That's my cell number. It takes calls anywhere in the world. Just call. Anytime. For anything."

"Thank you," Alex said. Lena was her father's daughter in more ways than she could count.

The meeting was over.

"До свидания," Lena said.

"До свидания," Alex answered. Good-bye, good-bye.

Lena turned and walked away. Alex stared at the card and

considered crumpling it in the ashtray. Instead, for more reasons than she could count, she slipped it into her wallet. To her right, she saw Sam, his eyes rolling. On her other side, the federal marshal was leaning back and pretending to survey the lobby as he watched Lena depart.

Many eyes were on Federov's daughter as she disappeared through the revolving door that led onto Park Avenue. Many thoughts were in Alex's head, not the least of which being that Lena surely was Yuri's little girl, all grown up, and that the apple never fell far from the tree.

Alex remained where she was sitting. She watched Sam at the bar as he continued to nurse his drink. Alex waited five minutes. Then she left the hotel by the passage that led to the secure area in the garage, the federal marshal twenty feet behind her as she walked.

Later that evening, she received a message on her phone. After lingering between life and death for more than a day, Frank Gonzales had died at the hospital.

NINETEEN

Friday evening, a man in dark Armani glasses came through customs at Bogotá in Colombia carrying a European Union passport issued in France. He was in his midsixties, trim and agile, dressed stylishly in a dark blazer, open-collared light blue shirt, and the best custom-tailored tan slacks that a Roman tailor could make to order.

As a courtesy, as a veteran of immigration procedures, he removed his dark glasses as he came to an immigration inspector's station. He gave his name as Antonin Debray, the same name as on the passport. Nonetheless, he spoke perfect Spanish, with a lilt that was more Mediterranean than Parisian. There was a similar quirk to his English. The immigration inspector at the airport asked perfunctory questions. The visitor said he was from Toulouse, where such strong regional accents were not uncommon, though he lived now in Paris where he worked. He also said he was visiting Colombia on business.

Ever vigilant for the wrong type of visitor coming to Colombia, those seeking to do business in narcotics, the inspector pressed the issue a little and inquired as to the nature of the arrival's business.

"Music," said the European. He explained that he was there on business as a representative for a major entertainment conglomerate. It was his business to scout emerging musical talent from Latin America and bring the artists to the attention of his bosses back in London, Geneva, Rome, Madrid, and Paris. From such discoveries, stars were born. As two of the top performers in the world were currently Colombian—Juanes and Shakira—such visits to the Colombian capital were hardly unusual.

The inspector, himself a man with an extensive music collection, looked up with more than cursory interest. "I envy you your job," he said.

The visitor shrugged. "I'm one of the lucky ones," he said. He glanced behind him to see if he was holding up a line. He wasn't. Quickly, he reached for his wallet. He flashed his business card, which did list him as a vice president of a music conglomerate. Then he separately flashed a photograph that he kept in plastic in his wallet. "Look at this. This is from Rome last year. You like this?" He showed a picture of himself with Shakira, impressively flat bare midriff and all: Shakira's, not the arriving passenger's. The picture looked as if it had been taken at a private party, maybe something post-concert.

The inspector raised his eyebrows in appreciation. His eyes widened. "Indeed! *De veras! Impresionante!*" he said.

"As I said, I'm one of the lucky ones. I love my work."

Debray grinned and tucked away his photographic character references.

The inspector laughed. "You are, sir. I wish I could say the same," he said with an ironic smile. "But at least I'm working." He stamped the EU passport and admitted the visitor to Colombia. "Gracias, señor," he said. He moved on to the next person in line, ever watchful for someone jittery and suspicious.

The visitor took a private car from the airport into the city and registered at the Hotel Cesar, not the more comfortable Alamagne or Generalissimo, which he might have preferred and where he had stayed before. He figured to be in Colombia for a week, maybe more if his girlfriend could join him later. He wished to be comfortable, but he was well known at the other, better hotels. The last thing he needed was to be spotted by someone who knew him. Some of the work he was to accomplish in Colombia needed to be discreet.

An hour after check-in, shortly before midnight in Bogotá, the front desk phoned the guest's room. "A package for you, señor," the clerk announced. "A gentleman just left it for you. Should we send it up?"

"I'll come down for it," the guest replied, pleased. The drop had been prearranged with a man named Vicente, whom he had never met personally but knew as a trustworthy contact. Debray expected the parcel from a contact. Nonetheless, it was good that things seemed to be proceeding as planned.

Debray took the elevator to the lobby and retrieved the parcel, rather than allow extra hands upon it. He brought it back to his room, locked the door, and made sure the blinds were drawn.

He examined the package carefully. One never knew what was booby trapped these days. He turned it upside down. In the bottom right corner were three small lines plus a circle, made with a green marking pen. This was a signal from his contact that this package was as expected. If anyone had tried to slip something harmful to him in its place, it's doubtful that an enemy would have known the proper coding. It changed each day, according to the date.

So he opened the box, still with some caution. As he had

anticipated, there was a small pistol within, a Walther PPK 9mm short. He checked it immediately to make sure it wasn't loaded. It was not. He hefted it in his hand. It would conceal well even beneath the clothing he needed for warm South American weather. With it came its companion pieces, a box of three dozen bullets and a nylon holster, the type a man could attach to a belt and wear under a jacket. *Perfecto.*

Also perfect was the location of the hotel, right in the center of La Zona Rosa, where visitors and local people found the best places in the city to hear live music and new performers. On Carreras 11 and 15 and Calles 81 and 84, one found a vast array of cafés, pubs, clubs, and live music venues.

The visitor could see many of the clubs from his window as he edged the curtains aside and peered out. Part of him urged him toward a few minutes out on the town that evening. But the more rational part of him took priority. He was tired and jet-fatigued, exactly the state in which a man could make a foolish small mistake.

So instead, he packed the pistol away and ordered a light supper from room service. He was ready for business and was set to proceed on the following day.

TWENTY

In her office, Alex looked at her watch. It was twelve fifteen. Early lunch hour. Her timing was good. She closed her office door and locked it. Transformation time.

She reached into the duffel bag she had brought from her home. She laid her gun and its holster on the desk, then pulled off her jacket and skirt and kicked off her shoes. She crouched down beside her desk wearing only her undergarments and pulled from the bag a complete change of clothing. She pulled on a heavy navy-blue sweatshirt and a pair of jeans. She looped the belt. Nice fit. She patted herself on the head. Size ten. She was in good shape at five foot nine. Hadn't gained an ounce. Ducking all those bullets, she mused, kept a girl in shape.

She adjusted the jeans so the fit was comfortable. She looped the holder with the Glock onto her belt. From the bag she pulled a light parka and, in case she needed them, a pair of gloves. Outside it was in the high thirties. She had a good pair of running shoes, new Nikes. She pulled them on. In the bag, she found a pair of final items: a New York Yankees cap and a big pair of dark glasses. She was ready to blend out there in the general population of New York, no bodyguards or chauffeurs this time around.

She popped her wallet into a pocket of the parka, zipped

the pocket, and then pulled on the parka. She emerged from the office and drew a double take from Stacey.

"Well. The new Alex," Stacey said.

"How do I look?"

"Like a graduate student," she said. "More Columbia than Adelphi."

"Perfect."

Alex was out to the elevator in another minute. In the elevator downstairs, she pulled back her hair, plopped the cap on her head, and donned the sunglasses. She was out on the street and down into the subway at the Wall Street Station. Moments after that, she was speeding uptown in an IRT express, eventually to get off at Fifty-Ninth Street and disappear into the lunch-hour crowds.

Fifteen minutes later, from the Lexington Avenue exit of the subway, Alex took a short walk westward across Fifty-Seventh Street. She had always enjoyed the area of Manhattan, its excitement, pace, and fascinating, if expensive, shopping. There was no shopping on her lunch-hour agenda today, however, other than shopping for insight and advice.

On the front steps of the Pierre Hotel, she spotted the man with whom she wished to rendezvous: Sam Deal.

Sam was huddled on the far side of the steps, positioned where he could eye everyone passing. His felt hat was pulled down across his forehead, and he too sported dark glasses. His hands were plunged into the pockets of his overcoat. He looked chilled and agitated, but his expression warmed when he saw the attractive brunette walking toward him, obviously with her gaze upon him. Then his expression heated up yet another notch when he realized it was Alex smiling at him.

"Hey!" he said, looking her up and down. As he eyed her attire, the parka and jeans and Yankee cap, a small confusion reigned for a moment. "What's with you? The whole government is dressing down these days or did you lose your honest job?"

"Neither, Sam," she said. As she stopped in front of him, he took her arm and gave her a highly chaste kiss on the cheek. "I'm just dressed down to move around the city, ducking anyone that might be looking for me."

"Ha!" Sam said, releasing her. "I can feature that. Come on, let's walk," he said.

The walk took them into the southern entrance of Central Park. They bought hot dogs from a food cart and walked together.

"So what's on the agenda, Alex?" Sam asked.

She scanned in all directions and prayed that no one had a long-distance mic aimed at either of them from any of the thousands of windows that were within view. Then she went ahead.

"I want to talk to you about 'selective assassination,'" she said.

"Ha!" Sam said, a third of a hot dog in his mouth. "Are you going where I think you are?"

"Maybe," she said. "At least in terms of discussion." She paused. "You knew about some of those activities when you were in Latin America, didn't you?"

"Whoa! Maybe," Sam said with a smile.

"Regrets?"

"Who? Me?"

"You're the only one here other than me. Look, Sam, I'm not here to be judgmental. But the notion has surfaced two or three times of late that the only way I'm going to get to a resolution of Operation Párajo is to break some rules. You remember what that is, right? Párajo."

"I remember. You against that Dosi woman and her organization."

"That's right. Me against her. She launches attacks and assassination attempts against me, and I have to play by all the rules to try to lure her out from North Africa."

"That doesn't sound like much fun," Sam said.

"It's not. So there are a few little birds whispering in my ear with greater frequency. I should work outside the rules. The type of operations you used to do. Unofficial takeouts. So that's my first question. Any regrets?"

"Some," Sam said. "Actually, a lot."

"Share some details with me."

"Assassinations? Is that what we're talking about?"

"Yes."

Sam's attention and thoughts went far away for many seconds, then returned. "Okay," he said evenly. "I'll cite you some stuff I'm familiar with. I wasn't involved in the two cases I'm going to mention, but I'll tell you what I think. Game?"

"Game."

"Not to be repeated, right?"

"Of course."

"These hits, these operations outside the official way of doing things. You never know how things are going to end up, even if you make the kill," Sam said. "Look at what the CIA accomplished in Latin America with two cases: Salvador Allende in Chile and Trujillo in the Dominican Republic."

They continued to walk northward. Sam was in the habit

of looking over his shoulder every minute or so. Just scanning, just checking.

"September of 1970, Nixon was president and Salvador Allende was rising to power in Chile," Sam said. "You know what a glorious old Cold Warrior Tricky Dick was, right?" Sam didn't wait for an answer. They walked northward on a sidewalk that bordered one of the roadways through the park.

"Nixon told the CIA that an Allende government in Chile would not be acceptable and authorized ten million dollars to stop Allende from coming to power or to oust him if he did get into office. Nixon told the CIA to prevent Allende's election by financing the political parties aligned against him. It was a typical South American thing, mostly the white settler class in Chile against the descendants of the indigenous people. Class war, ethnic war, economic war. Allende was a physician, white European stock, but sympathized with the unwashed masses. He was also a Marxist. He got legally elected in 1970, the will of the people. But there was plenty of stuff going on behind the scenes. As soon as Allende was elected, the US went to high gear trying to get rid of him, killing him if necessary. Not that he didn't have his own domestic enemies. Much of the internal opposition to Allende's policies came from the business sector, companies that feared being nationalized. But the US also funded several strikes—miners, truck drivers—designed to cripple the economy and create public antagonism toward Allende. So then the Ruskies jumped right in to prop up their guy. It was the Brezhnev era, recall. During his election campaign, Allende had made a personal request for Soviet money. The Russians came up with half a million dollars, channeled through the Chilean Communist Party. The money from the KGB was probably decisive because

Allende won by forty thousand votes of three million cast. So after the elections, Allende is in the Soviets' pocket, or at least that's how Nixon and Kissinger saw it. He stated his willingness to cooperate with the Russians on a confidential basis and provide any necessary assistance, since he considered himself a friend of the Soviet Union. He willingly shared intelligence information against the United States. That sent Washington over the top. But things were really just starting to get hot. Political and moral support continued to flow, mostly through the Communist Party and the Chilean trade unions that were run by Marxists. Allende received the Lenin Peace Prize from the Soviet Union. He was their new hero, their new Che, their new Fidel, all in one. Any wonder Washington put a price on his scalp?"

"None," said Alex, who finished her expensive lunch and properly discarded the wrappings in a trash can. Sam crumpled his similarly, including the final part of the bun, and shot it basketball style at the same can. *Swish.*

"Now, there were some rocky patches between Allende and the Soviets. Moscow believed that some violence was in order for Allende to hang on to power in Chile. Allende didn't want to do that. He was unwilling to use force against his opponents. So he kept leaving the door open to being deposed. In June of '73, a rebel colonel surrounded the presidential palace with his tank regiment but wasn't able to depose the government. El Tanquetazo, they called it. The "tank putsch." For all local intents and purposes, it was organized by the Patria y Libertad, a nationalist paramilitary group. It was followed by a general strike at the end of July that included the copper miners of El Teniente. All of this trouble was financed and engineered by the CIA. Langley's fingerprints were all over everything. The Russians kept telling him that without establishing an iron fist over all the machinery of state, his hold on power would always be elusive. They tried to help him. In mid-1973 the USSR had approved the delivery of artillery and tanks to the Chilean Army. However, when news of another attempt from the Army to depose Allende through a coup d'état reached Soviet officials, the shipment was redirected to another country. Maybe the Russians could feel what was coming and knew they were going to come out on the short end of this one. It was just a matter of time. Not long after, the endgame began. The US poured more money into the pot and financed a group of army people in Chile, led by Augusto Pinochet, to stage a coup. This was September 1973. The armed forces surrounded La Moneda, the presidential palace. Allende gave a speech on live radio. He knew the end was near, but refused to resign. He also refused safe passage to another country. He talked about himself in the past tense, went on and on about his love for his country. He said he intended to fight to the end. Another hour or so and the soldiers came into the presidential palace. There was gunfire; you could hear it outside. Live radio caught it. Shortly afterwards, the army announced that Allende had committed suicide with an automatic rifle. Prior to his death he had been photographed several times holding an AK-47, a gift from Fidel Castro. He was found dead with this gun. There were pictures. The gun had been set to fire automatically. The first shots tore off the top of his head. Some gift from Fidel, huh? Rumor had it that it was gold plated."

Sam paused.

"After General Pinochet assumed power, Kissinger told

Richard Nixon that the US didn't do it, but we helped the army do it. What's the difference?" He paused. "Then there was Rafael Trujillo in the Dominican Republic. We've talked about him before, you and I. Before his assassination on a dark highway on 30 May 1961, Trujillo ruled with an iron fist for thirty years. Trujillo's rule is considered one of the most brutal periods in the history of the Dominican Republic. Taking power in 1930, his hold over the country was absolute. He brooked no opposition. Those who dared to oppose him were imprisoned, tortured, and murdered. Their bodies often disappeared, rumored to have been fed to the sharks. Ever heard of a man named Antonio Imbert?"

"I don't think I have."

"I think he's still alive today, Alex. He must be past ninety. Fifty-odd years ago he was one of the seven gunmen who ambushed and killed Trujillo." Sam lit a cigarette and continued.

"The lights went out for Trujillo in May of 1961. He was on the way to a late-night visit with his mistress. He was on the road that leads from the capital to San Cristobal, where the girl lived.

"In their vehicle, Imbert and three other conspirators were waiting for Trujillo's chauffeur-driven Chevrolet to come past. Imbert was driving. Other gunmen were stationed further up the road. Trujillo and his chauffeur were armed, and fought back. Imbert and one of the others got out of the car to get closer to their target. Trujillo got out of the car, wounded, but was still walking, so Imbert shot him again. At the end of the gun battle, the dictator, commonly known simply as El Jefe, was left sprawled dead across the highway.

"The hit was sanctioned by the CIA, if not carried out by them. The feeling was, the only way to get rid of him was to kill him. That's how it is sometimes. Apply that to the Dosi woman if you want. She's your Trujillo, your Allende."

Alex was silent. Traffic passed them.

"By the way, years after the assassination, Imbert was given the military rank of a general in the Dominican army to enable him to receive a state pension. He's officially a national hero. How do you like that? You're a roadside assassin one day, a national hero years later. Go figure. Ah, but Trujillo was trash. This guy was so bad that our CIA station chief once wrote to Washington, 'If I were a Dominican, which thank heaven I am not, I would favor destroying Trujillo as being the first necessary step in the salvation of my country and I would regard this as my Christian duty.' And this from the ambassador of the country that was keeping him in power.

"During his rule, Trujillo collected medals and titles, and expropriated property and businesses for himself and his family. He renamed the capital city Ciudad Trujillo, and the country's highest mountain Pico Trujillo. And as a US ally, there is no one more loyal. You can still go online and find a picture taken in 1955 showing him in a smiling embrace with then US Vice President Richard Nixon."

Alex grinned.

"Here's the bottom line, Señora Alejandra," Sam said. "Look at the backward logic of what happened. We take out a pro-American dictator who the CIA supported, Trujillo, and the country prospers for five decades. Compare the Dominican Republic to Haiti, the neighbor on the same island. Then we arrange the downfall of a duly elected Marxist, Allende, prop up a brutal dictator named Pinochet for a couple of decades, and we watch Chile teeter on the precipice for three decades. You go around whacking people, and it often buys you exactly the opposite result you were looking for. That's just my opinion, but I've had an up-front view of a little of this. Honestly, I'm not buying into it anymore. The world is too complicated. You asked me, so I told you."

They continued to walk.

"What I was actually inquiring about, Sam," she said, "were hits on what might be called private citizens. You know the Dosi history."

"Yeah. I know it. You got a mess on your hands."

"More than one person recently has alluded to solving the problem through unconventional, unofficial routes."

"I'm not surprised. That might be the only way you get it finished. Or not. Keep in mind, what you're talking about is murder-for-hire. Just because it's state sanctioned or Justice Department sanctioned doesn't mean it's not—"

"It's not sanctioned by anyone, Sam," Alex said quickly. "I'm just examining the parameters."

"Sure you are," he said. "And there's only one reason you're doing that. If it weren't on the table, if you weren't giving it at least halfway consideration, we wouldn't be here talking about it over frozen hot dogs in Central Park, would we?"

Alex cringed but let it go.

"Whose idea was it for you to go into this line of work, Alex?"

"My own."

"And you didn't know what you'd be getting into?"

"I sure didn't know the direction things would take," she said. "Why did you get into it?"

"I don't remember. Or maybe I just don't care to remember," he said. "Hey, listen, LaDuca," he said, taking her hand as if to draw her into confidence, and then releasing it, "the problem is that you come to some points in this type of work where you have to make decisions. New lines to cross, new morals to compromise or jettison, if you want to think of it that way. Look at me. I spent a lifetime in that world. I'm very happy to be retired, working in New York, still chasing down petty shoplifters to stay in the game. But I get a check from the government every month for social security and another one for retirement. Work done. If I had it to do over again, know what? I wouldn't have crossed those lines. Would have done a lot of things different. You haven't gone over those lines yet. But you sure as heck are getting there. Watch where you step."

"So what should I do about the Dosi situation?"

"You won some battles against them. Don't make it your life's mission. Maybe take another operation, see where you are, then hand it off to your successor."

"What successor?"

"Ah, no one stays in a job like yours so long. If you do, it eats you alive. Look at your boss. I'm surprised he's alive."

"You know Andy?"

"I know who he is," he said. "I think he was an assistant to someone who sent me a subpoena twenty-five years ago. I never forget names."

Alex laughed.

"Alex, look," he said. "About these executions: I wouldn't want to put my spoon in that soup. With me, it was a different time, different generation. If you can't get Dosi in a reasonable amount of time, hand it off to some other sucker. You're not obliged, not obligated. Those of us on the side of right, we only do what we can. Chances are, when you walk from your job, she'll lose interest in you. It'll be on to the next. Reach out and smack her illegally, you never know the ramifications down the road. That was my point about Trujillo and Allende. Play whack-a-mole with them in one generation and twenty years later, you're sitting in front of Congress. Want that when you're fifty years old? I doubt it."

They emerged from the Park at Seventieth Street and Fifth Avenue. Sam glanced at his watch. "Hey," he said. "I got to get back. Anything else?"

"Not today. Thanks."

"Gotta run," he said.

He gave her a quick hug, lingered with it, and she caught more than enough of the Sam Scent: cologne mixed with tobacco. Well, there was nothing froufrou about it. Alex knew how to go with it or let it go.

"You know what? We should have a brief affair, you and I, Alex. It'd do you good. I could teach you more in a month than you've already learned in your life. How's that? How about if I buy two tickets to San Juan for the weekend? Drinking, gambling, getting to know each other . . ."

"You flatter me. And I've got a boyfriend, Sam. Remember? Broadway."

"Oh, him."

"Him," she laughed.

"Tactful way of shooting me down, Alex. Again."

"You didn't really think I'd accept?"

"I thought I'd give it my annual shot, Alex. You're worth the long-shot roll of the dice."

"I'm flattered again. Take care of yourself, Sam."

"Yeah," he answered. "No one else is gonna."

Sam stepped back, gave her a quick wave, turned, and hustled back down Fifth Avenue, weaving in and out between other pedestrians. Alex watched him go until he disappeared. Then she turned and quick-stepped in much the same way, hustling back to the downtown IRT at Fifty-Ninth Street.

She was back in her office thirty minutes later.

"Mr. De Salvo went home early," Stacey said to Alex as she walked past.

"Problem?" Alex asked.

"Indigestion or something," Stacey said. "He said he didn't feel good."

"Oh," Alex said. "Okay."

She settled into her office. Since she had no appointments or conferences scheduled, she indulged in the more relaxing clothes.

The afternoon went smoothly, but Andy, her boss, remained on her mind. It was most unusual that he left early. In fact, as long as Alex had worked there, he had been the ultimate workaholic: in before everyone else, last to leave, rarely missing a day. Well, as almost everyone was telling her, these things took their toll.

How could anyone *not* have indigestion on this job, Alex wondered to herself. But she quietly turned the afternoon to her advantage, poring over Dosi links and Dosi material again until it was suddenly six thirty and time to head home. She would go, she decided, by way of the gym in Chelsea she had just joined.

Her old friend Ben from Washington, who now lived in New York, had joined the same gym. The two of them had fallen into their old evening ritual of playing pick-up basketball games again. She managed to get there once a week, usually Tuesdays. It was like old times, back when she lived in Washington and was in love with a different man.

TWENTY-ONE

In preparation for Alex's visit to Honduras, both De Salvo and McCarron had organized another packet of hard copy reading for her. So this morning, Alex had a series of briefing booklets, a collection of blue-jacketed documents, each one consisting of several dozen pages, all folded into a sealed file with a gray cover.

At nine a.m. Alex broke the official seal on the packet and withdrew the contents. She scanned the opening pages that warned of endless legal recriminations for talking outside the office or to anyone in the office without a security clearance about what she was about to read.

The confidentiality agreement. The loose-lips-sink-ships document. At the top was the usual "steam-rollered eagle," as she called it, the flattened bird that was the Great Seal of the United States. Olive leaves in one talon and arrows in the other.

Then the content:

I, Alexandra LaDuca, have today read the declarations of United States Justice Department Intelligence dossier HON/US-243-8-19-2011. I warrant that I will not divulge any part of this report . . .

Yeah, sure. She signed it and asked Stacey to return it to the boss's office. Stacey came for it and went. Alex leaned back in her desk chair like a graduate student attacking new material for an important course.

In some ways it was riveting.

Honduras had 82.1 homicides per 100,000 residents last year, the highest per-capita rate in the world, according to a global homicide report published by the United Nations in October that included estimates for Iraq and Afghanistan. Security concerns prompted the US Peace Corps to announce last week that it would pull all 158 volunteers out of Honduras.

As in Guatemala and El Salvador, Honduras's neighbors in the Northern Triangle region of Central America, the homicide problem goes back decades. But as Mexico's billionaire drug mafias expand their smuggling networks deeper into Central America to evade stiffer enforcement in Mexico and the Caribbean, violence has exploded, as if the cocaine were gasoline tossed on a fire.

Honduras's grim tally reached 6,239 killings in 2010, compared with 2,417 in 2005, and researchers say the count will be even higher this year. The largest number of homicides occurred here around San Pedro Sula, a once-booming manufacturing center that is fast becoming the Ciudad Juarez of Central America. That troubled city on the US-Mexico border and San Pedro Sula share more than a reputation for low-wage assembly plants and fratricidal violence. They are at opposite ends of the billion-dollar smuggling chain that extends from the north coast of Honduras to the United States.

"San Pedro Sula," she thought to herself. "Never been there and I'm not so sure I ever want to go." What am I doing in this job? she asked herself for the tenth time in a week. Self-doubts began to bark at her even worse than usual. Why am I messing with these sleazebags? I'm not going to change the world.

Sam was right.

Sam is usually right.

"If you're smart in life," she said to herself, "you learn by your mistakes. If you're really smart, you learn by other people's mistakes. Why am I reading this stuff?"

The traffic starts on the isolated beaches and jungle airstrips of Honduras's Mosquito Coast region, where 95 percent of the suspected drug flights from South America to Central America land, according to US narcotics agents. US radar detected 90 such flights into Honduras last year, compared with 24 in 2008, marking a major shift in trafficking patterns that indicates a strong preference for the country's rugged geography and feeble institutions.

In March of this year, Honduran authorities with US advisors raided a cocaine processing lab in the mountains near San Pedro Sula. The facility was the first of its kind in Central America, capable of churning out a ton of powder each month by combining imported coca paste with hydrochloric acid and other chemicals. Then, in July, a semi-submersible "narco submarine" with $180 million worth of cocaine was caught by the US Coast Guard in international waters off Honduras, the first such craft detected in the Caribbean. Since then, three more have been interdicted, two reputedly sunk, losing cargo and crew.

[Inquisitor's note, Langley/DCIA; Salvage operations in operation currently via United States Navy. See File USN-Hon/Int./Op-18r/6.24/12].

The mind boggled. Were there no limits to criminal ingenuity? She was also haunted by the opposing opinion yelps in the earlier files: your country consumes all these drugs and establishes the markets. Then you come down here and wage your wars. The snarky agent had a point.

Wars. War. Well, that's what it was, wasn't it? A war. It had all the earmarks of a war, complete with soldiers, death, and up-to-date weaponry. To her shame, she skimmed several pages when each entry started to resemble the previous one. Her overriding urge suddenly was to flee this whole operation. Yet a sense of duty, a sense of seeing an unpleasant task through till the bitter end, kept holding her.

Bitter end. She wondered why the phrase was used so commonly. Were all ends bitter? Was God telling her something? Was there a bitter end in store for her if she persisted?

She came across a recent incident that encompassed almost all the worst elements of this whole undertaking:

The pilot of a suspected drug flight killed in an antinarcotics operation in Honduras earlier this month was shot dead by two US Drug Enforcement Administration agents after he refused to surrender, an agency spokeswoman said Sunday.

At the time, Honduran police said the twin-engine plane arriving from Colombia with a load of cocaine crashed while being chased by government aircraft. One pilot died in the

July 3 incident and the second was badly injured. Officials did not say how the death took place.

When police arrived at the crash scene in eastern Honduras, they found the plane's two pilots. The injured pilot was arrested and the second was shot by the American DEA agents after he ignored orders to surrender and made a threatening gesture. It was the second time a DEA agent had killed someone in Central America since the agency began deploying specially trained agents several years ago to accompany local law enforcement personnel on all types of drug raids throughout the region.

US officials say that in late June an agent shot a suspected drug trafficker as he reached for his gun in a holster during a raid in a remote northern part of Honduras. That operation resulted in the seizure of 792 pounds (360 kilograms) of cocaine, the officials said.

A similar raid on May 11 killed four people, whom locals claimed were innocent civilians traveling a river in Honduras at night. Honduran police said the victims were in a boat that fired on authorities. The DEA said none of its agents fired their guns in that incident. The deaths come amid an aggressive new enforcement strategy that has sharply increased the interception of illegal drug flights in Honduras, which has become a major trans-shipment point for drugs heading to the United States. The country's remote Mosquito Coast region is dotted with clandestine airstrips and a vast network of rivers for carrying drugs to the coast.

The strategy involves a special team of DEA agents who work with Honduran police to move quickly and pursue suspicious flights, a US official has said. Honduran and US drug agents follow flights they detect of unknown origin and work with non-US contract pilots.

While US officials laud the strategy's successes in seizing cocaine and arresting traffickers, it has come under fire from human rights groups.

"It is quite impressive that the DEA is directly involved in the killing of alleged traffickers in Honduras, especially since it is a repeating incident. It looks like an escalation with the sense of a lack of accountability and overstepping their boundaries in Honduras. We are just getting the DEA account of events and it looks like there is no real inquiry," said Alex Mayo, a senior associate in the Center for Economic and Policy Research.

International crackdowns in Mexico and the Caribbean have pushed drug trafficking to Central America, which is now the crossing point for 84 percent of all US-bound cocaine, according to Joint Task Force Bravo, a US military installation in Comayagua, Honduras.

Midway through this report, an IM flashed on Alex's computer screen. It was from the boss. "Come in here right away," it said.

Mildly annoyed at being interrupted when she was on a good roll through some bad material, she rose from her desk. The IM seemed brusque. She went down the hall to the big office with a faint taste of anxiety in her mouth.

The door was slightly open and he obviously recognized her footsteps. "Don't even knock. Just step in here, Alex!" he said.

He was agitated. He was standing behind his desk, jacket off, flush in the face, and there were faint rings of sweat around his armpits. He looked like a man with blood pressure of three hundred over two fifty.

"Close the door but don't bother to sit down," he said. His mood wasn't just frosty. It was outright hostile. It was the first time she had ever seen such temperament directed at her, though she had witnessed it many times going in other directions to other unlucky recipients.

"I want to ask you one question, eye to eye," he said, his voice rising in inexplicable anger. "And you need to answer it for me with complete candor. Do you grasp that? One hundred and ten percent honesty. Ready?"

Taken aback, her own indignation quickly rising to rescue her, "Sure," she said. "That's how I answer anything."

A moment, then, "Is there *any* event in your background while you were working here, or immediately before, that I do not know about, that we haven't discussed, that could suddenly surface, become an issue, and bite our heads off?"

"What?" she asked.

"You heard me, Alex," he said in equally harsh tones. "Is there *anything* I need to know, don't know, should know, will wish I had known, or be sorry I *didn't* know that I don't currently know involving you and your involvement in this office?"

There was a pause as she thought hard and ran through everything she could think of. Meanwhile, her indignation simmered quickly to a boil. "Is this a bad joke?" she asked.

"No, it most certainly is not!" he said. "I just got a phone call from the attorney general himself asking me that question and reading me a few lines of the riot act. Your name was sprinkled liberally through the discussion. So, if you please, answer my question."

"The answer is *no*," she said. "Categorically and emphatically, *no!*" She held her own pause. She sensed a quick boiling and then a deflation of the tension in the room, as if she had vanquished his worst fears, whatever they may have been.

"Please think hard," he said after another painful delay.

"I already did!" she snapped. "The answer doesn't change. And frankly, I resent the way you're posing this to me. What does 'one hundred ten percent honest' mean? Do I ever answer anything here with anything less than the complete truth?"

"Well, that would seem to be the underlying context of my question, wouldn't it?" he said.

"Then I resent it all the more!" she shot back. "What's going on, Andy? What's this about?"

"Anything that could be at variance with bureau regulations and proper operating procedures. *Anything at all?*" he insisted, but in a more conciliatory tone.

"Andy, you know as well as I do that I do everything by the book, almost religiously so. There's nothing lurking anywhere. Granted, we get involved with some strange stuff now and then. But I try to toe the mark on everything and leave a proper paper trail for my own good as well as yours and this office's, just so we won't have a problem. Could I possibly be any clearer?"

He blew out a long breath and then sighed. "No, you probably couldn't be," he said.

"You never spend the night with him or anything like that?"

She seethed. "No," she said flatly.

De Salvo eased a little. "Okay," he said. She stood before the door, waiting patiently for him to speak again. "Aah, sorry, Alex!" he said. "I should have known better."

"So where's this coming from?" she asked again.

He turned away, looked out his window toward Wall Street, and then turned back. "I have spies in the Justice Department," he said. "A couple of dear old Republican ladies who keep quiet at their jobs but watch out for me. For us, I should say. This agency. They always have an eye on things for me and keep a lookout for our well-being here. These are ladies I worked with years ago. Let's call them Heart and Soul. They tip me off from time to time and I reward them and their families big-time with Yankees and Rangers tickets when they visit the Big Apple. Well, Heart just started to scream Holy Murder over your c.v. file at the Justice Department. I just got off the phone with her, and two minutes later the AG himself called me. Turns out your c.v. got pulled by someone way up high on the Capitol Totem Pole."

Alex thought about it. "Well, I'm supposed to testify next week. Is that unusual?"

"The inquiry isn't unusual. Not at all. But the process is. Someone sent the bloody Sergeant at Arms from the House of Representatives over to grab the complete file, including the highly classified stuff. Whoever did it used a 'Congressman Doe' request."

"What the heck is that? Never heard of it."

"No fingerprints," De Salvo said. "It's a Congressional perk and held anonymously. Any of those forty hundred and thirty-five zipper heads in Congress could have done it. That's the point. Can't tell who's snooping. Or why. It's like someone looking in your window at night when you're stepping out of the shower," he said with his occasional gift for a creepy metaphor. "No way to know who it was. No way to know whether to be thrilled or chilled. And we wouldn't even have known that it happened, this sneaky look-see, if Heart hadn't snitched."

"Should I be worried?" Alex asked.

"No. Not if you've done nothing amiss. But those people in Congress . . . don't even get me going about their idiocy, duplicity, and arrogance. They could make a federal case out of cleaning out a sock drawer. So be on guard."

"I already am."

"Be even more so. Be on guard even about being on guard. Ah, you know? The time is coming when we should just do all our deals direct with the Chinese. They already own us, anyway."

"Not funny, Andy."

"It wasn't meant to be." He settled back into his chair. The landing was awkward. He looked a wreck. His hands had a twitch and tremble. Alex had never seen this before. It wasn't good, not by a long shot.

"You okay, Andy?" she finally asked.

"Sure," he said quickly and with a tight, fake smile.

"You don't look okay."

"Portugal. Five months," he said. "It keeps me going. That's all, Alex. Thank you."

She turned and left, leaving the door open, just in case.

She returned to her office and settled in to work. It was only a half hour later when a bitter realization was upon her. She *had* once spent the night with Federov. Several nights, in fact. It went back two years to Switzerland when she had been abducted from her hotel in Geneva, brought to his home, and held there.

She knew she had mentioned it in her debriefing after the Madrid case was closed, but she wondered if it had ever gone into the official report. Now she was stuck in a mistruth. Should she tell Andy and Sarah Fedderman and have to retract what she had told them? Then again, if it was *not* in the official report, who could know? Why bring it up?

It wasn't so much that she was caught in a lie, but she was caught in the appearance of one, which in a way was worse. She had no idea how to play this point. She wondered if she should run it past Eric, but would he—a man she was falling in love with, a man she wanted a future with—be able to understand the bizarre nature of what had happened?

She shivered at the implications if she misplayed this.

Maybe she should run it past Rizzo, she thought to herself. He understood such things. Or Sam?

Sam, she snickered. Sam would tell her to keep quiet and keep her head down. That was his way of doing things. Sam's advice was always scurrilous. But sometimes, she reasoned, in an imperfect world, scurrilous worked best.

There. There was her decision, she told herself. She would keep quiet and hope the point never arose before Congress. Otherwise, her career would be cooked. Life, she concluded, was getting much too complicated.

She called it a day and left work.

TWENTY-TWO

Alex and Eric shared a late supper in the theater district at a little French place named Le Champlain on West Forty-Eighth Street that served supper till one a.m. for the late theater crowd. A balding stocky Frenchman named Jerome from Marseille ran the place and took special care of the actors who came in after their shows. For them, there was a small upstairs dining room. Jerome was an expert on who was feuding with whom on Broadway and the other important tidbits such as who was dating whose ex-wife; he seated his clientele accordingly and kept the tabloid press at bay.

They dined simply but easily. Alex felt herself decompressing just by being in Eric's presence. He had that effect. He was a good listener and a sympathetic, decent soul. Once she had needed liquor and prescription drugs to deal with tensions or depressive moments—now, the presence of the right person could attain an even better effect. If she had a secret fear, it was what would happen if he were suddenly removed from her life. It had happened once, so it could happen again. Emotionally, she sometimes felt like a child of the Great Depression: she could never completely trust prosperity or believe in it. She was always prepared for it to vanish in a heartbeat. Again.

Toward a quarter past midnight, Eric signed the check. Le Champlain was almost empty, just a few late stragglers. The staff was setting tables for the next day's lunch.

Eric and Alex ambled out into the cold night. Maurice was waiting. Eric held her hand.

"I wouldn't mind walking a little," she said. "I'm still kind of wound up."

"That can be arranged," Eric said.

She turned to him and snuggled close. His arm found its way around her.

"How?" she asked.

"I'll have Maurice drop us off short of West Twentieth Street," he said. "We can walk the rest of the way."

"Really?"

"If that's what you want, if that's what you need, that's what we'll do," he said.

I love you. Those were the words that came to her lips. But she bit them back. She didn't say them. She didn't have the nerve. Instead, "That would be fabulous," she said.

"Then let's go."

He gently pulled her along. Maurice held the door open to the limousine until they were safely and comfortably within.

Following Eric's instructions, Maurice dropped them off fifteen minutes later on Eighth Avenue a few blocks from where they lived. They had separate apartments in the same brownstone; Eric's was on the third floor, Alex's was on the second, hers behind specially installed bullet- and bomb-proof windows, a special and dubious perk of her employment.

They walked the rest of the way. They both loved to walk in the city, even on a frosty winter night. Maurice followed from a distance of thirty to fifty feet, the limo staying close to the side-walk on the other side of parked cars.

They arrived on the corner of Twenty-Second Street and Eighth Avenue, their home block. Eric peered down the block and Alex followed his gaze. They saw a small knot of people waiting in front of their building, maybe four or five of them, a little self-chosen reception committee.

"Uh-oh. Fans. My adoring public," he said in a low voice with a hint of irony. This had been happening with increasing frequency and pushed Eric's level of tolerance and privacy. "They can't get enough, bless them. But I'm not really in the mood for it."

"You don't want to just sign a few things and get rid of them?"

"No," he said. "Not here. Not in front of my residence. It's a don't-feed-the-bears situation. They'll keep coming back. I know. Come with me," he said.

He turned and signaled Maurice, who flashed his headlights to indicate that he read Eric's message. Alex had no idea what they were about to do, but it was clear Eric had done it before. So she went with it.

Eric gently pulled her hand. They turned away from their home block and went south on Eighth Avenue, a conversation in motion. "It's not so much the signing but the turf situation. My home is my home. I'm not comfortable with people staked out in front of it. Outside the theater, near a film set, if I'm in a restaurant. Okay, those are public places. I'll service the public there and don't mind doing it. But I believe in boundaries," he said. "You ever read the Robert Frost poem 'Mending Wall'? 'Good fences make good neighbors.' I believe in that."

"I remember the poem. From boarding school," she said. "In fact, I think Frost visited the school in the mid-sixties, toward the end of his life. He was Poet Laureate of the United States at the time."

"How on earth do you know that?"

"Just the type of thing I remember," she said. "I have a waste-basket of a mind," she added.

"You've got *that* right," he said.

They both laughed.

"Trivia," she said, trying to dismiss it.

He winked to her. "I could fall for a woman who carries a gun but knows poetry," he said, and took her in his strong arms and kissed her.

They walked past a Greek coffee shop, an all-night place where Nick, the night manager, knew them both. Nick had a signed picture of Eric on display. Eric waved. Nick waved back. They passed several closed storefronts and a pizza place. At the pizza place, a couple at a stand-up area noticed Eric at the same time and nudged each other. Alex's hand left his and she held on to his arm. She liked the feeling. He spent three mornings a week torturing himself with weights and exercises at the nearby McBurney YMCA. It was strong.

"So where are we going?" she asked. "Right now, I mean. Are we circling the block toward home so they'll be gone when we come back from the other direction?"

"Ha! Certainly not," he said. Then he frowned. "You don't know the other access to our building?"

"No," she said.

"Well then, you'll see something new," he said. "Okay?"

"Okay."

"I draw the line at my front door," he said, returning to the initial topic. "And I avoid people hanging out there so that they don't hang out there again. Is that so mean? I'm entitled . . . *we're* entitled . . . to some personal privacy, are we not?"

"Absolutely," she said. And at least the people who stalk you aren't trying to kill you, she thought to herself. Thought but didn't say. Then, with a cringe, she dismissed the thought, thinking what had happened to Robert, how things had turned out the first time she had given her heart away and fallen in love. The cringe was followed by a shiver, full body, and Eric picked up on it.

"Hey. What gives? You okay?" he asked.

"I'm fine. I'm just a little cold." True, but a fib.

"Ah, well. We'll be upstairs in two minutes," he said.

She changed the subject.

"Monday I have an attorney coming into the office," she said. "I won't get any real work done Monday or Tuesday. I have to go to Washington in a couple of days for that Congressional hearing on Russian organized crime in the United States. Remember?"

"Ah. *That* thing," he said, as if it were a snake to be killed with a stick. "How could I forget?"

"I know I couldn't," she said. "Much as I'd like to."

"Well, best to get rid of it," he said.

"Lousy nuisance."

"It's all of that," he agreed. He offered to have Maurice take her to the airport, but she planned to take the afternoon train from New York when her one-day notice finally came in advance of testifying. The train was effectively faster and one of the security people from FinCEN would make sure she got to Amtrak Station on Thirty-Second Street.

"Well, good luck with it," he said. "You haven't done anything wrong, so you'll be fine."

"Yeah," she said, unconvinced. A Congressional committee,

she knew, could make a federal issue out of anything they wanted to. She cringed again, thinking of the nights in Switzerland that she had spent under Federov's roof. No matter how she ever explained that, no one would believe the truth. In her darkest moments in the last few days, she thought of the public spectacle she would turn into if some ambitious member of Congress threw that one at her. She shuddered.

"Hey," Eric said, feeling her movement. "What was that?"

"What was what?"

"I thought I felt a shiver," he said.

"It was nothing," she said. "It's cold."

He held her closely. "You sure?" he said. "You seem a little off tonight. Not quite yourself."

"You're perceptive."

"Thanks. I have two ears. Want to talk about something?"

She considered it. No, not now, she decided. "No. I'm okay. Just work stuff."

"I'm a good listener if you change your mind," Eric said.

"I know you are." She leaned to him and kissed him on the cheek.

They turned on Twentieth Street and walked east, following a path parallel to the one that led to the front of their building. Halfway down the block was a narrow corridor between two old brick buildings, about five feet wide. There were exits from two brownstones that flanked the lobby, a dim overhead light, and a Dumpster. Eric gave Maurice a wave to tell him that everything was fine. Maurice was dismissed for the evening.

"Scenic route," Eric said. "Come along."

"Yes, sir," she said, starting to laugh. "I'm assuming you know what you're doing."

"Never assume that," he joked.

He led her by the hand. They went down the alley until it gave onto another pathway, one that led in both directions, with high brick walls on both sides. Eric led her another few feet, then came to a steel door in the brick wall that was locked tightly. There was no marking on the door. The wall was about sixteen feet high, topped with barbed wire. There was a security camera and Alex wondered if it was operative.

Eric produced a pair of keys from his pocket and fumbled with them for a moment. Alex's hand instinctively slipped onto her pistol, and she scanned the surroundings for danger. She saw none.

Eric unlocked the door. They walked through. He closed the door and relocked it. They were in a small courtyard that Alex now recognized but had never visited. It was the back of the building where they lived. A few more paces, down a half dozen steps, and they were at another door, this one also strongly reinforced. Eric used one of the same keys. They entered the basement of their building, passed the utility room, electrical room, storage lockers, and laundry, and came to the steps that led upstairs to the first floor. Moments later they were in the lobby, which was warm and bright compared with the cellar.

"I'm impressed," she said, teasing.

"You should be," he said with a sly smile. He glanced at his watch. It was well after midnight. "Should we call it a night?"

They rode the elevator, stopping first at the second floor. As the door opened, Eric took her in his arms and kissed her. Then he kissed her again. They exchanged good nights and she stepped out. As was his habit, he waited till she was in her apartment with the door closed and the lock dropped before he took the elevator up to his apartment on the third floor.

From inside her apartment, she could quickly see that all was secure, no intrusions, no signs of trouble. She went quickly to her alarm and disengaged it. But she was still thinking about Eric. She had never seen a man who could move around the city with such ease, such grace, such *savoir-faire,* and such confidence.

Distantly, she heard his door close upstairs.

She showered and was in bed within another half hour, carefully placing her Glock in its usual position on the night table by her bed. It was five minutes later and she was almost asleep when her eyes snapped open again. Upon her was a notion that was monumental and ethereal and frightening all at the same time.

For the first time since Robert had been killed in Kiev, and for only the second time in her life, Alex realized how deeply she had fallen in love.

She remained uneasy with it. She hadn't told Eric the depths of her feelings, out of fear more than anything, fear that she would crowd him, scare him off, or lose him. And he had not expressed those deep emotions to her. She had even taken pains to avoid the subject of marriage. And yet, just when everything seemed to be falling into place, just when her life seemed to be going in the right direction again, just when their relationship seemed to be growing, now—with his impending absence to go make a film in Europe—it seemed that all that order was being pulled away.

A film in Europe? Three months away? She suddenly realized what a fixture he had become in her life. A wave of sadness rolled over her as she thought of two months without him. What would she do on nights like this when she just needed to be with that special person?

She thought back to how it had been before they had met, and she realized what a lonely person she had been, immersed in work, afraid sometimes to even come up for air.

And what if he met someone else?

She didn't understand why it had to be that way. What was her life destined for? she asked herself. Was she always to be chasing down crooks and cutthroats? Was there no personal side to any of this, no reward to having always tried to be a good, moral person? Had the only true love of her life been cruelly whisked away from her in her twenty-ninth year on a fetid gray afternoon in Ukraine? Was there never to be any recovery from that?

Did God really have a plan?

Was God really there?

Sometimes she just didn't have answers. This was one of them.

Earlier in the month, last week she guessed it was, she had resented Eric's advice about easing out of the job. But maybe he had had a very sound point.

"But this job of yours. Man! If I were your husband, I don't think I could handle it."

What had he meant by that? Was he hinting? Suggesting? Despite his incredible self-assurance, was he, too, afraid to make the first declaration of genuine passion?

In many ways in this relationship, she was frozen in the present: afraid to drop back, afraid to rush forward. It was, to say the least, the ultimate in precarious positions.

Fatigue overtook her. She slept fitfully, but she slept.

TWENTY-THREE

At shortly before three p.m. on a snowy Thursday afternoon in February, Alex LaDuca leaned into a pair of microphones that were before her on the witness's bench. She sat in an overheated hearing room of the United States Capitol in Washington, D.C. The televised hearing in progress, to which she had been subpoenaed as a witness, was the joint House and Senate Congressional inquiry, convened to investigate the growing influence of Russian-based organized crime in the United States.

Russian influence on and participation in organized crime in the United States was a subject about which she knew plenty, perhaps more than she cared to, perhaps more than was healthy. But that was the path upon which life had taken her. By this time, it was what it was.

The physical layout in the Congressional Hall was imposing. The joint hearings, the type that had originated with the Iran Contra Investigation that had brought an obscure Marine lieutenant colonel named Oliver North into public view, was so large as to be almost unwieldy. There were too many members for a single dais. A two-tiered dais had been constructed. With seven senators, eleven House members, and numerous staffers, they were arrayed in a semicircle on two levels. To a casual observer it looked like a firing squad aimed at a lone victim who had been subpoenaed to testify.

Alex took a final moment to steady her composure and looked up at the congressmen who would question her—there were seven men and two women—and the television cameras. A row of press photographers sat on the floor beneath the congressmen. The television lights were hotter than she had anticipated. Her insides felt as if they were going to explode.

Alex began by reading a brief formal opening statement, introducing herself to the committee.

"Thank you for inviting me here today, Congressmen and Congresswomen. My name is Alejandra LaDuca. I work as a Senior Investigator and Administrator with a division of the US Treasury: the Financial Crimes Enforcement Network, or FinCEN. Our agency enforces laws against domestic and international financial crimes that target US citizens and corporations. To be clear, I'm also a Special Agent of the FBI. But I'm currently on permanent loan to FinCEN as part of a joint interagency effort to combat international financial fraud. My reports go to the FBI, the Justice Department, as well as to FinCEN in New York, where I am based."

She paused for a sip of water and felt her nerves settle. She felt all the eyes of the room upon her, plus who knew how many sets of eyes on the other end of the TV cameras. She glanced up at the eleven committee members watching her without emotion, each of them flanked by eager-beaver aides and counsels who sat right behind her. She spoke a little of her qualifications for the job she held and her background before coming to FinCEN.

"Currently," she concluded, "I am number two in command

in our New York office. My most recent assignment, and what occupies all of my time at this stage of my career, aside from my visit here today and its preparations, is an effort called Operation Párajo, a battle against a cocaine-and-money-laundering cartel, most recently of Panama. My previous assignments, however, included an operation in Nigeria and then more recently an assignment that took me to Ukraine and subsequently brought me into an operation against elements of the so-called 'Russian-American mafia.' With the proliferation of the internet, financial fraud in the cyber world has gone global and high tech. It frequently provides the fiduciary underpinnings of other criminal 'growth industries' such as narcotics, counterfeiting, gambling, human smuggling, and money laundering, not to mention bank fraud. I welcome your inquiries and stand ready to answer them openly, truthfully, and to the best of my ability."

She looked up. So far, so good. At least she hadn't stumbled in her opening statement. She knew she looked calm and collected, but her insides felt as if they were going to explode. There was sweat forming under her blouse. The fabric was already sticking to her ribs. Distantly, she wondered how Eric went out and performed every night and didn't have performance anxieties. What a skill it was, what training! She moved to the next thought. Thank God she had worn a blazer, she thought idly, as she felt the attention shift from her back to the committee. How, she wondered, had she ever landed in a place like this? Note to self: live lower key in the future.

Next to Alex, Sarah Fedderman, her attorney, sat and waited. Sarah, who knew the Washington landscape, had caught some rumors about Representative Henry Sawyer of Florida, a committee member, as being eventually "a hostile." Alex had not forgotten.

The questioning began with Rep. Justin Thomas of California.

"Ms. LaDuca," he began, "other witnesses here before you today have focused on the operations of Russian racketeers on our economy and our banking system. You've been in a position to look at the larger picture of financial frauds from all venues. Are the Russians doing something more often than anyone else? Are they guiltier than any other crime group?"

"I don't keep statistics on such things," Alex answered. "But I think you can say that fraud and money laundering, financial crimes in general, are not the monopoly of any one group. It comes at us from all directions."

"In your opinion, is it any worse today than, say, five years ago?"

Alex thought about it for a moment. "Guardedly, I might answer yes to that, Congressman," Alex answered. "The worldwide financial crisis which started with the deflation of the housing bubble in the United States and Europe has become an engraved invitation for the higher-tech components of organized crime. As I'm sure you are aware, a number of recent scandals have uncovered the links between some of the biggest global banks and some of the people who are their best customers: smugglers, drug traffickers, and arms dealers."

"Why do you call them 'best customers'?" the congressman asked.

"Well, I use the term with some irony and facetiousness," Alex answered. "But American banks in addition to the off-shores have profited greatly from money laundering by Latin American drug cartels. At the same time, the European debt crisis, particularly in

Greece, Spain, and Italy, has strengthened the hands of the loan sharks and speculators. Those same people control the underground economies in those countries."

"Surely cozy profitable relationships between the underworld and gangsters are not new," Rep. Thomas said.

"No. Not at all. What's new, however, is the reach of these various underworlds into the highest levels of global finance."

"What's changed? Is there a reason for this?"

"In my opinion, the spread and growth of the worldwide narcotics industry is responsible. During the various global financial crises at the end of 2008 and the start of 2009, in many instances, the profits from the narcotics trade were the only sources of liquid investment capital available to some banks. Hence, interbank loans were funded by money that originated from narcotics cartels and ancillary illegal activities. Some banks that are alive today and eventually paid fines for their 'bad behavior,' so to speak, were rescued that way."

"And these profits were laundered?"

"Almost entirely. I saw one statistic that estimated that close to two trillion dollars was laundered globally in 2009, of which about half was related to drug trafficking."

"And we're talking about the offshores? Those places in the sun like the Cayman Islands, the Bahamas, and Bermuda?"

"Not entirely. Plenty went on domestically here. Two years ago, Wachovia admitted that it had essentially helped finance the drug wars in Mexico by failing to identify and stop illicit transactions. The bank, which was acquired by Wells Fargo during the financial crisis, agreed to pay $160 million in fines and penalties for tolerating the laundering, which occurred between 2004 and 2007. And you're probably also aware that a previous

Senate investigation uncovered the fact that one bank had for a decade improperly facilitated transactions by Mexican drug traffickers, Saudi financiers with conspicuous and continual links to Al-Qaeda and Iranian bankers trying to circumvent United States sanctions. The bank set aside $700 million to cover fines, settlements, and other expenses related to the inquiry, and its chief of compliance resigned. Just to bring that back out to where we began, let me remind you that there was not a single Russian who was a major player in that routine."

"Anyone else you could mention while you have the spotlight?" he asked.

"I could mention that ABN Amro, Barclays, Lloyds, ING, and Credit Suisse have all reached settlements with regulators after admitting to executing the transactions of clients in countries even more disreputable than Russia."

"It's hard to imagine a country more disreputable than Russia," Rep. Thomas said to laughter from his peers and from the gallery. "What nations are we talking about?"

"The usual suspects, as far as I can recall. Iran, Iraq, and Cuba, Libya, Myanmar, and Sudan. Many transactions preceded the events of 2008. But continuing turmoil in the banking industry created an opening for organized crime groups, enabling them to enrich themselves and grow in strength. In fact, some of our studies have shown that the vast majority of profits from drug trafficking in Colombia were reaped by criminal syndicates in rich countries and laundered by banks in global financial centers like New York and London."

"How can that be?"

"Bank secrecy and privacy laws in Western countries often impeded transparency and made it easier for criminals to launder their money." She paused. "I should also point out again that none of this is anything new. It's only the reach and power of these criminal enterprises which is new. The financing of criminal activities via otherwise legitimate banks has ebbed and flowed over the years. In the early 1980s organized crime, which had previously dealt mainly in cash, started working its way into the banking system. This led authorities in Europe and America to take measures to slow international money laundering, prompting a temporary return to cash."

"Thank you," Rep. Thomas said.

Next, Congresswoman Maria Ruiz from Texas took the microphone.

"Ms. LaDuca," Rep. Ruiz began, "you stated earlier that even American banks are used to channel massive amounts of illicit funds, to 'launder' them as it is known. Could you tell us how that is done while still remaining illegal?"

"Of course," Alex said. "It's a complicated process for most individuals, but actually very easy for those with enough legal advice, financial resources, and criminal intent. The laundering occurs in three stages," she began. "First, illicit funds are directly deposited in banks or deposited in banks in dummy corporations which don't provide any service or produce any product other than to serve as a conduit for currency. The accounts are often maintained by attorneys for their clients and exist only on paper. Sometimes the money is made illegally in the United States, smuggled out, and then physically smuggled back in in cash and dumped into these accounts."

"What would be an example of that?" Ruiz asked.

"Money laundering is a 'cash-intensive' business, Congresswoman. Suppose you have a business in the United States that generates vast amounts of cash from illegal activities. Street sale of narcotics, for example, where payment takes the form of cash in small denominations. The cash is smuggled out of the country. Or it is placed into the financial system or retail economy in dummy corporations. The aims of the launderer are to first remove the cash from the location and means of acquisition so as to avoid detection from the authorities. That's the first step of the laundry cycle. The second is to transform the value into other assets: for example, travelers checks, postal orders, stock certificates, bonds. After it is deposited outside the United States, the process of 'layering' begins. In the course of layering, there is the first attempt at concealment or disguise of the source of the ownership of the funds by creating complex layers of financial transactions designed to disguise the audit trail and provide anonymity. The purpose of layering is to disassociate the illegal monies from the source of the crime. The launderer creates a complex web of financial transactions aimed at concealing any audit trail. Typically, layers are created by moving monies in and out of the offshore bank accounts of shell companies through electronic transfers. There are over half a million wire transfers, representing in excess of one trillion dollars, electronically circling the globe daily. There isn't enough information disclosed on any single wire transfer to know how clean or dirty each dispatch of money is. Given the sheer volume of daily transactions, and the high degree of anonymity available, the chances of transactions being traced are almost nonexistent."

Rep. Ruiz sat with her arms folded. Alex paused and sipped some water.

"You mentioned a final stage," the representative said.

"The final stage is what's known as 'integration,'" Alex said.

"Once the criminal profits are separated as far from their origins as can be arranged, they then become wealth that is accessible to the criminal enterprise. At this step, the tainted cash is integrated with legitimate business transactions. Legitimate transactions create a cover to hide tainted profits. Methods popular to money launderers at this stage of the game are the establishment of anonymous companies in countries where the right to secrecy is guaranteed. They are then able to grant themselves loans out of the laundered money in the course of a future legal transaction. Furthermore, to increase their profits, they will also claim tax relief on the loan repayments and charge themselves interest on the loan. The final stage in the process. It is this stage at which the money is integrated into the legitimate economic and financial system and is assimilated with all other assets in the system. Integration of the 'cleaned' money into the economy is accomplished by the launderer making it appear to have been legally earned. By this stage, it is exceedingly difficult for any regulatory or oversight agency to distinguish legal and illegal wealth. And at this point the money moves around with relative ease, covered by the sending of false export-import invoices overvaluing goods, which allows the launderer to move money from one company and country to another with the invoices serving to verify the origin of the monies placed with financial institutions. An even simpler method is to transfer the money to a legitimate bank from a small bank owned by the launderers. These are what are known in the sophisticated underground economy as 'off-the-shelf banks.' They are stocked and ready to go and are easily purchased in many tax havens."

"So by using such strategies, foreign criminal enterprises can integrate themselves into the United States?" Ruiz asked.

"Exactly. One could say the Russians have raised it to an art form. And in my opinion in the past, regulatory agencies have too often focused on the cultivation, production, and trafficking of an illegal product, such as narcotics. In the meantime, they miss the bigger, more sophisticated financial activities of crime rings, and how the profits create an even larger menace or cancer in our financial systems."

"Thank you, Ms. LaDuca," Congresswoman Ruiz said as her time expired. "You've been most informative."

"You're quite welcome," Alex answered.

A congresswoman from New York threw Alex some friendly questions. A congressman from Michigan added a few more, and Alex did fine with some easy add-ons and clarifications from a pair of representatives from California. All this time, she kept an eye on her watch. Representative Harvey Sawyer was positioned last. It would also be the final testimony of the day. Why? Was he going to hit her with something incendiary? Why was he saving it?

She answered questions as best she could. Her attorney kept quiet and refrained from distracting her. Things went smoothly. She soon found herself on autopilot.

She also noticed that the House members of one party were taking their fully allotted time and killing it. If Sawyer was last, they were leaving him with his allotted time and no extra. Politics? Coincidence? What was going on? The longer the charade went on, the more suspicious she became.

She kept reminding herself, as she politely answered the other representatives, that she was clean, that she had nothing to hide, that there were no skeletons in the closet. Why then did she feel an onset of dread? Momentarily distracted, once or twice she let her eyes drift from the speaker to Representative Sawyer. Sawyer's eyes were unwavering upon her: fixed and focused. His two aides were doing the same, but their gaze seemed light by comparison. Alex looked away from them but still felt the gravity of their attention.

Congressman Sawyer readied his microphone.

He began with forty-five seconds of small talk, mostly as a soliloquy, and then took it directly to where he wanted to go.

"Ms. LaDuca, in reviewing your personnel records at FinCEN, I noticed that a central event in your career there was your involvement with a Ukrainian-Russian gentleman named Yuri Federov."

"That's correct, Congressman."

"For the record, could you summarize your initial involvement with him?"

Alex began. "Mr. Federov, who is currently deceased, was an individual who was involved in various business enterprises, some legal, and some illegal. He was based in Kiev but had interest in Moscow, in the international natural gas business, and various other enterprises in Europe and the United States, notably New York. I first heard his name when there was an impending visit by the President of the United States to Kiev, in Ukraine. I was asked to establish contact with Mr. Federov, under an umbrella operation of FinCEN, the US State Department, and the FBI."

"No CIA?" Sawyer asked. There was some laughter around the hall.

"They knew what we were doing, but I had no direct contact that I know of."

"So what was your assignment, simply stated?"

"There were steady rumors of impending trouble, violence, from Ukrainian dissidents in anticipation of the presidential visit. I was to keep a lookout for anything, while at the same time perhaps initiating the terms of a legal settlement between Mr. Federov and the United States government."

"Settlement? Of what sort?"

"He had a tax bill of ten million dollars, approximately, and no outstanding assets in the United States that could be seized. There may have been some smaller issues, state by state, civil and criminal."

"A bit of a mess. A bit of a nefarious character," the Congressman said.

"You could say that."

"Would you agree?" he pressed.

"I don't think he was anyone's idea of an upstanding citizen," Alex said.

"You indicated that Mr. Federov owed the United States government ten million dollars," Sawyer said. "Am I correct?"

"I only know that the Justice Department and the Treasury Department had presented him with a tax bill for approximately that amount. If there were any other debts or obligations, I was unaware of them."

"Aside from criminal warrants, you mean."

"Those were on the state level, as best I can remember. I don't remember the specifics."

"Mr. Federov had been in prison in the United States at one point, had he not?"

"That's correct, sir."

"Do you recall what for?"

Alex processed the question quickly. She hadn't thought about this point for months. She searched for an answer. "I believe it was for assaulting a police officer in New York," she said. "If memory serves me, he was sentenced to four years."

"Very good," Sawyer said, consulting a paper that his assistant placed before him. "Your memory is as sharp as a tack today, Ms. LaDuca."

"I'll take that as a compliment, Congressman. Thank you."

There was a small tittering of laughter and a little wave of relaxation. The questioning seemed cordial so far, if not friendly. Alex remained on guard.

"Do you recall what line of business Mr. Federov was in? His main business?"

"He was involved in more enterprises than I could count, Congressman, but the main enterprise was something called The Caspian Group, which ostensibly held some heavy interests in the natural gas industry in Ukraine."

"And the whole concept and operation of shell companies, currency laundering, Russian transfer of criminal profits . . . Caspian was involved in that?"

"It appeared so at the time, though I'm not sure any of that was ever established in a court of law."

"But it was your impression?"

"It was."

"A firm impression?"

"In retrospect, Congressman, dealing with Mr. Federov was my first direct exposure to a criminal enterprise of that nature and scope. So if you're asking me if I believed I witnessed activities such as those described here today and which your committee is examining, the answer is yes."

"Thank you. Now let's go back to the ten million dollars.

That's a lot of money. Ten million dollars," Sawyer said. "Wouldn't you say?"

"I think we could all agree on that," Alex said.

"Was Comrade Federov ever indicted?" the Congressman asked.

"No, he wasn't," Alex said, allowing the misleading "Comrade" to slide by.

"Did he ever pay the back taxes owed? Or did his estate pay them?"

"Not to my knowledge."

"And we know that he's deceased. Did his estate pay any?"

"You'd have to ask his executor," Alex parried.

Sawyer shifted positions in his chair. "Ms. LaDuca, I have the impression here that while you're answering my questions, you're not answering them fully. Let me ask you directly, while reminding you that you're under oath, if you know the final adjudication of Mr. Federov's tax bill."

"I believe the Department of the Treasury wrote it off."

"Why would they do that?"

"In exchange for Mr. Federov's assistance during a crisis in Madrid about two years ago," Alex said. Her lawyer tapped her on the shoulder and whispered advice in her ear. Alex nodded and came back to Sawyer. "I'm advised that operation, or much of it, remains classified. I'm not at liberty to discuss it in detail. Only in an overview."

"All right. So then let's skip along to *your* knowledge, Ms. LaDuca, what you know. What you're free to discuss with us. We are here to discuss Russian criminal influence in the United States, how it comes about, how it perpetuates itself, and paths of corruption. You've stated that this Yuri Federov arranged a settlement with the federal government that permitted him to escape paying any part of his tax bill. In fact, this arrangement had his taxes expunged."

"I wasn't party to that agreement, but I did know about one such," Alex said.

"Pretty good deal," Sawyer said, grandstanding. "Most honest folks, if they owe the IRS fifty bucks, Uncle Sam comes looking for them. Now here you have this mobster who walks on ten million dollars."

"As we both know," Alex said, "it's an imperfect world. Sometimes the government makes arrangements with some unsavory people for the greater good."

"But I'm just puzzled that this man was able to escape paying. Can you shed any light on that?"

"Well, to start with," Alex couldn't resist saying, "he died, not that his death would spare the estate. But even before then, there was a major case that FinCEN was involved with in Europe. It involved international terrorism and there were several American targets. Mr. Federov was in a position to assist the United States government and save several American lives and many tens of millions of dollars of property. As a result of his cooperation, agents of our government ran a successful operation to counter the terrorism threat. A deal had been struck: in appreciation of Federov's help in resolving the situation, the US government had arranged a tax pardon."

"I'm told this event took place in Spain. Would I be correct?"

"You wouldn't be incorrect. It stretched across several countries."

"Is this something *you* arranged?"

"The event or the tax arrangement?"

"Well, either."

"I didn't arrange the event. I was on R & R following the Kiev incident when I was asked to look into a matter in Madrid. As for the tax relief, Congressman, I was an intermediary."

"Why were you chosen?"

"Again, I knew the individual. I speak Russian and Ukrainian in addition to Spanish."

"And it was known that Mr. Federov had an eye for attractive western women, isn't that the case?"

"I resent that line of suggestion, Congressman," Alex said.

The chairman interrupted and the question and statement were withdrawn from the record.

Sawyer continued. "Did you promote his interests in any way? Act in his behalf? Suggest a kinder and gentler treatment to your superiors?"

"Absolutely not," she said evenly. "I only filed my reports of what I knew."

"Why *you*? I'm fascinated."

"I had access. I had developed his trust."

"Personal relationship?" he asked.

"Professional relationship," Alex replied.

Rep. Sawyer glanced at his watch. He folded away his notes into a file. He scratched his head in what Alex took for mock confusion. She could tell he was now going for the main event.

"Ms. LaDuca," he said. "Once again, we're talking all around the point. The objective of this committee is to learn about the involvement of Russian organized crime groups to penetrate our banking system and the regulatory bodies that oversee them. It would seem to me that you enjoyed a very cozy social relationship with the late Mr. Federov."

"I've explained what the relationship was," she said.

"Yes, yes. We've heard you."

She snapped. "Despite what you're insinuating or suggesting, there was no personal involvement."

"None?"

"I wasn't sleeping with him, if that's what you're suggesting."

There was a wave of reaction around the committee room. Alex kept her eyes tightly on her adversary and listened to all the cameras snapping in the row of photographers who sat on the floor beneath the chairman's bench.

"I wasn't suggesting that, Ms. LaDuca."

"It seemed that way to me, sir. You were leading the questions in that direction."

Alex's counsel leaned to her. "Ease down," she said.

"I know where he's going on this," Alex whispered back, covering her microphone with her hand. "He's out to make me look bad."

"He's succeeding," Fedderman said. "He's getting you to lose your cool."

"If he's going to dish it to me, why can't I dish it back to him? I'm supposed to sit here and look like a patsy?"

"If you look angry it looks like you have something to hide. Be careful, Alex, I'm warning you. This could blow up."

Alex drew a long breath and tried to settle herself. She tried to balance her lawyer's advice against her anger and desire to defend herself. She spent more time than necessary taking another sip of water.

Then Alex's attention returned to the front. "Sorry, Senator," she said with more calm and bearing than she thought she'd be able to muster. "Please proceed."

"Ms. LaDuca," Sawyer continued, "did you ever receive any gifts from Mr. Federov or anyone representing his interests?"

Suppressing a sigh, Alex moved to the tricky part.

"What I suspect you're referring to, Congressman," she said, "was a bequest from Mr. Federov's will several months ago and several weeks after his death. He left me an amount of money."

"Could you tell us how much?"

Alex's counsel leaned toward her and whispered again. "Answer completely," she said.

"Two million dollars," Alex said. "After taxes."

There was a rush of reaction around the room.

"Well! Quite a gift! Why would he do something like that?"

"I couldn't begin to guess," Alex said. "It came as a surprise to me."

"No *quid pro quo*?"

"Mr. Federov was deceased," Alex said. "There was nothing I could do for him."

"But his interests?"

"I've been away from any cases that might have touched upon his interests," Alex said. "I'm not even sure what his interests are anymore. His wealth has passed into other hands and is no longer the concern of FinCEN or any other branch of government."

"But you chose to accept the bequest?"

"I reported it to my office and the matter was referred eventually to the Department of Justice. While it was highly unusual, I was advised that I would be within protocol to keep it as long as I was never working on any case that would affect any of his interests. So yes, I accepted it."

"So you're a wealthy woman due to your involvement with Mr. Federov?"

"Life takes some strange turns sometimes, Congressman," Alex said. Here her attorney again whispered advice. "I'm also reminded that if I hadn't accepted, the money would have reverted to the state of New York. There was no way I could, for example, direct it to a charity. With all due respect to the state, having cleared the matter with those who employ me, I chose to keep it."

"And the appearance of impropriety? It doesn't bother you?"

"It was a concern," Alex said, "and still is. But all I ever did was do my job well. Whenever a man does his job well, he's a hero, gets rewarded, his valor is praised. A woman gets the job done and all people want to do is suggest she slept her way there."

"Welcome to the big leagues."

"I've been in the big leagues for several years, Senator. Same as yourself."

Alex felt her attorney wince.

Sawyer looked down at a sheet of paper in front of him. There was silence in the chamber. Alex could feel disaster brewing. The line of questioning was getting ever closer to the issue of her having stayed for several nights at Federov's home in Switzerland. Innocent as it may have been, it could now emerge as a career-breaker if Sawyer spun it right. The question remained: What did he know?

He looked back up and stared her in the eye from thirty feet away.

"Ms. LaDuca," he said, "my duty to my constituents compels me to ask a question that is perhaps more personal than I'd prefer. But I need to pose it. My apologies in advance."

"Go ahead, Senator," Alex said.

"In your memory, in your recollection, taking into account your entire relationship with Mr. Federov, public and private, can you think of anything that might have carried with it the appearance of impropriety?"

Alex considered the question and the wording.

"It seems as if you're asking me to do your own investigation for you, Senator," she parried.

There was laughter in the chamber.

"I still believe in the Fifth Amendment, Ms. LaDuca," Sawyer said when the laughter subsided. "I wouldn't think of asking you to do that."

"I can't think of anything, Senator," Alex answered. "If there's something specific on your mind, please ask about it. I'll explain it to you as best I can."

A moment followed frozen in time. Sawyer glanced down to his papers, then looked back up.

"No," he said. "Nothing specific." There was another pause of several heavy seconds. "No further questions," he said.

Then, at about six o'clock, Senator Norman Daniels dropped the gavel on the hearings. "The committee," he declared with unusual flourish, "will stand in recess until nine a.m. Tuesday morning to receive the testimony of Lieutenant Colonel Noah Remington."

Senator Daniels' gavel ended the day.

Mercifully, Alex's hour of national exposure ended with it.

Sarah Fedderman leaned to Alex.

"Nice work," she whispered.

"Mostly damage control," Alex said in return.

"Whatever it was, I think you survived."

TWENTY-FOUR

With great enthusiasm, the man known as Antonin Debray was out to the Zona Rosa on the second night of his stay, a Saturday. When he didn't like the first club, he moved along to the next. All the top spots were situated right beside each other. The pink zone was also one of the safer areas of Bogotá, but Debray packed his weapon anyway.

In several places, Debray ingratiated himself, dancing with young girls and middle-aged women who equally were knock-outs, many of them on their own hunt for men with European or American passports. He considered taking one or two back to his hotel, if they were willing, but, in an odd gesture of morality, decided not to: he was involved with a young woman already back in Europe and found little appetite for romantic games tonight.

On his third night, keeping an active book of personal reviews and notes on the various bands he saw, he ventured beyond the Zona Rosa and hit the discotheques located on Calle 94 and Pepe Sierra Avenue. These were among the most popular venues in Bogotá. They played an eclectic mix of reggae, salsa, hip-hop, and funk. The crowds were friendly and the cover charges were reasonable, less than two American dollars.

Because most clubs and bars closed at one a.m., Debray found, the after-party scene in Bogotá was huge. These rambling raves could cost anything from a hundred to twenty thousand pesos, but they were popular and well attended among young revelers of the city. So Debray tagged along, more to get a handle on the city and what was going down—the rumors, the scuttlebutt—than anything else. He passed himself off as a foreign businessman, which was truthful to a point, there to make some deals. He fell in with a crowd of Brits one night and spoke English with them, some French another night. It never ceased to amaze him how much strangers would tell him if it afforded them the opportunity to show off their ability in another language.

Most parties lasted until dawn. There were a great deal of drugs in use—it was Colombia, after all—through no one forced anyone to partake. So Debray kept clear of that territory. Being arrested here would be messy.

All this time, Debray was also more than careful to watch his back, on guard for anyone who might be following or track-ing him. By the time he saw the sunrise three mornings in a row, he was convinced he was clean and that he was not under any surveillance.

So from a public phone at noon on the fourth day, he con-tacted a prearranged local number, one not unrelated to the parcel that had been delivered to his hotel room.

"*Debray aqui,*" he said. "*Todo va bien.*"

There was a pause. Then the voice of a young man answered abruptly in Spanish. Debray assumed it to be Vicente. "You like Caribbean? I suggest Club Caliente," the young man said. "*Esta noche, a la medianoche.*" Tonight at midnight.

"How will I know the right place?" Debray asked.

"In the rear, there's a painting of Havana," the voice said. "Give your name. Find the painting."

The young man hung up with an abrupt click before Debray could utter another word. But he had said enough.

Caribbean music was very popular in the Colombian capital. There were several clubs that offered both salsa and reggae to its patrons, but the Club Caliente was among the most plush and expensive. So on this fourth night of his visit to Bogotá, Debray opted for something with a tropical rhythm. He set off to Carrera 5 between Calles 26 and 28. There, many clubs offered music from Jamaica, Barbados, and Cuba. He easily found the Club Caliente on the corner at the end of a block of Calle 26. He wandered in and checked out the scene. The bar was packed with beautiful young women, more bare limbs than any man could count or appreciate at one glance. A group of young men, some in jeans, some in suits, orbited around them.

Debray flirted with the hostess, a stunning brunette in a short blue dress. He gave his name and she led him to a table reserved for him at a quiet place in a back room. Above the table was a striking mural-sized painting of Havana, obviously recalling a day in January of 1959. In the painting, joyous citizens were welcoming Fidel Castro's revolutionary army as their tanks rolled into the city.

Debray ignored the political message, if there was one. He sat with his back to the wall where he could see the door. He sat in a way that would permit him to quickly access his Beretta if necessary. There was a nice noise level, just enough to cover conversation, not enough to annoy him. He assumed that's why Vicente had chosen this venue. He relaxed as best he could.

The tone of the Club Caliente was Bohemian and informal, a quaint touch for the most expensive place on the block. Waitresses wore sunny yellow T-shirts and denim short shorts, radiating youth, charm, and good looks, and an attitude of party-tonight-and-who-cares-about-tomorrow. Debray settled in comfortably with a tall Cuba Libre made with a double play of the real stuff: Coca-Cola from the United States and dark Havana Club from Cuba.

A quarter hour passed. When he had a pleasant buzz from a second drink, a dark-haired young man in a tan suit emerged from the crowds in the next room, scanned quickly, and locked his eyes upon Debray. The young man wore a stylish fedora, and flicked it off. He carried it in his hand as he strode toward Debray's table. He slid into the empty chair and seated himself.

"I'm Vicente," he said in Spanish. He offered a firm handshake and a tight smile. Debray accepted both. "And you are?" he asked.

"I'm exactly who you're looking for."

The visitor from Europe moved his left hand to his inside jacket pocket, slowly and carefully so the gesture would not be mistaken, and pulled out his European Union passport, the one he had arrived on. He laid it on the table.

Vicente put a hand on it and opened it to the identification page. He did this without lifting it from the table. His eyes scanned the picture and the name. He glanced up, uttered a small laugh, and then closed the document. "Of course," he said.

"Of course," the European answered. He took back his passport and put it away.

"So you're here to talk business?" Debray asked.

"Absolutely. And with great pleasure."

"Then let's get to it," Debray said.

But, as if he had eyes in the back of his head, Vicente fell silent. Debray saw why. A waitress appeared with a gin and tonic and set it down next to Vicente's left hand. Vicente looked up and gave the girl a warm smile. She reciprocated. Obviously to the European, the younger man was known here, if not by name, by sight. The girl walked away after a moment of pleasantries.

"And let's cut quickly to the main event," Vicente said, sipping the drink and looking back to Debray. "You started making inquiries about me about two months ago from your offices in Europe. You know as well as I do that inquiries of that sort quickly get back to the subject of the inquiries. So I made my own about you. Who you work for, who you have worked for in the past, who your friends are. It didn't take me long to have a notion of why you might require my services."

Debray tried to identify the man's Spanish. Surely it wasn't European and it didn't seem Cuban. Very possibly it was local, Colombian, but it could have been Bolivian or Venezuelan, also. But, trumped for a moment by the brazenness of his guest, as well as the accuracy, Debray was silent for a moment. Then he recovered as Vicente opened a pack of American cigarettes and lit one.

"Since you are so well prepared," Debray said, "why don't *you* tell *me* what this is about? Then we'll see how smart you are."

"Operation Párajo," Vicente said. "Let's just say you have an important dog in that fight. One of the top two dogs, if you'll excuse my expression."

"No apologies needed. You're correct."

"Then maybe you can give me some further details," Vicente said. "Things I wouldn't know by reading newspapers on the internet."

"Very well," Debray said. He brought the younger man in on Operation Párajo, the operation launched in New York by the Americans who sought to crack down on a vibrant money-laundering and smuggling operation that provided money and jobs all over the western hemisphere. It was remarked during their conversation what hypocrisy the Americans dealt with, since their own nationals were the major consumers who kept the Dosi operation afloat. Over his own drink, Vicente grinned. It amused him the way the visitor phrased things, even as he spoke so authoritatively of the events of the last two years from New York to Panama. Aside from that, he betrayed no emotion.

Nonetheless, Debray continued. "The personal war between Alex LaDuca in New York and Yardena Dosi, late of Panama, now of Morocco," he said, "has escalated into what now resembles an old-fashioned Italian vendetta, something from the sixteenth century. Alex LaDuca in New York has all the power of United States law and influence on her side. Señora Dosi, in faraway Morocco, has all the powers of the underworld on hers. LaDuca has to play by certain rules. Dosi has no such limitations. It would be out of the question for the LaDuca woman to arrange for an underworld hit on her nemesis, and even if she *could* order it, she is personally bound by a certain sense of religious morality. So she would *not* do it even if she could."

"Pity," said Vicente, still with no emotion whatsoever.

"It *is* ironic," Debray continued, rambling slightly. "Both women live their existences barricaded by different forms of walls and protective coverage, yet both live in trepidation of taking the slightest misstep in public, for fear of being fatally brought down by the other."

"Excuse me," said Vicente. Vicente spoke Spanish with an unusual but distinctive accent, Debray noticed. It sounded as if it might be from the southern cone of South America. Not quite Argentinian, but maybe Chilean. "Let's get to the point of this interview," Vicente continued. "You are here to arrange an execution. You and I both know which of these two women you are going to ask me to kill. I'm familiar with the battle going on between the two of them. And I believe the job can be done, particularly if it is an assignment for a small team as you suggested before we met. But I wish to ask questions."

"Very good," Debray said.

"There is a man in this woman's life. Is he a target also?" Vicente asked.

"Ancillary perhaps. Collateral damage. Not primary. But if he's in the way or if killing him would move you closer to your ultimate goal . . ." His voice tailed off. "Why not?" he continued, thinking it through further. "He could be a target as well. It might serve as a warning to other men who get involved with women like that."

"So *al fondo*, the bottom line, the man is a target for execution as well?"

"Yes," Debray said. "As long as you get the woman also."

"Very well. So then," Vicente continued, "now let's skip quickly to the question of barricades and protections. As I said, both these women live behind walls of various sorts and have built-in layers of security and counterintelligence that would be difficult for anyone to easily penetrate. From what I know of the battle, for example, between these two *mujeres*, Señora Dosi was able to elude capture when the initial Párajo arrests were being made. She evaded apprehension again in Rome. She obviously has her own sources, perhaps even within American law enforcement and intelligence. She knows when extreme plans are afoot against her." He drew heavily on his cigarette and blew out a long stream of white smoke. "Then, more to the point of what we are discussing here, the woman in New York evaded a sniper firing at her through her window. She avoided a man with a bomb on a motorcycle, also in New York. So the failure rate is quite high, even among professionals." He snuffed out his cigarette. "I will tell you this: it would cost about a million and a half dollars for me to assemble a team to arrange the type of ambush you want and to get it done effectively."

"That would not be a problem," Debray said. "The money."

Vicente raised a hand. "And the victim would have to be lured out into a vulnerable situation in a country other than the one where she resides. LaDuca has the full protection of the United States government. I would be unable to readily bring a team into the United States and successfully exit again with current immigration policies. Similarly, Dosi has the full protection of the Moroccan government and her own hired forces in that country. Home turf, you could call it, for each of these prima donnas. I prefer a level playing field, or one sloped to my advantage. I'm not stupid. That's why I'm still alive in this business."

Vicente took a moment to light a new cigarette. He watched two young women at the bar, coyly encouraging a pair of men. He eyed the women up and down, overt lechery in his eyes. Debray followed his gaze. When Debray looked back, Vicente's brown eyes were upon his again.

Vicente spun further. "Location? Forget about Asia or Africa," he said. "There are too many variable and the logistics would be a nightmare. The assignment that you require would need to be set up and completed in this hemisphere," Vicente continued. "That's where my people reside, that's where they have their homes, and that's where they have their own friendly contacts in law enforcement. Mexico is always possible and the drug cartels would get the blame. Same with Colombia, but I would go no farther south than Colombia. Central America would be ideal," he said, thinking. "There's not one government that isn't corrupt or a single police force that can't be bought, except possibly Costa Rica, which I would avoid. So there's a partial answer to your question. I can arrange for an ambush on your troublesome female, but I would need to set up a team and lure her into a vulnerable situation. How is that?"

"Acceptable. Fine, in fact."

"Then how will you lure her there?"

"It is very simple," Debray said. "The woman will be drawn out from her coverage. She will be made to move around the globe in order to further the interests of her own career. First she will learn that these trips are safe if she makes them carefully. Then she will relax slightly. When a trap is finally set by you, she will not recognize it and she will walk into it."

He paused.

"Already there are forces in motion that will lure her out into the open," Debray said. "Situations which she will find too tempting to resist, opportunities to win the game against her adversary. It will be your job to have your operatives ready, say, within the space of a month, and ready to move on relatively short notice."

"In what country?" Vicente asked. "That part is critical."

"Panama," Debray answered.

Vicente nodded and calculated. "Knowing what I know, I suspect I will need four people in addition to myself. Maybe five. I intend to be the lead gun and I intend to do it from in close.

That way I will be sure to succeed. Two others will support me with assisting fire, two others will be charged with our getaway. And I may have one in a 'fail safe' position to finish the job if I miss, or provide covering fire if either I or my people come under unexpected resistance and return fire." He paused. "You expect that the target will be in a vulnerable position within two months."

"Yes," Debray said.

"Excellent," Vicente answered without emotion. He fell silent and pulled out a small notepad. On the top page, he wrote a short note, focused around two lengthy numbers. He tore the sheet off and handed it to Debray.

"This first number is the cell phone at which I can be contacted," he said, indicating as Debray received the paper and looked at it. "The second is the routing code and account number for my financial institution in the Cayman Islands. You'll give me the important details on the location for the ambush when you have them. Use this number," he said. "But first, of course, my fee, our fee, must be received. As soon as the bank alerts me as to your deposit, I will begin this task in earnest. I have people who always stand ready, for the right price and situation. We will coordinate what we need to. Beyond that, I don't need to know anything else this evening."

"Very well," he finally said. He accepted the numbers and folded them away.

Then he stood, smiled for the first time, and held out his hand to his contact.

"We will be in touch. You will have your money within the week."

"See that I do," Vicente said. "I don't like wasting my time with meetings like this. And, frankly, this is an assignment I will enjoy. Like Señora Dosi, I have a personal agenda as well as a professional one."

Vicente released Debray's hand and briskly popped his hat back on his head. He gave a final touch to Debray's arm, then turned and left. Debray watched the man disappear, vanishing into the crowd of young revelers as abruptly as he had appeared.

Debray sat again. He let go with a small shiver. Men like this never failed to give him the creeps, even though he had been dealing with men like this—and worse—for the better part of his adult life.

He stood and laid some cash on the tabletop to pay for drinks. He was gone a few minutes later.

Two mornings later, his business concluded, he caught the morning flight to Paris from Bogotá. He had heard enough music and seen enough of the local sites.

Once he was back in Europe, he reported the substance of his meeting with Vicente to his own superiors. They seemed very pleased. They, too, had their own agenda here. So they launched the million and a half dollars toward the bank account in the Cayman Islands. The plan was a go.

Alex LaDuca, they all knew, would never have an inkling of what was up until she was in a vulnerable position and the guns were drawn and the shots were fired. And by that time, it would be too late to change anything.

Debray, who too had some personal interests in the matter, was more than pleased. He was delighted.

TWENTY-FIVE

Alex escaped Congress and the press that night in Washington. While scores of reporters searched all the likely hotels for her, looking for a follow-up interview, she managed to rendez-vous with her old friend Laura Chapman. She had a private dinner at Laura's apartment, slept over, and returned to New York the next morning by rental car.

There was a small armada of reporters waiting for her outside the FinCEN building in Manhattan. She stood with her lawyer outside in the cold and answered questions, defusing the situation as much as possible. No, she had not spent the two million dollars and no, just as she had testified, she had not been Yuri Federov's mistress or a conduit for favors, other than the arrangements that the Department of Justice and the IRS were willing to grant.

The two daily New York tabloids took their shots at her, the New York *Daily News* on page three, the New York *Post* on page one, under the mortifying and screaming headline, Money for Nothing? And then in smaller type, Russian Thug Leaves $2MIL to G-Girl. The more sedate—comparatively at least—*New York Times* gave her an eight-inch story that started on the front page also, breaking the story with a low column on the left side.

All three newspapers carried her photograph, just what she needed to dodge potential assassins.

Andy De Salvo came downstairs and stood behind her as she fielded questions. Sarah Fedderman, her attorney, had joined her also. Andy and Sarah helped pull her away from the press after fifteen minutes, hot questions on a cold afternoon. Two federal marshalls blocked the lobby of the building. Andy led her into the elevators as Sarah followed. They arrived upstairs on the FinCEN floors, entered the suite, and Alex was met by applause from her peers, which buoyed her spirits. Beneath it all, however, she felt the job was getting away from her.

But not for long.

Rick McCarron called that afternoon toward three p.m.

"Hello, Rick," she said, answering.

"I loved your TV performance."

Alex sighed. At least he was friendly and she knew he was gently kidding her. "I'm glad someone did," she said. "I sure could have done without it."

"Ah, hold your head up high," McCarron said. "The politicians bring you on because they want a target. You did well. Nothing should be dragging you down about the appearance."

"Nothing is dragging me down. It's that it won't go away. I could do without the celebrity."

"I hear you," he said. "So you won't mind if I segue quickly to another subject."

"I wish you would," Alex said. "Go for it."

"Honduras. You are needed there," he said.

"When?"

"Maybe Tuesday or Wednesday of next week," he said. "The agreement is going to be signed tomorrow. Suarez is sitting in a stinking cell in Nassau sweating it out. I can have my colonel in Nassau by the day after tomorrow. You should arrive the day after that. If I were you, I wouldn't waste much time on this. Things could go off the rails very easily."

"I hear you. Travel details? My contact in Honduras?"

"There's a Colonel Acosta who's our man on the ground in Honduras. He will be in touch," McCarron said. "I'll forward to you his most recent memo of the situation there. There will also be a private charter flight for you out of Miami." He paused. "Final answer? Are we doing this, Alex? We are, right?"

Alex felt something seize up in her gut. Why did she have such bad feelings about this? Her free-floating anxiety was floating everywhere and dropping down on anything she looked at.

Still, she steeled herself and marched forward.

"We're doing this," Alex said. "If you want to know the truth, suddenly I can't wait to get out of town."

"I thought you might be thinking in those terms. Hang in there."

"Thanks," she answered.

She closed her office door and returned to her desktop monitor.

There was a new email in her inbox. She clicked on it. It was from McCarron and included the joyous new document from the previously mentioned Colonel Acosta in Honduras.

She braced herself, tried and tried to dig into what was another background document on Honduras and the situation she was being asked to visit.

Colonel Acosta was not bearing great news.

"We know from past history, the Reagan years in particular, that the infrastructure of a Central American country like

Honduras is not strong enough, is not corruption-proof enough, is not anti-venal enough to be a bastion of democracy," wrote the colonel. "One wonders sometime if anything we do accomplishes anything. For all the interdictions we make in the field, as long as sound financial underpinnings support the cocaine trade, one wonders how we will ever have any success."

And yet at the same time, Alex read, the American military was starting to engage on a larger scale. They had brought lessons from the past decade of conflict to the drug war being fought in the wilderness of Miskito Indian country. A remote base camp named El Campo de los Santos had been built with little public notice but with the support of the Honduran government.

In past drug operations, Acosta noted, helicopters transporting Honduran and American antinarcotics squads had launched operations from Tegucigalpa whenever an intelligence task force identified radar tracks of a smuggler's aircraft. Three-hour flights were required to reach cartel rendezvous points. That did not leave much idle time to spot airplanes as they unloaded tons of cocaine to dugout canoes, which then paddled downriver beneath the jungle canopy to meet fast boats and submersibles at the coast for the trip north.

In creating the new outpost, Campo de los Santos had been patterned on the forward bases in Iraq and Afghanistan that gave troops a small, secure home on insurgent turf. There were spartan but comfortable barracks, complete with five-thousand-gallon tanks of helicopter fuel, food depots, and solar panels to augment diesel generators.

The site supported two-week rotations for sixty people, all less than thirty minutes' flying time from most smuggling hand-off points.

"Now, in addition," Acosta wrote, "Honduran Special Operations forces, with trainers from American Special Forces, the Green Berets, are ferried from the outpost by Honduran helicopters to plant explosives that would cut craters into smugglers' runways. Honduran infantrymen provide security for the outpost, which remains nominally under Honduran command. To my mind, this mission smacks of many reminders of the 'dirty wars' of the 1980s—El Salvador, Nicaragua, and Honduras. The more things change," wrote the soldier, "the more they remain the same."

And this was what Alex was sent to visit in Honduras. This was where Suarez was being held, at El Campo de los Santos.

Alex's cell phone rang. She grabbed it from her desktop. She recognized Sam Deal's number.

"Hello, Sam. I guess you saw me on television," Alex said.

"Ha. Wouldn't have missed it," Sam said. "I thought you did pretty well. Lousy politicians," he said.

"I felt like I had a target on me."

"What did you expect?"

"Some fairness and civility," she said.

Sam grimaced. "That's the trouble with you, Alex. You got morals, you got principles. It's the irony, you know. You are in justice and you have a sense of fair play. You shouldn't. The whole world's a dog fight." Sam unleashed a torrent of profanities, but that was Sam, the way he wanted to comport himself. "Ah, excuse me, I get teed off and carried away. You know what you got to do, LaDuca, and I say this to you as someone who likes you. Who was your enemy on that committee? Sawyer, right?"

"So it seemed."

"When did this committee thing start? When did it get started?"

"I have no idea."

"Okay then, when was the first you heard of it?"

She thought back. "It was maybe eight months ago."

"Right. And Federov is dead by now, pushing up daisies in Switzerland, right?"

"He died in November of 2011, correct."

"So he's not the target of this inquiry. *You* are. And why's that? Wake up, pretty woman. You got your Dosi operation going, your bird operation, right?"

"Yeah."

"You ever see that movie with the girl whose head spins around and she spits pea soup?"

Alex needed a laugh and Sam was giving her one.

"*The Exorcist*, Sam. Yes, I know it."

"Well, the young priest starts saying he's identified three different enemies and the old father shuts him off and says there's just one. Remember that?"

"Sort of."

"You're the young priest. I'm the old priest. Get it?"

"Just one?"

"Just one enemy," Sam said. "People from those Congressional Districts aren't elected by their constituents. They're elected by oil companies, Israel, electric companies, big banks, labor unions, what have you. Corporations. You'd be surprised."

"Sam, if I thought that there was some Dosi link to that inquiry, I would have checked it out."

"No, Alex, God bless you, that's the problem. You're just not venal enough to see it. It's got nothing to do with political parties. Look what happened. They blew your personal cover, they outted you, they embarrassed you, and they made you a public face for any trigger-happy Latin American hood who wants to turn a few bucks. There's a target on your butt, in Sam's humble and contrarian opinion. And that Congressmoron Sawyer put it there."

It started to fall into place for Alex. And she wasn't pleased.

"Follow the money, Alex. I'm just putting forth a theory, a hunch with lunch. See what you find."

Then, before she could follow up on Sam's tip, her phone rang again at the end of the day. This time it was her favorite new author, Colonel Acosta himself, phoning on a secure line from the US Embassy in Tegucigalpa. He assured her that he had "Suarez" in tight custody and he reconfirmed that he was expecting her.

"I can be there Monday night of next week," she said. "I've made the arrangements to Miami."

The colonel said he in turn had arranged for a military escort and bodyguard to meet her in Miami, a guy named Ken, and get her safely the rest of the way.

She said that was good and signed off, amazed at the lack of enthusiasm she heard in the echo of her own voice.

TWENTY-SIX

Two nights later, a Sunday evening, Alex sat with Eric again at Il Trovatore, their favorite late dining spot in Manhattan. Sometimes at "Il Trove," as Eric had nicknamed it, he got the private room if he requested it in advance. Sometimes he didn't. Generally, Eric didn't care for the affectations of stardom in most instances and preferred to dine just like any other New Yorker. There were the occasional autograph seekers, whom he usually indulged. More often than not, he was left alone, aside from many sideways glances from other diners.

Tonight, he was in a fairly good mood. There had been a bizarre occurrence onstage, but at least no one got hurt and he could laugh at it.

"Priscilla Kim," he said, "the actress who plays Liat, Bloody Mary's daughter. She came running over to me during her entrance into the song 'Happy Talk.' I picked her up, as I always do. At this particular performance tonight, however, I was wearing a new pair of shoes and I stepped on a freshly waxed part of the stage. Overwaxed, I might say. Well, it was as if I had stepped on a banana peel and all the girl's weight was right on me. We went up in the air, then straight down. Hard. I mean, hard. With a tremendous thump. My butt can still feel it," he laughed. "Jimmy Snyder, who plays Emil, was upstage facing the audience, and when he turned to face us, he was laughing so hard. I managed to find a graceful way to pull myself back up without making it look like it was an accident." He took a sip of wine. "Well, it seemed as if the audience bought it. The only people laughing were the four of us onstage. Oh, most of the orchestra was laughing, also. But the music continued. I don't think most of the audience realized." He shrugged and sipped again. "Always march forward in life, I guess. If you louse up, maybe no one will notice. Or care."

"Maybe," Alex said.

The waiter appeared and they ordered.

"So. Alex," he said. "Amuse me with some stories about that place where you work."

"I was coming to that," she said. "I have to make a trip next week."

"Where to?"

"Can't tell you."

"What will you be doing?"

"Meeting with someone. A few people, in fact."

"Can you give me any idea who?"

"Not really."

"Oh," he said.

"Sorry."

"I am, too."

"What's that mean?"

"Well, you know," he said. He offered her bread from the bread basket. She declined. He started a piece.

"I'm under very specific instructions. I'm not to tell anyone where I'm going. Even if I were married and had a family, even then I wouldn't be able to let you know."

The statement was no sooner out of her mouth than she

realized that she had misspoken. Inadvertently, she had amped up the discussion, taking it to a place she wasn't yet ready to discuss.

"That's a questionable way to live, Alex," he said.

"Someone has to do what I do."

"Do they? You bring down one hoodlum, there's going to be what, ten, twenty, to take his place?"

She sighed. "Maybe," she said.

"Then why do you do it?"

"I don't know. Maybe I don't even remember why I do it."

"Then if you don't remember, maybe it's time for you to stop doing it."

"What does *that* mean?"

"Nothing. Just a thought. Just an old-fashioned notion. I'm an old-fashioned guy from time to time. If I'm involved with someone, if I care about her, I like to know where she is, what she's doing. Not because I'm prying or possessive. But because I care. I like to know she's safe."

"Oh, Eric."

"You're never safe, it seems. It could drive a man nuts, Alex. In fact, I'll let you in on a secret. It does drive a certain man nuts, the one who by coincidence is sitting across the table from you."

"You sound angry."

"I am. Not necessarily at you. But at the situation." He paused. "I guess I should have discussed this earlier."

"No. It's all right. We can discuss it now."

He sighed. "There's not a lot to discuss," he said. "I miss you when you're not here, when I don't see you every day. Knowing you're off somewhere dangerous . . . I assume the place you're going to is dangerous, right?"

She thought about Honduras. San Pedro Sula. Murder capital of Central America.

"It's not *un*-dangerous," she said with a half-smile.

"Tactfully put," he said, almost with a laugh. "I rest my case."

They both fell silent.

"Look," he said. "Talk to your boss. I know I met him. What's his name?"

"Andy."

"Andy. He seems like a reasonable man. See if at least you can tell me where you are and give me a time frame in which you might be back. Or a way we can talk while you're away. Is that so much to ask?"

She sighed.

"Trust me on this. Let me do this one time and I'll do my best not to ever do this again. Would that help?" she asked.

"That would help quite a bit," he said. "Tremendously, in fact."

They embraced and he kissed her.

"Then it's a promise?" he asked.

"It's a promise," she affirmed.

A short time later, they were stepping out of the elevator on her floor in their home building on Twenty-First Street. Eric embraced her, kissed her, and then stepped back from her.

Alex picked up a vibration, one she didn't like. "Eric?" she asked. "Something else?"

He looked sheepish. "Yeah. There is. One thing. It might upset you so I haven't mentioned it. But I need to now. Don't read anything extra into it or take it the wrong way. Okay?"

"Okay. What is it?" she asked.

"Priscilla Kim. The young lady who plays Liat."

"What about her?"

"When the producer of the film was in town to sign the contract with me, he came by the show. Wanted to see *South Pacific*, naturally." He paused. "Well, he liked Priscilla and her performance. So he signed her for a small role in the same movie."

After a moment it sank in. "So Priscilla's going to be in the same production with you? Again. The film. *Flowers from Berlin*."

"That's correct," Eric said.

"That's quite something," Alex said. "Nice career move for her."

"Yes. It is."

Alex nodded. "I'll see you when I get back from Honduras," she said. "Then we'll see where we are."

With that chilly note, she ended the evening.

TWENTY-SEVEN

On Monday morning, Alex boarded her flight from New York. She booted up her laptop and plugged in a USB stick with background on Suarez. There was a sketchy history of some criminal activity in Florida, with many edits to protect the ID of Suarez, should the stick be lost. It made, nonetheless, for good reading at thirty thousand feet.

Alex's flight from New York arrived in Miami shortly after eleven a.m. Alex slung her carry-on over her shoulder and walked quickly through the terminal, always an eye out for trouble, not expecting any here. She moved to the next terminal to find the gate for her escort and her connecting flight to Honduras.

Gate 17. She spotted her escort immediately: an escort and bodyguard, just as Colonel Acosta had promised. He was a burly white man with closely cropped gray hair, a dark green sports jacket, and arms folded across his chest. Baby face. Fiftyish. He looked ex-military or ex-cop. He spotted Alex a moment after she spotted him. He gave her an up-and-down glance.

She approached. "Ken?" she asked.

"Yeah. Alex?"

"That's me."

"Good timing. How was your flight?"

"It arrived. What more can I ask?"

"Yeah," he snorted. "I hear you."

"Follow me," he said. "We have a private gate." With his head, he signaled. She walked with him to a distant point in the same terminal. They went through a couple of doors for which he had passes, and then hit the waiting area for the connecting flight.

"Let's sit," he said.

"Sure."

"Sit" meant sit in silence apparently, as Ken had very little to say.

"So you're my bodyguard?" Alex asked, breaking the ice in a low voice.

"Call me that if you want," he said. "I'm here to get you there and make sure you get back. I know the other people on the ground in Hondo. If any shooting starts, duck and cover 'cause that's what I'm going to do."

"That's a joke, right?" she asked, joining his banter.

"Did I offend you? Sorry. Let's hope there isn't any."

"No offense taken," Alex said.

She sat and gathered herself. More small talk. The flight boarded in half an hour and was in the air bound for Tegucigalpa, the capital of Honduras, by fifteen minutes after noon.

They sat next to each other. Ken didn't have much more to say here, either, which was just as well. Alex disappeared into her iPad and listened to music. She was in the mood for light classical and connected with Murray Perahia, the brilliant Israeli pianist. Good backdrop, grand and calming. Beethoven piano concerto: a 1980 recording. Simultaneously, she clicked into her Kindle, selecting a ghost story, *Loose Ends*, by a new favorite author, Terri Reid. She was ready to roll—or fly. In the back of her mind, the previous evening with Eric kept replaying itself. Well, if she lost him, she lost him, she told herself. Then she realized again that that was the last thing she wanted. She sighed. It seemed out of her control at this point.

Three hours later, they passed through Honduran customs and immigrations and into the lobby of a moderately sized airport, moderate for a secondary city in Central America at least.

"Okay," Ken said in English. "Follow me and stay close."

Barely though the arrival gate, Ken made eye contact immediately with two men wearing reflector sunglasses and dark slacks in the airport lobby. They stood close together but almost at an angle with each other, a couple of conspicuously big men, both well over six feet, one thicker than the other, one with a salt-and-pepper mustache, one without, studying arrivals but eyeing the lobby of the airport, too.

The thick man had hands on hips; the other held his arms folded behind his back. They were watching arrivals. They spotted Ken and Alex immediately. They fell into formation to walk toward them and meet them, the second man holding back by fifteen feet with a hand poised under a jacket.

"These are our contacts," Ken said, everyone simultaneously spotting everyone.

"Got them," she said. The thought recurred to Alex that she could have been walking into a major league trap. Surely the Dosi cartel had spread plenty of cash around this section of the world. She wished she had jawboned enough to bring Rizzo along. Then she rejected the notion, whispered one of those little prayers that was either a residual reflection of faith or just a recurring habit from girlhood, whatever it was these days. As she ventured forward, she watched the second man and his hands.

She felt naked without her own weapon.

For half a second her mind swam and bounced around from image to image like a pinball. Her world, which had approached a sensible pace, suddenly careened wildly: she wondered how her friend Ben was doing back in New York, how his new romance was going, and, aware of the time, wondered how Eric's performance was going on Broadway that night.

She wondered with a shiver what women were throwing themselves at him these days and further realized that there wasn't much she could do but trust him, anyway. She wondered if she was still the story of the moment in the press thanks to the Congressional probe, which made her remind herself once again that she was glad to be out of the country where she would not be asked for the sixtieth time if she had been Yuri Federov's mistress.

Then they were a few feet in front of their contacts.

The two men were even bigger close up. The man on the left raised his dark glasses, smiled, and extended a meaty hand. He had a massive torso that barely differentiated his stomach from his chest. The collar of his shirt could barely contain his muscular neck.

The second man was leaner, more angular, and more cadaverous. He was also taller, maybe a full six-four to the other man's six-three. Alex read the faces. They were both Latino, pale beige skin, coffee with cream, common in this stretch of Centro America.

They spoke Spanish as they greeted their arrivals. Low tones, hushed intonations, not much above rumbling mumbles.

"*Soy Luis,*" said the thick man with the mustache. He gripped her hand. "*¿Se habla espanol, si?*" he asked.

"*Carlo que si,*" Alex answered. "*Yo domino el español.*" Fluently.

"*¡Excelente! Es mi compadre, Carlo*," Luis said, introducing his companion, the one with the ominous hand under the jacket. When Carlo's hand moved, Alex caught a glimpse under the jacket. He had an automatic pistol the size of a cannon.

Alex and Ken shook hands with Carlo.

Mucho gustos? all around. Everything was copacetic.

Then it was a conversation in motion as Alex reprocessed her homework and thought back. Luis was the American. DEA. Carlo was the Honduran. Army. A major. Her age. Lean and tough. What he lacked in polish, to her initial assessment, he made up for in muscle and macho. Mentally, even as they moved, she frisked Carlo.

She found the slight lump in his jacket on the right side where he was wearing his gun.

In contrast, Luis's shirt was tight and formfitting. If she knew anything about the male anatomy, his shoulders were forty-forty and his waist thirty-four. A good equation. Obviously he spent several hours a week working at it. She figured the gun was on his ankle. These guys didn't walk around unarmed.

"Let's get moving," Luis said. There also was a small brigade of soldiers in the airport. Fatigues and dark green berets, occasionally a red beret. Three of them, two greens and a red, a junior officer, all armed with assault rifles, followed them through the gate: extra security.

They hit the doors and were outside. A blast of midday heat rolled into Alex like a giant hot towel. There was a gray van waiting, engine running. The driver came around quickly and slid the doors open. Luis offered Alex a hand. She accepted it as she stepped up into the vehicle and slid to the far side of the second row. The three men climbed in around her, Ken beside her, Luis and Carlo in the third row. The van was over AC-ed. The temp dropped from ninety to seventy, airport driveway to van interior.

Then the van was moving. From the backseat, Luis handed each of his guests a small canvas bag. Alex opened hers and found a pair of useful travel gifts. Two of them, in fact, just as Colonel Acosta had promised.

The first was her usual weapon, a Glock-12. Someone had done his homework to know what she usually carried. As the van moved, she checked it and found it to be both new and in good working order. The second gift, a second pistol, was more of a museum piece. She recognized it as a Baby Browning, a small semi-automatic pistol. It had a 6-round magazine capacity, a striker-fired, single-action, blow-back mechanism. Browning had been making these little killers for decades. This weapon looked to be about twenty years old, but in excellent condition: a perfect second weapon, complete with ankle holster.

No words were spoken; this was how business was done and this was how a woman from New York would be wise to dress for her evening meeting. She examined her weapons one by one as the van moved. She loaded magazines, dropped the safety catches into their proper positions so that a bump in the road—and there were already plenty of them—didn't result in her shooting off her foot or a piece of her hip. Then she clipped the Glock in its holster to her left side. A moment later, she drew her left leg up to her, lifted the hem of her khakis until her calf was free and exposed, and placed the second weapon in its holster on her ankle. By this time, the van was on the access highway to the city.

Ready to roll, she thought to herself. She felt better being armed again.

Carlo, the Honduran, began a backstory in Spanish from the backseat, updates on where they were going, who they would be seeing. Alex turned to listen. Her eyes floated away from Carlo, and her gaze settled through the rear window of the van and on a vehicle that was following. Luis caught her gaze.

"Parte de nuestro equipo," Carlo said, without even looking. He switched to English, even though it wasn't necessary. "Part of our team. Don't worry." Carlo, she now noticed, had a semi-Bronx rasp to his Spanish.

They veered from the highway several minutes later and traversed a working-class neighborhood of shops, small millinery workshops, and homes. The movement of the traffic was stop and go, the feeling nonstop infuriating. Their driver laid off the horn and the escort car that was following remained right behind them, its nose consistently almost to the rear bumper of the van.

Then, as conversation within their vehicle continued, the follow-up car stopped and held its position, blocking the traffic from the rear. Seeing this, Alex knew they were about to make a move, and they made one, indeed. To their right was a steel door to what appeared to be an auto repair shop. The door rose. Within, a man in oil-stained coveralls pulled a chain that lifted the door.

Their driver did a quick scan of the sidewalks and streets and then turned to his right so sharply that all his passengers lurched to their left. He gunned his engine and the van rolled into the repair shop. The gate went down so fast that Alex wondered how it missed the rear of the van, but it did.

"Hurry along," Ken said, opening the sliding doors.

Two big young men, nominally "mechanics," helped with the van door. One had an automatic rifle across his chest, aimed downward. Ken stepped out first, Alex followed. The positioning was awkward, and she was still dragging her carry-on and making sure the gun clipped to her belt was secure. The second mechanic, a clean-cut Honduran boy in workman's coveralls and an army haircut, offered Alex a hand to steady her and a polite smile to reassure her. She accepted both.

Their host led them through a warren that passed through the two neighboring storefronts, then to another garage. He indicated another vehicle. It was an ambulance with a red cross icon and the words Cruz Rossa Hondurena emblazoned on its side. Alex admired the touch as they all climbed into the back. There were small tinted windows in the rear of the vehicle. Anyone trying to see in would be skunked.

The doors slammed, another garage door flew up, and they were out again on a parallel street going in a different direction. The whole transfer had taken less than two minutes. They rolled for another ten minutes, then went into a hospital parking lot, where they walked into an administrative building and out of it just as fast into another unmarked van. This one, Alex could tell as she settled into the back, was armor plated: police or army security or maybe DEA.

"Hope you didn't mind the little charade," Ken said in English.

"Not at all. I enjoyed it."

"Can never be too careful," he added.

"I agree," she added.

The van navigated a warren of backstreets of San Pedro Sula then emerged onto what passed for a highway, then onto a toll road that had police watching access points. The driver slowed and took a ticket from an attendant. Alex turned slightly in her seat and rode with her back partially to the side of the van. She saw, as they pulled from the booth, that they had acquired yet another escort vehicle that drove behind them.

"Army," said Kenneth in English, not even looking but picking up on Alex's apprehension and observation. "Someone somewhere is pretty anxious to have you returned to New York or Washington or wherever you came from in one piece. Not sure I've seen such a vigilant escort."

"Again, I'm appreciative," Alex said.

"As well you should be," he added, with the first slight suggestion of a smile.

They drove in silence for a quarter hour. By the remaining light in the sky, Alex could tell they were heading to the north, probably the northwest. She knew they couldn't go far, as the sea was the boundary.

"We're going to Puerto Cortes," Ken finally said. "Army safe house. That's where you'll find 'Suarez.'"

"I thought he was at one of your advance outposts."

"Too risky. They moved the prisoner."

"What else can you tell me?" Alex asked.

"What do you want to know?"

"As much as you're willing to tell me up front," Alex said. "I get the idea that you're more than Colonel Acosta's errand guy."

"I'm the colonel's second in command," Ken said. "So here's what I can tell you about you and Suarez. You're going to listen to the story, run the interview," Ken said. "Then you tell the colonel what you want to do. See, the thing is, you've put a pretty good dent in the Dosi operation in this area. That doesn't mean

NOEL HYND ★ 222

we're putting an end to the narco traffic. That will never happen until we legalize the junk and take the profit out of it. But that's my opinion and unofficial, and if you repeat that opinion up north, they'll think I've gone soft. About a year ago much of the Dosi organization in this area started to unravel. It was the same time as your operation—"

"Párajo?"

"That's the one. When you started to roll up their networks, the bottom ranks of the operation suddenly bought into a collective paranoia. There were defections and wannabe defections all over Honduras, Guatemala, and northern Nicaragua. A lot of the big shots went down with the first wave of arrests, while some cashed in their chips and moved to safer places for them. Friendly retirement in Mexico, say, or Bolivia. Take your million bucks and run. But that left the small fry behind. The drivers. The airplane mechanics. The chauffeurs. The phone people. The warehouse people. The runners, the bagmen. A whole bunch of small-timers suddenly wanted to jump sides."

It was dark out now. The van was driving toward a halfmoon that hung above the horizon at the far end of the highway. The moon was bright yellow and almost looked as if it were marking a target.

"We formulated three categories for the people who were coming to us," Ken said.

"Category C: If a potential turncoat didn't have good enough information, we'd give him a few bucks just to keep him liking us. It's the American taxpayers' money, not mine, so what do I care? Then we'd just leave him in place. No harm, no foul. Tell him or her to keep his ear to the ground and come see one of us adults if he sniffs out anything good in the future."

They hit a bump on the highway, a heavy one. The occupants of the van bounced with the jolt and a couple of hands went for guns, even if the pothole was nowhere near as threatening as a bullet might have been.

"Category B," Ken continued. "These are people in sensitive positions within the smuggling or financial organization. Bank employees. Radiomen. Monitors. Drivers. People with access to ongoing material and logistics. We work them back into the system as paid spies, assuming no one is onto them and they're not going to get whacked some morning over coffee. They get a cash stipend and keep working. Must be nerve-wracking stuff. Never know when someone's going to snitch and you're going to be fitted with a piano wire around your throat."

"Have you lost any of these people?"

By the yellow glow of car lights passing in the opposite direction, Alex watched Ken's face pucker in thought. "Not yet," he said at last. "We do what we can, but these people are taking their own chances. Then there's Category A. If an informant has top-grade stuff, we buy him or her outright. We download him of all the information that we think we can glean, then we re-settle him somewhere. US if it's possible, though some of these people want to go farther afield. Spain is popular. So is Paraguay, so is Peru. That's usually the case with one-timers, people who have one big piece of info and need to make one big sale."

"Like Suarez?"

"Like Suarez," said Ken. "The only trouble with this informant," he said, "was that more than once agency had claim on Suarez. The Honduran army wanted Suarez, so did the national police, so did the DEA. So far, the Justice Department has trumped them all. You've got the juice. Suarez is your asset as long as you want."

"You can hold him there indefinitely?"

"No. We'd have to move Suarez for more reasons than I can even begin to count. But it will be your call after the interview, after you hear what Suarez has to say. I'll let you know what the options are. Those are my instructions. You tell me what you need, I tell you what I can do. It doesn't work the opposite way. Orders," he said.

"Okay," Alex said, understanding. "Orders."

The van left the highway. They were on broken asphalt, then dirt, then gravel. Foliage rose on both sides of the van, vegetation that was thick, dark, primitive, and foreboding. After winding slowly on a narrow dirt driveway, they approached a gate with a cement guardhouse. A single light burned inside. Beyond, in the center of a well-lit quarter acre, was a single-story edifice that appeared to be midway between a prison and a military installation.

The driver rolled to a halt and gave a soft low toot of the horn. Two men emerged from the house, both soldiers in uniform. One had a sidearm, the other an automatic rifle. The one with the heavier weapon stood about ten yards away. The soldier with the pistol approached the gate and unlatched it. The van rolled forward. There was a low concrete building at the end of the driveway, painted green, no marking. Alex heard the gate slam shut behind them.

They stepped out into a humid night. There was the sound of insects and moisture ticking on a nearby stand of trees. The soldiers remained behind them and watched the gate. Fortunately, there was no trouble. Ken led the way and the party of four went into the wide, low building that looked like a military outpost. It had the feel of a bunker, bars across the windows, deeply tinted glass. Lights were everywhere to illuminate the grounds within.

Kenneth led Alex into the reception area, which was more in the way of bunker architecture. The place had been built to withstand a shelling, or at least a few bombs. There were two flags by the door, an American and a Honduran one, just to add to the confusion of who was running the place. Two more young soldiers stood quietly at the door as everyone filed in.

There was a tall man in camouflage fatigues standing in the center of the room, arms folded behind his back. He was tall, six-feet-two she guessed, with a shaved head and spectacles. His eyes, dark and smart, found Alex right away, which probably wasn't difficult, Alex guessed, as she figured she was the only woman within a mile.

He offered her a smile. She searched his lapels for a rank and saw the eagles. She wondered whose army. Then he answered all her preliminary questions at once.

"Alex LaDuca, I assume," he said in English. "FinCEN, New York, correct?"

"Correct, all of that," she answered.

"I'm Bill Acosta, US Army, Anti-Narcotics Division, Central America," he said quietly.

They exchanged the pleased-to-meet-yous.

"Do you need food? Water? Refreshment before you meet our prisoner? I thought you might want to start the interview tonight. Then we can continue in the morning."

"Just some cold water, then," she said.

Colonel Acosta switched into perfect Spanish and dispatched one of the young soldiers to a pantry. Then the meeting moved

along. Colonel Acosta led Alex and the other guests down a corridor, while the driver stayed behind. He unlocked a steel door
with a key and a combination, then a hand image swipe, and they
walked into what was obviously to be their interrogation chamber. There were a table, chairs, and, as Alex scanned, a security
camera, which obviously took in everything.

"Thanks," Acosta said to the boy soldier when he appeared
with water bottles. "Get the prisoner."

"Yes, sir."

He didn't say which prisoner, Alex noted, suggesting there
was only one. Or only one important one.

Alex settled in at the center of a table, wondering what to
expect next. Several minutes passed. Acosta attempted to fill it
with small talk. He was from Texas, he said, and was due for
leave if he could ever get away from this place, which was sure
to blow up immediately without him if he dared to stray for two
days. Alex commiserated. Sometimes, she agreed, a good steady
job was like a pair of custom-tailored handcuffs.

Then a second door opened, one that led obviously to a cell
area. Alex flinched, gasped, not ready for what she saw.

The young soldier returned first, followed by a prisoner in
an orange jumpsuit. Behind them came another soldier. Alex's
eyes went to the prisoner.

So much for Alex's on-the-fly theory of being the only
female within shooting distance. The prisoner was a *woman*,
small framed, about five-two, light brown hair, and an Anglo
face. She walked with a pronounced limp. She was hard to
connect with the legend of cunning and violence that had preceded her.

Colonel Acosta confirmed everything.

"This is the individual we call Suarez," he said. "We played with the gender, obviously, to not tip off anyone. Her real name is Judith Moreno and she's from Fort Worth, Texas."

Alex eyed her up and down. The prisoner remained standing. Her eyes rose. Deep blue.

"Judith Moreno," Alex said, looking the young woman in the eye. "'Judy,' would it be?"

Judith waited a beat to make sure it was safe to answer. Her eyes shot back and forth from the colonel to Alex and back again.

"Yeah, you can call me that if you like," she said.

Her English was native. She spoke with a soft Texas accent, a touch of Latina. Alex took a second to study her. She had a pretty face with delicate features: light brown hair pulled back, a small jagged scar on the lower left jaw, blue eyes that were half-vacuous and half-cunning, with a heavy insolence quotient tossed in. Her forearms were heavily designed with bold tattoos. Alex took them as gang markings.

A trailer-park Venus.

Alex had seen the type before, often in jails or juvenile detention schools. They had the look of Girl Scouts but the spirit of hellcats. Never turn your back: an emery board could turn into a shiv in half a heartbeat.

"Why don't you sit down, Judy?" Alex said. "Let's get to know each other."

"Okeydokey," Judy said. Her tone was almost grudging. The chair squealed on the floor as the soldier dragged it back. He allowed the prisoner to sit.

"Thank you, ma'am."

Ma'am. It sounded far too formal for the setting. But for the moment Alex let it ride. She drew a breath and ordered cans of chilled coffee. Yes, she decided, with a witness like this, anything was possible.

TWENTY-EIGHT

At the steel table, the prisoner folded her manacled hands and faced Alex. Her gaze was straight on Alex, but Alex sensed Judith Moreno still had one inner eye on an inner world, or a world beyond the prison and the current situation. Colonel Acosta sat to the other side of the prisoner at the same table.

Judith was rake-thin and fidgety. A twenty-year-old would-be, wannabe gangster. She was affable but hyperactive, or maybe she had consumed too much white powder. Sometimes her eyes seemed to track an invisible fly.

"You're in a bit of trouble, aren't you?" Alex began.

"How do you mean?"

"Well, from what I hear, a bit of an orphan. I read some reports on the flight coming down here. You went up to the US, a job blew up, you couldn't stay there, but you're in hot water here, too. I understand that if I take a pass on you, if for some reason I don't feel you can help me, the DEA is prepared to turn you over to the army. Or, maybe worse, put you back out on the street in San Pedro Sula. That wouldn't be very nice, would it? I suspect there are some very rough people out there who'd take a few pieces of you, then have you shot."

"I'm used to taking care of myself," Judy asserted.

"Not very well, from what I can see. You're not walking very well, you've got a bounty on your pretty head in the real world, and you came into this room in handcuffs, just a few signatures away from being remanded to the Honduran army. I'd say you need a friend."

"Maybe."

"Well, you know what?" Alex continued. "I'm not your friend. Not now, not ever. I don't like you or think much of you. I don't really care if someone cuts your throat, except you might have some use for me. Follow?"

Judith only glared.

"What I can offer you, though, is a lifeline," Alex said. "It's going to be your own choice whether or not you cooperate with me, but I'd guess that you either come under my wing this evening, after which, assuming your truthfulness and cooperation, you'll have safety and a new life. Or, failing that, in three days, three weeks, three months, you'll be dead. Or worse, if there *is* something worse than dead." Alex turned to Colonel Acosta. "Would you agree with me, Colonel?"

Acosta scoffed. "I'd give her three days max on the outside before the Dosi organization cuts her throat. There's a twenty-five-thousand-dollar contract on her, cash payable to whoever can bring her head and one of her hands to the right Dosi operative in a box."

Judy was silent.

"My guess is that they'd disfigure her before they kill her. That's how it works down here. Cut off her hands or arms. Slash her chest. Then leave her."

Alex, suppressing an inner cringe, shrugged.

"See what I mean?" Alex said.

"He's lying," Judy said, meaning the colonel. "I don't scare so easy."

"Should we turn you over to the army, then? The soldiers? Tonight, maybe. And we'll see how it goes?"

"I didn't say that," Judy said.

"Wise," Alex said. "My name is Alex, by the way. And the rules are very simple. I tell you the truth, you tell me the truth. You help me, I help you."

"Okay."

"If you jerk me around, if I catch you in lies, I drop you like a live wire. And whatever your situation is now, it will be worse."

"I get it."

Alex offered a hand. They exchanged an awkward handshake, the prisoner's manacles weighing down the moment. The young soldier returned with chilled cans of coffee, Starbucks knockoffs. He gave one to Alex and one to Colonel Acosta. Judy received a bottle of non-caffeinated cola.

Alex turned to Bill Acosta. "Is there any reason Judy needs to remain handcuffed?"

"None that I know of," Acosta answered. "She's not going anywhere and the matron did a full search."

"Then where would we find the keys?" Alex asked.

"*Llaves,*" the colonel said to the young soldier. The young man produced a steel key from a pants pocket. He unlocked the manacles on the prisoner's wrists.

"Thank you, ma'am," Judith said.

Alex watched as the steel cuffs came away from Judith's wrists. The prisoner flexed her fingers first, then the entire hand, and then the wrist. The cuffs had been quite tight: Alex watched the blood rush back. Alex also noticed calluses on the prisoner's thumbs and palms. She wondered where she had once done manual labor—prison, maybe?—and what sort it might have been.

Judy's eyes rose and she caught Alex looking.

"Better?" Alex asked.

"Yeah. They was kinda tight. Hurt a lot," Judith said.

"I'm sure."

"Good to have them off," Judith said.

"That's your real name, is it?" Alex asked, opening a can of coffee. "Judith Moreno?"

"Yes, ma'am."

"I'm told you murdered a young man in a motel room in Jacksonville, Florida," Alex said. "Is that true?"

A long pause. "I shot him, yeah."

"That wasn't very nice of you. Why did you do that?"

Judith shrugged. "Money."

"You were smuggling, right? You were on a run delivering some cocaine, I'd guess, and you murdered your partner, took off with the drugs, and sold them somewhere else. Do I have that pretty much correct?"

"I guess."

"Look me square in the eye and give me a yes or a no."

"Yes," she said.

Alex started to shake her head. "I find your stupidity to be of world-class proportions, Judith," Alex said. "Coke smuggling and murder. That's enough to send you away for life in Florida. But then you whack one of the couriers for a cartel financed by the Dosi syndicate. That's enough to make the prison sentence in Florida look like Club Med, if the coke boys catch you."

"They haven't yet," Judith said defensively.

"But it could be arranged," Alex said. To which Judith had no good answer.

"I hear you got busted in the Bahamas," Alex said next. "Trying to take money out of a bank account that wasn't yours."

Judith gave a snickering little laugh. "Yeah," she said.

"It was an account belonging to a Dosi corporation, wasn't it?"

"Uh-huh."

"How did you know the numbers?"

"I used to be a cash courier," she said. "I knew all the names and all the numbers."

"And you still remember them?"

"That's why you got me here, isn't it?" Judith asked.

"It's one reason." Alex paused. "How much were you trying to withdraw?"

"Fifty thousand dollars," she said with nerve.

"What went wrong?"

"I got the signature off. The teller called bank security."

"And security called the police, I would assume."

Judith nodded.

"Not your lucky day, was it?" Alex asked.

"Maybe not."

Alex made a few notes in her notebook. Then she leaned back. "How did you get there?" Alex asked.

"Where's 'there'?" Judith answered.

"Freeport. Bahamas."

"Ha! That's a story!"

"I'm listening," Alex said.

"Buses," said Judith.

"You took a bus from the United States to the Bahamas? That's a good one. Do tell."

"Buses and boats," she said. "When all that stuff came down in Jacksonville, I turned around. I was gonna go to Miami, but I figured there was too many bad vibes there. So I lit out for Texas. My old hometown, you know. I get there and there were already people looking for me."

"How did you know that?" Alex asked.

"I had a few old friends. I used to work in a music store in Galveston. I went in. Saw an old girl-buddy. First thing she says is, you better pay your bills. I say, what? I don't have no bills. Then she said there was a guy looking for me. Guy named Tito. Said I owed him a few Franklins. That was bull, Miss Alex. I didn't owe nobody no money."

"Do you know who this 'Tito' might have been?"

"Yeah, maybe. A local Dosi guy." Then, "Can I smoke?" she asked.

"One cigarette," Alex said.

"I don't have no smokes myself," Judy said.

Alex looked to Bill Acosta, who shrugged. Then he made a smoking gesture to the soldiers, drawing on an imaginary cancer stick. The soldier with the pistol produced a soft pack of Kools. Alex motioned to Judith, who flirted with the young solder and got him to light it for her.

"So we left off in Texas, Judith," Alex said. "But now you're two or three borders away."

"Yeah."

"Normally, that implies a passport."

"Uh-huh. Yeah, it does, Miss Alex." She looked to the colonel.

A moment, then, with the air of confession, "We've been holding a few personal items for Judith," Colonel Acosta said. "Just in case she got a wanderlust and wanted to bolt. Or in case you need to move her quickly."

"That remains to be seen," Alex said. "I might just throw her to the wolves here," she added for effect.

"Yeah, well, she's got the traveling papers," Acosta said.

The colonel reached to a jacket pocket and pulled out what appeared to be a United States passport. Blue with the gold lettering, the flat eagle that looked as if it had been run over by a steamroller, with the arrows, the olive branches, and the Latin phrase that most people couldn't remember.

He tossed it onto the table. Alex picked it up and examined it.

"I got to thinking," Judith said, "I'd done some heavy-duty work for the organization. I had killed one of their importers and delivered a million dollars' worth of goods for them. And I was still living on nothing. So I wanted to rip them off. I figured I'd raid some of their bank accounts. Give myself some retirement dough. Then disappear."

Alex laughed. "After a stunt like that, where did you think you could go where they'd never find you?"

"Way out west somewhere, maybe. Wyoming. Montana. Change my name. Live in a cabin."

"Sure," said Alex, turning over the passport, looking at the bindings and the inking. "Where's your real passport, Judith? This one's a fake. Real name, but a fake passport."

"I figured the real one was hot, you know?" Judith said. "So I trashed it."

"Trashed it how?"

"Burned it."

"This one *is* actually very impressive," Alex said. "Must have cost you a few dollars."

"Yeah. It did."

"I suppose you bought it with the proceeds of the drugs you stole in Florida. Would I be right about that?"

"Sort of."

"Where did you say you got it? The passport."

"I didn't say."

"Why don't you say now?"

"Miami," she said.

"Miami's a big city. Where in Miami?"

"I'm not here to rat people out," she said, some anger coming into her voice.

"I didn't ask for names."

"A friend does some printing. He ran it up for me, knocked it off."

"Does the passport number work?"

Judith was silent. She shrugged.

"She's used it twice in the Caribbean," Acosta said. "That's how she got to the Bahamas."

"Interesting," Alex said. "It probably works in some friendly places but not others. Well, who knows?"

Alex flipped the passport back onto the table. "I would call this a professional forgery," Alex said. "An authentic replica. A legitimate alchemist. A bull heifer. I've always had a grudging admiration for forgers," Alex said. "Most of them could have been fine artists, if only they didn't have that dishonest gene working against them. Here's the deal, Judith," Alex said. "It's your career as a runner of cash from the United States to the

Bahamas that interests me. That and wherever else you plied your trade. You indicated that you know the company names, where the banks are, and the account numbers. Is that correct?"

"It's correct."

"And you've got this all memorized, do you?"

"Yeah. I know the numbers. And the names," she said. "I was always, you know, ready."

"In case you ever wanted to turn against them, right? Or try to clean them out."

"You could say that."

"How many do you know?"

"Maybe fifty to seventy. If I reach."

"Let's start with the easiest ones," Alex said. "I'm going to leave the room. You're going to write down corporate names, banks, and account numbers on that pad. When you're ready, I'm going to collect it. Then I'm going to check. If everything's right, I'll get you back to the US and put you in protective custody, and we can start attacking the remnants of the Dosis' financial empire. If a single number is wrong, I will probably leave you here."

Judith nodded. "Okay."

Alex prepared to stand.

"There's another part of this," Judith said.

"What's that?"

"That guy I shot in Florida. Mrs. Dosi put me up to it."

Skeptically, "Why did she do that?" Alex asked.

"His name was Pete Jimenez. I don't know. She had it in for him. And she trusted me. That's how I knew all the account numbers. I was supposed to keep half the money from the drugs, but, I don't know, I got greedy. And scared. I thought it was a trap."

Alex stood. "You'll testify to that if I get you to the US and into protection?"

"Yes, ma'am," Judith said.

Alex indicated the pad. "Work on the names and numbers, Judith," she said. "We'll talk homicide later if your numbers work."

TWENTY-NINE

I 'd love to offer you a fancy dinner at a nice place," Acosta said. "But we only have a small officers' quarters here. Want to join me, even for a club soda?"

"Sure," Alex said. "I can use the opportunity to unwind."

"I'll have the sergeant take your bag to the barracks. We're always under siege conditions here," he said, "but the traffickers have more profitable things to do than attack us. They prefer to just avoid us as best they can. But there's always the possibility, particularly with Miss Universe in there," he said.

"Do they know she's here?"

"Good question," he said. "You have a weapon, right?"

She nodded.

"You've been in places like this before," he said with a smile. "I can tell."

"More than a few times," Alex said.

"Keep it near you at all times. You never know when we might have visitors."

They were halfway between buildings. The humidity was thick and oppressive, noisy insects everywhere. Alex slapped her arm twice on the short stroll of no more than fifty feet. With the second slap she killed a mosquito that had been the size of a dime until she nailed it. There was blood in the remains.

"Anything that flies or crawls is potentially poisonous," Acosta said. "So be careful."

"I'm trying to be," she answered.

"I'll get you some antiseptic for that," he said, looking at her arm.

Ahead of them was another bunker-styled building. Two US Special Forces MPs stood outside, bearing assault weapons. They came to attention as the colonel approached. They saluted. The colonel returned the salute.

"At ease, men," he said softly. One of them withdrew a step or two and opened the door. Alex gave them an appreciative nod. They entered a well-fortified entrance hall. Colonel Acosta used a card to swipe a security point and entered a five-digit number. Then they were in a hallway. More concrete within concrete.

"Suarez mentioned a group called the 'Maras,'" Alex said.

"You know who they are?"

"I did a lot of homework before I flew down here. Local gangbangers, right?"

Acosta snorted in agreement. "You could say that. Las Maras Salvatruchas. Big-time gang. Very big-time. They're power players here. Suarez used to play for their team, which is unusual for an American female. It's probably why she popped that Mexican kid in Jacksonville. Trying to prove she was as tough as any of their male hoodlums."

"They were mentioned in several of the documents I read before I flew down here," Alex said. "Can you give me any more specifics?"

"Plenty," he said. "Drink? Food?"

He motioned to a large refrigerator. When he opened it, she

saw it was well stocked. "Just some bottled water," she said. "And something to eat. That would be great."

"Coming up," he said. "Sure you don't want something with more pop? We got whiskey. Gin. Vodka."

"Just water, thanks."

He grabbed some bottled water for Alex and two cans of beer for himself, plus a handful of packaged pretzels and nuts and a package of processed meat. Cordon bleu it wasn't. Survival stuff it was.

He led her from the dispensing area to a small adjoining lounge. It was sparsely decorated, no windows. There were a few pictures of local operations, an American flag on a stanchion, a self-service bar, and a microwave. Tables and chairs were arranged around the room.

"Okay, the 'Maras,'" Acosta said as they pulled up chairs and sat at a table.

There were two other small groups of soldiers in the lounge. Junior officers, she noticed. They talked quietly and ignored the colonel and his guest. "Or 'Mareros,' as they're sometimes called," Acosta continued. "You've probably seen pictures. Members mark themselves with tattoos covering the body and often the face."

"So that was a Mara tattoo on Judith's forearms?"

"Would appear to be," Acosta said. "She's got them all over her body. Disgusting stuff, if you ask me. You can have a look if you want. We have pictures."

"I'll take your word for it," Alex said.

"The Maras and the other big hoodlum gang, the *Dieciochos*, are notorious for their violence. They're from Salvador too, the other people. Dieciocho. That means 'eighteen' in Spanish."

"I speak Spanish," Alex said.

Acosta forged on. "The Dieciochos are from Barrio 18 in the city. Their moral code, both gangs, them and the Maras, consists mostly of retribution. No mercy for anyone. Do I need to soft-soap this or mince words? You can take the ugly stuff, right? If they want to get back at you, make their point, if they don't kill you, they'll do something worse. Last week I heard of a case where they cut off an enemy's testicles and sent them to the man's wife in a jug of homemade rum. They love to disfigure women who cross them, also. Now their excesses have earned them a path to the bigger time. They've been recruited by the Sinaloa Cartel battling against Los Zetas in the drug wars up in Mexico. It's all about machismo and narco-trafficking. Drugs. Extortion. High-tech weapons and violence. They began with planeloads of Central American gangsters deported from the US. The gangs originated in the United States. LA. Between 1998 and 2009, the US dumped seventy-five thousand young convicts out of their jails back to the native countries of their parents in Central America. Children of illegal immigrants. Most had never set foot in Central America until being deported. Some didn't even speak Spanish. But they were quickly recruited because they'd learned gang tactics in Los Angeles. Oh, the tattoos?" Acosta asked, sipping a Budweiser. "They usually include one with three points. Symbols: the stopping points of a Mara life. Hospital, prison, and morgue."

"Silly question," Alex said, "but with destinations like that, why does anyone sign on?"

"Some kids join just to get away from their families, others to hang out with friends. The gangs offer the things all of these young Latino punks crave. Drugs, guns, cars, and sex. They also rob buses and raid each other's territory. That's when the rifles and Uzis come out," said Acosta, forming his hand in the shape of a gun. "That's when there's real trouble." He threw back more beer.

"It's an attractive package, with the power and pseudo respect wrapped in," said Acosta. "Their business is drugs, extortion, and they don't lack for stupid young men. The estimates are from one hundred to two hundred thousand of them just in Central America. They're fueling death rates to match the years of guerrilla warfare and counterinsurgency in Nicaragua and Salvador." He started a new Bud. "You may only last one or two years in a gang, but it makes you someone."

"Why would a female join?" Alex asked.

Acosta seemed to take the question as a challenge. "Why don't you go back in and ask her?" he shot back.

"I might," Alex answered steadily. "I'm not questioning that she was a member. I'm trying to wrap my head around it, why a woman would subject herself to that."

"Females do a lot of nutty things," Acosta said.

"And men don't?"

"Power trip," he said. "For that girl in there, for anyone. Belonging to something, even if the something is a pile of crap to us. The illusion of wealth," he said. "More of them wind up dead than empowered. But try telling that to an eighteen-year-old who comes from nothing, has got nothing, and sees nothing in the future but roadblocks. You got a strong stomach, Alex? I'm not giving you too much, am I?"

"No," she said. "Not at all."

"My chat is going to get gross and dirty and disgusting. Let me know when I'm giving you too much."

"With all due respect, I don't think you could."

He grinned. "We'll see," he said. "The gangs have initiation rituals. That usually means stripping naked and getting a group beating if the recruit is male. In Judith's case in there, it meant sex with every male in her chapter. That probably meant fifty or sixty of those tattooed, disease-ridden young punks. And this is voluntary, mind you."

The notion sickened Alex, but she didn't outwardly react. It didn't surprise her. She had seen enough of this stuff to not be shocked at anything. But she found the concept deeply repellent nonetheless.

"Most of these local punks grew up in the streets and entered the gangs very young. One day you're Fabian, Miguel, Carlito, Luis, Omar, or Alberto. The next day you're el Demente, el Sombra, el Zorro Loco, or el Bestia. Then after the initiation, you're not a full member till you're ordered to do a kill and do it successfully. The kid she whacked in Jacksonville? He was probably one of her initiation sex partners, but he may have been her assigned killer, also, and she figured it out. So she iced him first. They know she's a turncoat now. So if they catch her, she gets this," he said, drawing a line under his throat. "They don't just shoot you. They cut your throat, then watch you bleed to death. And they let the newbies watch so they learn some fear and respect." He paused, then, indicating, he said, "Out there, beyond these walls, the Hondurans are putting their kids in cemeteries all the time. It's no big thing. There's always another ambitious trigger-happy punk to take the place of the one who got snuffed."

Acosta opened the packaged meat with his teeth, pulled back the wrapper, and pushed it to Alex. "Sorry we don't got anything better to offer you," he said. "We make do down here. If we all get out alive, we'll call it a success. If we don't get out alive, we won't be around to call it. So nothing to worry about, right? You got a husband?"

"I'm not wearing a ring, am I?"

"No, but you're smart and sassy. That's a compliment. You'd be wise enough to take it off before you flew down here."

"Thanks, and no. Not married."

"Got a guy?"

"A great one."

"Good for you. Do your duty, get your tail out of here after you've done your work, and take care of your man and have a happy family. Fifteen years ago I was a good Catholic and a new dad. Now I'm twice divorced thanks to this job and have two kids who hate me."

Alex helped herself to two slices of something that resembled turkey.

"We're starting to see the same type of activities that we've seen in Mexico," Acosta said. "Not just bloodthirsty killings, but mutilations. The cartels are taking their lessons from Al-Qaeda, I'm afraid, which makes them even more dangerous if you ever thought that these narco criminals and the Islamic fascist terrorists would throw in their lots together against US interests. The Dosis work hand in hand with both the Zetas and the Sinaloa cartel. It's the banking aspect that gives them a walk. The Mexicans aren't so smart with their money; the Dosis are brilliant."

"Exactly why I'm trying to close them down, cut off the twin heads of the snake."

"More power to you," Acosta said. "If it was up to me, I'd have them assassinated, but I don't make the rules. I just get stuck following them."

"Then we have that in common," Alex said.

"My point is that here in Honduras," Acosta said, "we're starting to see the killings and the mutilations. About a year ago, there were about sixty bodies dumped on a highway outside Vera Cruz. Work of the Zetas. All the bodies were decapitated, some were mutilated even more. There's a message behind the mutilations. If they cut out a tongue, it means the victim talked too much. Anyone who gave up any information on a cartel, no matter how small, no matter how insignificant, his finger gets cut off while he's alive and stuffed into his mouth after execution. This type of traitor is known as *un dedo*—a finger. There have been tens of thousands of them in Mexico over the last decade; now it's spreading here, across central Honduras. They castrate you if you have slept with a cartel member's woman or if you have, in the case of a government official, police, or the military, become too boastful about battling the cartels. A severed arm means you stole from your consignment of illegal goods or you skimmed profits off the top. Severed legs mean that you tried to retire, walk away from the cartel. You don't retire; you're in it for life no matter how long or short that might be. Decapitation, however, is an even bigger game. It is a statement of raw brutality, a warning to all, like the public executions of old. In other words, '*Somos los reyes aquí. Vamos a hacer lo que queramos.*'" We are the kings here and we will do whatever we want. His eyes narrowed. "A woman, it's even more horrific. There should be a special fire in hell for these people."

"Maybe there is," Alex said.

"Did you say any prayers before you flew down here?"

"Is that a serious question?"

"Yes, it was."

"I did. Several."

"Good. You'll need them. Let's hope they work for you."

"Thanks."

"Well, that's my good word. Stay close to us and hang on to your two guns. These are just a few of the symbolic 'messages' the cartels use. And if they catch you, you're law enforcement like anyone else. What happened to those bodies in Mexico, in Veracruz, that would happen to you. Or me. Heads have been thrown into nightclubs and one victim's face was skinned and sewn onto a football. There's been a resurgence in beheadings, thanks to cartel leaders inspired by Al-Qaeda execution videos. Every cut sends a message, and the extreme violence is intended to intimidate folks like us." He paused. "Ever been to Tegucigalpa?" he asked.

"Only to pass through," Alex said. "Like tonight."

"Even for Central America, Tegucigalpa's slums are beyond incredible," Acosta said. "Twelve-year-old tarts. Ten-year-old glue sniffers parked on rubbish dumps, even younger children begging amidst sewage and burned-out cars. And the gangs rule that turf like their own little kingdoms. They hit pedestrians, motorists, cabdrivers, store owners with a toll known as *peaje*. They extort a 'war tax' from big businesses. If you don't pay, your employees get shot at, your vehicles get torched, and your buildings take a fusillade of bullets every few days. So if you're not crazy, you pay. Honduras has the highest murder rate in the hemisphere, worse than Colombia, worse than Haiti. It averages twelve or thirteen a day, and that's just what's reported. Hey, there are seven million people in this country, and last year nearly seven thousand of them got murdered. And it's these gangs who are responsible. Know what was the most violent day of the year last year? Christmas. Christmas, can you believe it? God help us! Fifty-two people got killed. They like to drive home a point. Anyone who decides to quit the Maras has to live with a lifetime death sentence on them. It's a rule. No one can leave behind his Mara. To do so puts at risk the life of his family and friends. They'll come and hunt you down anywhere in the western world.

"Let me tell you a quick story, then I got to get some shut-eye and you should, too. There was a civilian man who worked here on the army base for a while. Honduran. Named Hector. I never trusted him completely, but that's a different issue. He had a daughter named Sylvia. Pretty little girl. Maybe fourteen or fifteen. Hector worked here and her mother worked in a sweatshop stitching T-shirts for one of the big US companies. So no one's home during the day, and the daughter stopped going to school. Next thing you know, she started running with some boys who were in some second-tier gang. Well, little Sylvia Rodriguez was never altogether convincing as a gangster. She had the filthy tattoos and walked the walk, but she was too slight, too fragile, maybe too pretty to really look the part. She adopted the slang and body language, you know? All slouch, loose limbs, and burn-in-hell attitude. She had a dream, her father told me. She wanted to go to America and be an actress. She liked Madonna. And that other one with the Latino name. Played the Tex-Mex singer but she got whacked by the head of her fan club."

"Selena," Alex offered.

"Yeah. That's her," Acosta answered. "She even started making herself up to look like the actress who played her. Who was that?"

"Jennifer Lopez."

"That's right. She told friends, told her dad. She said that playing an apprentice gang member felt like a role. So she was acting at it, see? Wasn't really a gang babe. She just played one for these second-string punks. It was her big role and her last one. Her gang ran up against the Dieciochos and must have teed someone off. So the Dieciochos decided to get back by going after some of the rival gang's girlfriends. One night last November, Sylvia disappeared. Two weeks later a girl's body washes up in Puerto Cortes, wired to the bodies of two other young girls, also gang girlfriends, who had disappeared hiking in the Manzanales Mountains. All three girls had been murdered and dumped, a real-life end for wannabe teenage gangsters in this country. The corpses were bagged by police and transported to the judicial morgue in the capital, Tegucigalpa. You should go over there. Take a look. See what we're financing down here, see what we're trying to keep away from our doorstep. Grim, grim, grim, Alex. The morgue's fridge? It's a battered, grubby factory container from 1970. Used to be used for meat. It's free- standing outside and surrounded by rusting ambulances that don't run anymore and discarded stoves and microwaves. It's in a hospital junk yard with weeds and garbage that hasn't been picked up in a year. It stinks of desolation." He finished his second beer. "Anyway, I went over there with Hector, Sylvia's old man. Me and a couple of other US soldiers. Her dad had gotten a call that there were some new female bodies over there so he had to go look, maybe do an ID. We looked in the morgue container and even I had to hold back from barfing. Nothing but a stack of young bodies, maybe a dozen, not even wrapped right or frozen right. Yellow decaying feet poking out from dirty sheets, most of them bloodstained, some of the feet mutilated. The faces were all clammy masks. All of them teenagers. And then we start picking through them, taking a look, until Hector starts to scream and then cry. Hector identified his daughter by her ear studs and a cheap two-dollar tin necklace that he had given her for her birthday. Sylvia's nose and half of her face had been eaten away by fish, vultures, and coyotes.

"The gangster culture. The drug culture. There you go. We all chipped in here at the base. Five or ten bucks each. We bought her a Catholic funeral and a grave in a maintained cemetery. What else could we do?"

There was a terrible silence that hung in the air for many seconds, neither Alex nor Acosta having the wherewithal to break it. Then finally, Alex spoke.

"If I take her, I'm going to want to bring her back to the United States with me," Alex said.

"Take who?" Acosta asked.

"Suarez. Judy," Alex said, motioning toward the interrogation room and the resumed cell where she was being held. "That's who we were originally talking about, wasn't it?"

"Ah, well, yes. Of course."

"I'll probably need two security people and my guess is we'll have to catch a military transport plane. Would I be right?"

"I think so," he said. "Can't just drive someone like that to the airport, board a commercial flight, and waltz through customs and immigrations, can you? Not by a long shot. I'll be happy to release her to you," Acosta said. "The longer she's here the worse our security becomes. I'd like to move her before anyone finds out. Don't forget, I got her from the Honduran army. How good do you think they are at keeping a secret? Not very, in my opinion. It's a matter of time before someone in the army tips the gangs that she's here. If it were up to me, I'd be just as happy to dump her on the streets of San Pedro Sula."

"Well, you can't do that," Alex said.

"No?" the colonel asked sharply. "Why not?"

"She knows enough to convict Dosi if she tells a court what she told me."

"And if the jury believes you."

"So do I arrange the release with you or with Washington?" Alex asked.

"Both," Acosta said. "And I'll be glad to get her out of here. She's just a distraction and potential target. I hope she's worth more to you."

"Only if we keep her alive."

He stood. "You can take her as soon as the arrangements are made. You sure she's worth the trouble?"

"I'm *not* sure," Alex said. "I can authorize it myself, but I want to check with New York and Washington just to be on secure footing."

"Feel free. There are secure phone lines. Call in the morning."

"I'll do that," Alex said. "I admit, it's overflowing with risks from my point of view. But it's the chance I have to take. If she's my only witness against Señora Dosi, there will be another set of contracts out on her life in addition to the Mara head-hunting. It goes without saying that she'll have to go into the federal witness protection program, so I hope she likes northern Arizona, not that it matters. And you're right: Who knows if a jury is going to believe her, anyway, Colonel? It's hard enough to believe what you see down here with your own eyes, let alone having to convince some twelve citizens in court that someone like this isn't inventing stories just to make a deal. I mean, that's what the defense lawyers are going to hammer at. But if her story checks, that's the chance I have to take."

All of this seemed beyond the colonel's pay grade.

"Like I said, to my mind, she's a piece of scum. I'll be happy to be rid of her. You want her, you got her. I hope you take her. I don't envy you, Alex. Good luck."

———

Colonel Acosta's wish came true.

Alex picked up a list of banking information from Judith late that evening. The next morning she sent it electronically to both FinCEN and Rick McCarron at the CIA. Responses came back like a pair of yo-yos. Alex, and Judith, had a sale. A team from the Treasury Department began with criminal legal proceedings against various bank accounts in both the Bahamas and other offshore islands. Secrecy was one thing, but if the US government could prove that the proceeds were the result of narco-trafficking, or financing thereof, the assets could be tied up for years, if not seized. It would be another profound blow against the Dosi cartel.

The homicide situation was trickier.

Alex sat in Andy's office along with a FinCEN counsel and discussed it two days later.

"Judith is not a potentially credible witness in court," Alex conjectured, "but her testimony would probably be enough to get a grand jury to indict Yardena Dosi. It gives us another tool. At the very least, it's an unused weapon."

"How so?" De Salvo asked.

"There's no statute of limitations on homicide. As long as Yardena Dosi knows we could bring a case against her, I doubt she'd ever dare show up in the United States. If you were she, would you even want to risk it?" She looked around and saw a consensus. "I say we proceed with it," she concluded.

There were no objections around the room.

THIRTY

Winter weather being unpredictable, Carter Wilson drove south from New Jersey, reaching North Carolina on the first day. He then turned southwest on his second day, driving all the way to Arkansas. He paid cash at fuel stops and cash at the fast-food places that he patronized. The weather cooperated and there was no snow, no ice. He drove no more than five miles over any speed limit. He didn't want a ticket that would peg him to a time and place, and a dark-skinned man, he reasoned, was more likely to draw an inquisitive cop than a white man. So the trip progressed smoothly, though more slowly than if he had been able to really press the pedal to the metal.

By day four he was in Texas.

By day five, he was in Arizona.

By day six, he had found the fortified hamlet known as Vista Del Lago. There was a guard booth at the entrance to the community, but Carter quickly noticed that the guard was careless. The cheapskates who administered this place didn't provide the guard a backup for bathroom time, so it was easy to slip past the gate in his car when the guard disappeared into an adjacent administrative building.

That allowed Carter to scope out the community. It allowed

him to do a drive-by on unit 303, the residence of the people he was there to treat to a special repair.

Late in the day, he even managed to lay his eyes on one of them, a scrawny-looking fifty-five-year-old white man who was Carter's primary target. The next day he caught a glimpse of his wife. Then, over the next few days, he noticed that they were in the habit of golfing and dining at a place called the North Tucson Golf Association. They lived on a golf course, for heaven's sake! Carter wondered why they needed to go off and pay to play somewhere else when they could have remained in their own backyard.

But he didn't pursue the question. No answer would have made any difference. They were, after all, making his assignment easier for him. He settled in, observed the "clients'" daily patterns for a few days, and began to feel comfortable.

As soon as he felt comfortable, he started to plan the how, when, and where of completing his assignment. Good carpenter that he was, he removed the bag with the wrench and the bolts from within the rear of the car's chassis. It was almost time to go to work.

THIRTY-ONE

When Alex returned to New York, within a few days a new comfort zone had developed between her and Eric. The film was still scheduled for the summer and his departure from *South Pacific* had been announced. The most immediate result was upon ticket sales for the show. Every single performance between the present and the time of his departure was now sold out.

But beyond that, Priscilla Kim seemed to recede as a potential enemy. It still rankled Alex to stand in the wings of the theater and see the man she loved embrace, kiss, and sing love songs to another woman. "Just acting," he kept saying. "Just acting, Alex. Please believe me." Maybe it was because she had so much on her plate at work, but in the end, she was actually starting to believe him. It was just acting. Very good acting.

"There's something I've always wondered," Alex asked Eric the second Sunday evening after her return from Honduras. It was nine p.m. They walked together on Madison Avenue in the Seventies. "How do you do it? How do you stay so calm, so collected, with a house full of two thousand people watching your every move?"

"I know my job, I know my role, I come in rested and prepared every day," he said. "I'd be a fool not to handle my job properly. There are thousands of actors who would kill to be where I am."

"I just . . . admire the way you do things," she said.

He looked at her and released her hand as they walked. They passed her church: St. James at Seventy-First Street. They had gone there together the first Sunday she had been back. Oh, how she had needed it.

He wrapped an arm around her. "Alex, listen," he said. "I'm going to tell you something about me you don't know. It will explain a lot to you, I think."

She waited. A Madison Avenue bus pulled into a stop and discharged passengers. He waited till the clatter had ended and till other people were out of earshot.

"When I was twenty years old, I first started making some decent money in films," he said. "It wasn't a fortune, but I was young. Unattached. I had some prominent appearances on TV to go with the movie, and everyone wanted to be my friend because that's how Hollywood is. You can go up or down faster in Hollywood than any other place I've ever seen. Well, anyway, I was cooking. I went out and dropped forty thousand dollars on a car. It wasn't just a car. It was a vintage Jaguar. XKE. Not in the greatest condition, but it turned heads. I used to tool around in it, drove around the San Fernando Valley, Malibu, up to Big Sur, down to San Onofre. Hit all the surf towns, the parties, the girls. Well, I'm driving home one night. I had a place in Malibu, a little apartment. Nothing fancy, just nice and hidden away. It's about two a.m. I'm on Mulholland Drive, it's all mountainous and windy, it's where James Dean got killed, and suddenly I see headlights behind me, coming up fast. I watch my speed. I'm okay, not speeding, but you never know if it's the cops, and I'm a young guy in a car by myself, so I'm liable to get pulled over. So then the car behind me starts acting like it's got a bug up its butt. It comes close, tailgates me, swerves a little, and I think, whoa, this guy's drunk or on something, or whatever. I glance at my dashboard. I'm doing thirty, maybe, and this guy is tailing me for a couple of miles. Then suddenly, it's as if I hear a voice. It was so distinctive and clear it was as if someone called out to me. And you know what it said? It said, 'Put on your seat belt, Eric, my boy.' And I suddenly notice, my belt had come undone. It was an old car, remember. So I buckle up, particularly just in case it is the cops, or a rogue cop, behind me. And I drive on ahead. The guy drops back and I think I'm rid of him. I'm almost off the canyon road when I look in my rearview again and he's racing up behind me. There's a stop sign up ahead and I slow down because I can't run it. But somehow I know he's not even looking and I hit the stop sign, try to get out of it quickly, but it's no use. He's drunk. Or crazy. Or something. He skids and slams into me in the rear left quarter, knocks my car off balance and off the road. He blasts his horn for some reason, then just merrily drives away as I go over the curb and tumble. I don't know how many times my car turned over. Maybe three or four, but I'm thinking I'm dead, I'm waiting to die, and then the car comes to rest upright in a clump of bushes, about ten feet from going over an embankment with a hundred-foot drop. And I'm surprised to be alive. I unbuckle and get out real carefully. I had some scrapes on my arm and on my head, but aside from that, nothing. I climb the hill, flag down the next car, which must have been twenty minutes later, and we call the police. The car was damaged, but I was unhurt. I was home later that day wondering if all of that had really happened, but I know it did.

I had the car repair bill to remind me, for example," he laughed. "But that's not the point." He paused. "I can only say this to you, Alex. Everyone else will laugh. Or does laugh. Or did laugh." They crossed Sixty-Ninth Street. "God was tapping me on the shoulder that day," he said. "That's how I looked at it. God was telling me to slow down, think about my purpose, think about God's plan for me." He grinned. "Crazy?" he asked.

I love you, she nearly said. Very nearly, but didn't. "Not crazy at all," she said.

"I began to read the Bible again. Just a little here and there. Enough to find a road map. Guideposts. My own plan. Stay away from the stuff that kills your body and spirit. Six months later, I got my first big role. It's been all good since."

"Not crazy at all," she said. A winter wind came up and nearly sliced them in half.

"You know what *is* crazy?" he asked.

"What?"

"Walking in this cold. Let's get a cab and go home."

"I second it," she said.

Eric had been leasing his apartment, but recently he had purchased it directly from the owner. No mortgage, no trips to the bank. The asking price had been $1.4 million, and he had paid it in cash. Well, in a bank draft, actually. Movie stars, Alex thought. Broadway stars.

Eric wasn't in any way flamboyant or flashy but sometimes the amount of money he made took her breath away. She knew he quietly redirected tens of thousands of dollars a year into various charities, from the Red Cross at home to microfinance agencies that provided seed money to fledgling capitalist enterprises in Central and South America, as well as Africa and Asia.

NOEL HYND ★ 260

She knew, not because she had asked or because he had ever brought the subject up. But she had seen the paperwork lying around his desk in his apartment.

"I like what you do," she said to him later that same evening, looking at a printout of Kiva receipts. They sat together in his apartment over mugs of warm cider. A fireplace crackled.

"What do you mean, 'what I do'?" he asked.

"Microfinance," she said.

"Oh. That," he said, almost dismissing it. "It's a habit I picked up from my parents. No matter how well you're doing, no matter how comfortable you are, always look over your shoulder. There's someone who needs your help." He shrugged again. "It's only money—only loans, even. You can't take it with you. I'm lucky, I have more than enough. So I try to spread it around."

"I like that, Eric," she said. "I mean, I *really* like that."

"You've told me about your interest in Venezuela. Your trips there in the past. You do the same."

"But not everyone does."

"Hey! Want to do some right now?" he asked.

"Like what?"

He flipped open his laptop. "Let's lend out five hundred dollars."

They went to the site and Eric called up his account. They sat together on the sofa, Alex leaning on him, as they found cases. Then Eric made five "loans" of a hundred dollars each across Latin America. Alex eyed the account. She could see that what he did was put his money in play. When it was repaid, he lent it out again. It was none of her business, but he had launched close to ten thousand dollars into these various endeavors.

Even in Panama.

"You're too much," she said affectionately. She still felt over-loaded from the office and exhausted. She leaned against him and closed her eyes. That was the last thing she remembered from the evening as apparently, she learned the next morning, she accidentally fell asleep.

Eric placed a pair of blankets on her and placed a pillow under her head. She awoke the next morning at seven by instinct, let herself out, and was at work by her regular hour.

THIRTY-TWO

Caracas, Venezuela, was often described as *el jungla de concreta*, the concrete jungle, by South Americans. The description is more apt than not. The city is rarely the top destination for visitors to South America or even to Venezuela—it is a congested, noisy, and polluted metropolis of three million and, in many parts, dirty and crime-ridden. Wandering safely through many streets is a challenge, even in daylight. But Vicente, coming off his meeting with Debray in Bogotá, was hardly a tourist. A Cuban by birth, he had emigrated in his late teens and settled in Venezuela. So the short flight from Bogotá to the Venezuelan capital was a homecoming of sorts. Further, his adopted city might display staggering inequalities of wealth, but it was also bound together by the warmth and happiness of its inhabitants. He also shared their love of the beach and partying. He appreciated the verdant avenues, the excellent subway that shuttled people about, the Parisian-style street cafés, and the cool, soothing visual presence of Mount Avila. The pleasant tropical climate resembled the best of Italy or Spain with very little variation of temperatures between summer and winter.

Vicente kept his home not in Caracas proper, but in El Hatillo, a little colonial town located at the southeast suburbs of Caracas in the municipal area of the same name. The town was one of Venezuela's few well-preserved typical colonial regions. It reminded a visitor of what Caracas was like in the nineteenth century. Much like every town in Venezuela, Bolivia, and Colombia, El Hatillo had its own Plaza Bolívar with a statue of *Simon, El Libertador* in the middle. It also had a well-preserved Roman Catholic church and many colonial houses. Even the municipal government, banks, and bookshops bore the look of *los siglos passados.*

Today, however, found a refreshed Vicente back in Caracas, where he would call on two or three contacts to further his most recent assignment, the one he had received from Debray in Bogotá. He sat in the front of a small coffee shop adjacent to the Parque del Este, a rare green paradise in the middle of Caracas. The park for many years had contained two items of endless charm and interest. One was a small zoo, The other was a replica of the ship *La Santa Maria*, one of the three used by Christopher Columbus in his voyages to discover America in the late 1500s. Vicente loved to play on that ship when he was a boy, recently arrived from Cuba with his parents, and would imagine himself as the vessel's swaggering captain. The replica had been recently destroyed by the government of Hugo Chavez, however, an act of wanton savagery that Vicente would never forgive. Vicente hated Chavez. If Vicente had had to concoct a short list of the world politicians he most hated, Chavez would have been near the top, with Fidel Castro a close second. Truth was, Vicente hated all Communists and hated them with a passion. He sometimes shuddered at the thought of what would have happened to him if he had stayed in Cuba. Here, at least, he could be his own entrepreneur, and one of the things he bought and sold was members of the national police. But that was a different matter and, strangely enough, very much part of the irony of Vicente living in modern-day Venezuela.

In Vicente's line of work, arranging for the untimely deaths of certain selected people, it was always a good idea to live in a country where one could keep his own arsenal and be beyond the extradition laws of most western republics. Venezuela was just such a place, yet close to the action in the western hemisphere. Hugo Chavez, whom Vicente so hated, was the reason for the quirky legalities. The world turned, sometimes, on a very strange axis.

Today Vicente was planning to spin that axis a little more on its side. As he sat in a wicker chair on a comfortable terrace, he watched the young girls walk by in their bright clothing and short shorts and skirts. He deeply admired female beauty and movement and couldn't get enough of it. Every woman in the world, after all, was someone's daughter, maybe even wife, mother, or *novia*. So it disturbed him in a small way that he was there to plan the earthly demise of a woman, and a powerful foreign woman at that. But such was life, such were the turns of fortune, such were the vicissitudes of fate.

He turned his attention to his problem, idly sketching and doodling in a notebook. His problem: Debray had hired him to assassinate a woman and anyone who happened to be with her. Plus, it was a given, there would be a driver-bodyguard involved. So the hit would be on three people with one as the actual target, the other two as collateral damage.

So far, so good.

The hit, he was also advised, would need to take place in Panama City, the capital of Panama. It would occur here even though the victim herself did not yet know that she was destined to visit that location. Here was where the assignment got a little messy. The hit would need to take place in the Casco Viejo, the historic Spanish Colonial sector of the city, which was also the cramped business district. There the victim would be lured. But she would also be traveling in an armored car, probably a Mercedes, a Hummer, or an Escalade, if previous trips abroad could be an indicator. The area was crowded and noisy with traffic and not far from the canal, which would make escapes trickier.

Those in charge of moving the target around the city would most likely be theorizing that she was most vulnerable when she was on foot in the open near other people. So any such moments would be rare and fleeting. Conversely, her security people would conjecture that she was safe in her vehicle. She would not necessarily be more vulnerable there, Vicente reasoned, but she would present more opportunity there.

He thus worked out the first detail of his plan. He would attack her when her protectors felt she was least vulnerable. Their overconfidence would translate into strength for him.

For him at this point, the equation was almost a textbook exercise. His ideal team would be comprised of three people with weapons, and then maybe a half dozen supporting personnel. He would need a sniper who was dependable at fifty to one hundred yards. He would then need pistol people at ten to fifteen yards. The latter might not even be necessary, but there was no point in taking chances. Plus, he knew on-the-ground trigger people who needed and wanted the work and were more than adept with heavy handguns. So there was no reason not to have them.

Additionally, he would need his escape team, maybe six

people waiting nearby with cars and cell phones that could not be traced, ready to get the gun people out of the area. Two escape-vehicle options for each shooter. They would be scattered around the perimeter of the target area. If one escape route was blocked, they could go to another. Each shooter would need to select a primary getaway before the event, then memorize where the others were. He himself would be within close range with an array of cell phones, keeping track of everything, perhaps even calling the first shot if he could.

From there, Vicente applied a dark logic. Hit the vehicle, damage the vehicle. Render the transport inoperable. Kill the bodyguard and driver. Then kill the passengers.

The rifleman would be known only to Vicente. The gunmen on the street might know each other and they might not. The drivers of the cars would be known only to Vicente, as well. The locations of the waiting getaway cars would be known to all the gunmen, but the identities of the drivers would not be known. Vicente would provide counterfeit Panamanian license tags for the automobiles, and the numbers alone would be known by the shooters.

They would know to go to Calle San Luis 16, for example, and look for a white Volkswagen with a plate ending in -548. Or it might be Calle Santiago, where a gray Honda with a -734 tag would be waiting. There would be a change of clothing in every car, also.

Backtracking for a moment, he also considered a "two-shooter" option, which would have one M14 shooter at street level shooting at the side of vehicle and a second M14 shooter at the front, rear, or rooftop shooting at right angles to the first M14. They would open up a simultaneous cross fire on the vehicle, two clips each. The first shots would blow out the windows.

The problem was the placement and concealment of the street-level shooter. He would clearly be visible and vulnerable— a suicide mission. Finding such a man would be a problem, as would paying the type of man who might be enough of a cowboy to try it. Vicente shook his head. The other problem was collateral damage. With eighty rounds fired, with hits and ricochets, there could easily be a bloodbath of bystanders. That would only make escape more difficult and apprehension more likely. No good, this strategy. No good at all.

Similarly, he thought further, a twelve-gauge shotgun firing one-and-a-quarter-ounce slugs would take out a windshield at fifty yards. Vicente owned a Mossberg 950A1 tactical shotgun with iron sights. A weapon like that was frighteningly more accurate than one at fifty meters with slugs. A sabot slug made of hard copper or steel would be dandy ammo, Vicente reasoned. A sabot slug was snugged into a split plastic sheath that fell away when airborne. It would work here. But the weapon was noisy and it, too, could leave a lot of collateral damage. He dismissed this method. Then finally, for a moment at least, Vicente considered using a rocket-propelled grenade. This would be very effective and even messier. And this, too, called for the one-shooter option with two shooters lurking, but available, in case of non-detonation of the grenade.

Vicente lit a cigarette. He smoked quietly for a few moments. On the sound system in the small café, the lovely tones of Myriam Hernandez flowed smoothly over the sound system. Myriam Hernandez, a charming, beautiful Chilean, was one of Vicente's favorites, the type of woman he would hope to claim for a wife someday. The sound of her, the thought of her, mellowed his mood and heightened his desire to do this job properly. He watched more girls amble by and thought even more deeply about what he was assigned to do. No man or woman in the world was safe against the proper team of assassins, he reasoned. The thing was, it was like a goal in football: the logistics had to be perfect, so did the strategy, so did the execution. If one of those elements was not perfect, failure was preordained.

So Vicente sipped the end of his coffee and drew up his strategy. His did this all in his head. Despite the notebook, he never made notes on his actions. Notes could fall into the wrong hands and be used against him. He moved to his conclusions. Once the vehicle was down, he would need to motivate the passengers, including the victim, to exit the vehicle.

From that point, envisioning the massacre of his civilian targets, Vicente lovingly considered his potential artillery. For a moment, he considered a "one-shooter" solution and what he thought of as the "Swiss cheese" option. In this strategy, the attacking gunman, shooting from an elevated spot and waiting in ambush, might be armed with an American M14, which fired .308 on full automatic or semi-automatic. Twenty-round magazines would be typical. Two magazines would cook the goose. This option would take less than thirty seconds and would require armor-piercing ammo for the reinforced vehicle. This option would perforate both the auto and its passengers.

For the armored vehicle, he decided, he would want to use a Remington 700 in .308 caliber with a scope. Iron sights work just fine at those ranges. Bolt action with four or five rounds in an internal box magazine. He had once used such a weapon on a hit in Brazil. He still owned it. It could drive a tack at six to seven hundred meters in the tender hands of a top shooter. Which ammunition? he asked himself. The first two rounds should be military-grade Armor Piercing. These rounds would shatter the windshield and dispatch the driver, if so aimed. The rounds would travel through the driver and, depending on the angle, could end up gut-shooting the passenger sitting in the rear seat. If the driver was still functional, the next round should be in the car's engine to ensure a stationary target. Then an incendiary round would follow, the intent being to start a fire in the car to motivate a panicked passenger to exit, assuming the passengers were still alive.

If they were alive, they would then be walking into two gunmen with pistols, probably Glocks. Vicente also had a passion for a larger weapon, however, and would offer them to his shooters: Springfield XDM's in .45 caliber. A head-shot at seven to ten yards would finish their business. Then his team would rush to their escape. They would want to leave the country quickly. Since the FARC, the Revolutionary Armed Forces of Colombia, had arrived in Panama a few years earlier, drug trafficking had significantly increased. Waterways were now being watched carefully by the Panamanian Naval Forces, but just as the FARC had adapted ways of smuggling narcotics across Panama by land, Vicente had overland ways of getting his people to Costa Rica to the north. Escape needed to be swift, but if all his people could get away from the assassination scene, he was sure he could get them out of the country.

That left only one problem to be addressed. In most parts of Central America, if such a hit was to be effected, an honorarium needed to be paid to whatever local gang claimed that particular turf. This was always a thorny step to Vicente. He had very little respect for most street gangs, considering most of them to be

petty rip-off men and dumb thugs. Plus, their ranks were noto-
riously infiltrated by cops and potential snitches. So why even
bother with them, particularly in a place like Panama where ridding the world of this troublesome female who stood in the way
of an unfettered drug trade might be seen as a public service?

For a moment he considered who he might be dealing with,
the people who were the powers on the streets of Panama City
these days.

The first Panamanian gangs had appeared during the late
1980s and increased in numbers when the Panamanian Army
was disbanded in 1990 due to the United States' invasion of
Panama, the invasion that had sent the thuggish Panamanian
president, Manuel Noriega, to a prison in Illinois. To Vicente's
knowledge, there were now scores of petty street gangs working
the city. But none of them had enough juice to control significant turf.

He had no respect for them whatsoever. They behaved like
two-bit punks and stick-up men. Their specialty was something called the "express kidnapping," which was a stunt
pulled on careless tourists, usually Americans and often
females. The procedure of express kidnapping consisted of
abducting the victim and taking possession of valuables such
as cell phones, watches, credit cards, cash, and jewelry. Besides
taking all of the victim's valuables, the kidnappers made the
victim withdraw money from different ATM locations. Once
the kidnapper was satisfied, the abducted person was usually
released. In other cases, the kidnappers would ask for ransom
money for the release of the victim. This long process of kidnapping was slowly decreasing, since most kidnappers wanted
a quick payoff without complicated negotiations with relatives.

Ninety percent of express kidnappings went unreported due to the threat that thieves imposed on the victim and relatives of the victim.

It was ham-fisted crude people like this who gave crime a bad name, Vicente snorted. He decided to ignore them. Then there was a final consideration.

In recent decades Panama had become an important connection for shipping narcotics to the United States and Europe. The international traffickers had smuggled narcotics through the country's uncontrolled transportation system, such as airfields, coastlines, containerized seaports, and highways. The FARC had also contributed to the increase. Many of the FARC soldiers who seek shelter and refuge from Colombian Armed Forces had crossed the border between Darien and Colombia. Some of these people were bucking their way upward on the streets of the Panamanian capital, and some of their organizations would be looking for a tribute also.

But Vicente had nothing but contempt for these people, also. They, too, would be ignored, he reasoned. Then, thinking it through, he factored in one other element and changed his mind. Most of the clubs in Panama City made payoffs to the gangs who controlled their turf. Part of the payoff was to employ goons at the door who would act as bouncers. These were invariably burly thugs, usually with guns, but also who could call in gang backups in the event of real trouble. The casino employed two such doormen. Unless neutralized, they could be a problem when the hits were made. And if they were accidentally injured, the wrath of the local gangs would turn toward Vicente, his employees, and all the way up the food chain to Debray. This could not be allowed to happen.

Very well, Vicente decided. He would find out who was to work that Saturday evening and each would receive a thousand American dollars in cash. They would be told that something was going to happen on their doorstep that evening and to stay out of it. The gangs would be fine with it because their people had been taken care of. That was how things worked in Central America.

Vicente finished his coffee, paid, and left the café. After a pleasant walk through the Parque del Este, he went to a secure internet café, plugged in his own tablet, and sent a secure encrypted message to Debray, whom he believed by now to be either back in Europe or somewhere in North America. In the message, he stated that he had worked out all the details and was ready to proceed. He just needed to know dates and a confirmation that the venue of the execution would be Panama City. His plans, he felt, were now airtight.

He launched his inquiry into cyberspace and left the café. He assumed he would hear back within the very near future. So, still tired from his trip, he settled in to relax at his home.

THIRTY-THREE

On Tuesday afternoon, Alex picked up her office phone to find Joshua Silverman, the attorney, on the line. Lena Smirnova's dazzling Jimmy Choo footwear was about to drop, or at least some shoe was.

Alex and Silverman spoke for a solid half hour. When the call was over, Alex walked down the hall to Andrew De Salvo's office and knocked.

"It's open," Andy called.

Alex walked in and pushed the door shut.

De Salvo looked at Alex. "You look angry," he said. "What's up?"

"Yardena Dosi wants to negotiate," she said, easing into a chair before his desk.

"What?"

"She's hired Joshua Silverman," Alex said. "Same pack of lawyers who represented Federov."

"Yes. Of course. I know them. Every time I deal with them I feel I should have a tetanus shot afterwards."

Alex folded her arms across her chest. "The Dosis are sitting in their complex in Morocco and talking to Silverman every day. They're willing to concede several legal points, forfeit a percentage of their offshore assets, and terminate their business dealings in exchange for a cessation of prosecution in the United States."

"Wow!" De Salvo said.

"Presumably she'll stop shooting at me in the bargain. I even raised that point with Silverman. He said yes, of course."

"Well, one would hope."

"So is this good or bad?" Alex asked.

"Are you kidding?"

"No. I can't focus on it. Nor do I know if I should take it seriously."

"It's tremendous, Alex. It's a complete victory for you. And if Silverman is calling, you have to take it seriously."

"Not to my way of thinking," she answered.

"How's that?"

"Andy, I want to put her and her filthy cartel out of business and I want to put her and her husband in prison for at least twenty years."

"Well, you've been around long enough to know that you can't get everything in life that you want. Right?"

"I can dream," Alex said.

"Dream, yes. Destroy yourself going for a hundred percent? What if we could get eighty-five percent? And it also meshes with stuff that I'm hearing."

"Like what?" Alex asked.

"We're getting some overtures. Back channel stuff. The good señora still has some powerful friends in Panama. They sounded out our ambassador about a plea bargain. A deal or such."

"I don't make deals with criminals," Alex said.

"Commendable and highly principled," Andy De Salvo said.

"And for the first five years that I worked here, I thought much the same way. Then I began to realize, be true to your principles. But let your first and guiding principle be flexibility."

"This is bull, Andy."

"It's not, Alex. It's the way the world turns. Look, you've done an exemplary job. You've destroyed seventy-five percent of their business. Apparently the government won't let their banks transfer any assets unless they return to Panama and do it themselves. And you've tied them up in the Caribbean, also." He paused. "I can see what's falling into place, Alex. I suspect they know you've got 'Suarez' in the wings and at the same time, the Moroccan government is warming up with the current administration in Washington. The Dosis must feel cornered."

"Then why not squeeze them?" Alex said. "Nail them to the wall."

"Because that will probably never happen. Right now, you might be looking at a win by a TKO. You keep the fight going looking for a knockout, and it might be you who gets knocked out." He thought about it for another moment. "What did you tell Silverman?"

"I said I'd talk to you."

"Well, you did. It's your case. But, heaven knows, if you could negotiate a wrap-up at this point it would be a blessing to all of us."

Quietly, Alex looked out the window for a full minute, taking in the gray, cold sky of Manhattan.

She looked back to her boss. "Here's what else Silverman said," she continued. "The government of Panama is willing to grant them unfettered free passage into the country for fifteen days. They're then going to be allowed to have access to their bank accounts long enough to withdraw a tenth of their money and transfer it to Switzerland. The rest will be ceded to the Panamanian government, meaning it's going to line the pockets of the crooks who run the place."

"Of course."

"During that time, Mrs. Dosi wants a face-to-face sit-down with me to discuss the parameters of an arrangement."

De Salvo paused. "Holy smoke."

"I don't know about this," Alex said. "I've got a bad feeling about it. Why would they keep their end of the bargain, for example?" Alex asked.

"Well, on one hand, why wouldn't they?" De Salvo answered. "It works for them. They're wealthy people. They're in their late forties. I suppose they can retire with ten or twenty million dollars in the banks and be free of any further action from US law enforcement. And no one else in South America or Central America is going to come after them. They've done a world of harm and they've paid everyone off."

"That's why I don't want to negotiate with them," Alex said. She shook her head. "Andy, I know you empowered me to run this case, but I want your input. What should I do?"

Now it was De Salvo's turn to gaze out the window in thought. He did so for a full minute. When he looked back to Alex, she could see again the deep fatigue not just on his face but in his spirit.

"You know what you should do, Alex? Let's face it. No one likes to live with the specter of his or her car blowing up at any given moment. Or bullets coming through the living room window. You don't really want to spend your life chasing this one down. Truth is, eventually FinCEN would say it's not worth it anymore and swap you out onto something else. So if there's a way to close it out, I'd say do it. See the wisdom in that?"

"Maybe."

"I knew you would," he said.

"What about going to Panama and sitting down with her face-to-face?" she asked.

"Your call on that one, Alex."

"I'm inclined to go."

He rolled his eyes. "I don't know whether to admire that quality in you or admonish you for it," her boss answered. "You're just as foolish as I was at your age. Ah, well. I survived. Maybe you will, too."

THIRTY-FOUR

O n a sunny afternoon in Caracas, during a long, solitary walk in the Parque del Este, Vicente mentally worked through the scenario of assassinations that would soon shake the law enforcement communities of North, Central, and South America.

When putting together such a team, he always tried to keep it as small as possible, just enough people to get the job done and then quickly escape. Fewer people meant fewer things to go wrong, fewer leads for police to follow. Vicente's father had been a gambler. In his earlier days he had been a successful casino manager in Cuba, Mexico, and Puerto Rico. The old man had a favorite saying: *"Nunca apostar a cualquier cosa que se puede hablar."* Never bet on anything that can talk. Translation: boxing and sports events were all off-limits. The old man had loved the games of numbers, the table games in Old Havana and Las Vegas and, on the occasion of vacations, in places like Nice and Monte Carlo. But that was all.

Vicente respected and remembered his father's wisdom. In a way, assembling an assassination team was like betting on people. Vicente didn't need anyone extra who might talk. He frequently thought about the John F. Kennedy assassination, for example. It had been perfectly executed, in his opinion. Fifty years later, no one had talked, no one knew what had really

278

happened. The ostensible gunman, the fall guy, was taken out within forty-eight hours, and the man who killed him was allowed to rot away in jail and never testify.

Perfecto!

It was Vicente's method to bring in his trigger people from as far away as possible while still able to blend in. Far, but near, was the way he thought of it. For this job, he would need Latino personnel. No point in having a suspicious Serb or a Pole hulking about attracting extra attention. Plus, South and Central America were overflowing with street trigger teams who were looking for action. He knew of an excellent team from Mexico. They had both been on the police force in Mexico City until retiring to pursue other interests, such as freelance assassination.

Vicente had used them to get rid of a troublesome leftist politician in Nicaragua a few years back. He knew through the grapevine that the team worked steadily. They knew each other's moods, moves, and sensibilities. Hiring them was like acquiring two men who had played together on an athletic team for many years.

For a situation like the upcoming event in the Panamanian capital, where a car was to be incapacitated and blown open and its occupants murdered, he needed two street gunmen who knew how to work in concert with each other, not get in each other's way, not leave clues or collateral damage, and, above all, get the job done effectively.

They were two men in this team and they were known as Rafael and Dominic. They were the people who would be down on the street and who would have to fight the instinct to duck and run when the shooting started. They would have to identify their target visually from ten yards away and hammer away with pistols, so they would need to know exactly who the target was and how to recognize her. So much the better to complete a head-shot. For some teams, that would be a problem: many professional gunmen drew the line at shooting women. But these guys, Vicente knew, would have no compunction about pulling the trigger on a woman, even a very pretty woman. Some men would, for some reason. These men had no such reservations.

For the shot that was to start everything off, the sniper position, Vicente had a hunch and an inspiration. He had been hearing highly complimentary stories in professional circles for the last few years about a young Latina woman who was frighteningly adept with a Remington, exactly the weapon Vicente was going to provide for this assignment.

She was a pretty girl in her late twenties. Vicente had met her once in the Dominican Republic through a mutual friend. He had been smitten by her. She was svelte and agile and spoke English and Spanish interchangeably. She had a very plain face, which was an asset, but an attractive body. She was romantically involved with some Argentinian hood at the time, however, so Vicente knew enough to lay off.

What more he knew was this: she went by the name of La Loba, the "she wolf," after the song by Shakira. *Sigilsa al para, Esa loba es especial.* She moved silently and lethally, and was special. Well, that was what he needed. She had grown up in a paramilitary family in Colombia, then later lived in the United States for a couple of years when her father had to hide out from the FARC. Through the grapevine, Vicente had heard that she had even been hired by the CIA to do a single hit with an RRG during the recent mess in Syria. The hit had been successful. Her skin was light mocha–colored and she could pass for native in the Middle East as well. It was also said that she had done a hit in Pakistan, knocking out an "A-" Taliban honcho for the US Army.

Vicente knew it wouldn't be difficult to draw his hired guns to Panama City. Monsieur Debray had access to good money, so he could pay well. That was a given. As for Panama City, the capital bustled with three million people these days, with Latin swagger, machismo, and a frontier mentality. There were countless bars and clubs where people could go out to have a drink, relax, listen to music, meet attractive people of the opposite sex, dance, and cavort. The people Vicente was going to hire if everything came together properly—Rafael, Dominic, and La Loba—were all in their late twenties or early thirties. Panama City was a much easier sell, Vicente knew, than Africa, the Middle Eastern sandbox, or the Balkans. It was even better than the remote places in South America that were crawling with narco gunslingers.

There were concerts and great boxing cards, particularly popular with Colombians, Venezuelans, and a rough-hewn American expatriate community. And then there were the banks and the financial wizards, including the small-time Meyer Lansky wannabe, all of whom had conspired to make Panama an exciting place in the first decades of the twenty-first century, particularly after the United States Army, under the lead of General Colin Powell, had done the country the service of ridding it of the clownish thug Manuel Noriega in 1994. The city was booming as never before.

Young Panamanians, both men and women, loved to dress well, impress, and be impressed when going out. They loved to find excitement and live on the edge. There were casinos throughout the city and no shortage of players, in any sense of the term. Trigger people fit well into such a town on a short-term assignment. It was also an easy place to get in or out of, by car, by plane, by boat. One could be from one coast to the other in a matter of minutes with the help of an ingenious pilot. It was, in short, a perfect fit for the team that had now come together in Vicente's head.

The plans coalesced. Rafael and Dominic would know each other and what the target looked like. They would not know La Loba, they would not even know where she was shooting from. She would not know them. After her shots were fired, she would not waste a second watching the aftermath. She would be all set to flee. There would, as he had planned earlier, be six cars nearby, equipped with cell phones. The drivers would be locals who would do their job if called upon and drift back into their daily lives instantly. All would have cell phones and would do a quick call to Vicente, reporting "un," "dos," or "trés," depending on whom they had picked up. The drivers would connect their trigger people to their next means of escape.

Pleased with himself, he left the park and walked to a safe house in downtown Caracas kept by some of his North American and European friends. Not only was the house secure with an armed guard, but it contained the latest technological advances in jamming devices for any bugging mechanisms that may have been covertly installed.

He set himself up with a whiskey in a quiet room. Then, through secure cell phone lines that traversed Central and South America, Vicente was making calls. He had decided upon the team he wanted for the assassination in Panama City. Now it was a matter of sending messages onward and making the hires.

THIRTY-FIVE

Carter Wilson sat in the car, waiting. The carpentry supplies remained on the backseat. Some of them were on the passenger's seat in the front, beside him. Low on his radio was a religious AM station, to better assuage the police if they stopped and questioned him about anything. Arizona was enemy territory and he knew, as a black man, he stood out. He probably scared some of these old white people.

Next to him, amidst the clutter on the front seat, was a small canvas sports bag. He had bought it that afternoon. University of Arizona. Gold and maroon. State pride.

He pulled on a pair of latex gloves. He unzipped the bag and opened it. From it, he pulled out what appeared to have the shape of an ornate yet compact monkey wrench, jet black and in steel. He then pulled a smaller pouch from the bag and from that poured eight objects into his hand. They looked like bolts.

But they were not bolts. And the steel object was not a wrench. One by one he threaded the bullets into a chamber of a forty-five-caliber pistol. And he waited, watching the entrance to the clubhouse of the Glendale Golf Association, his eyes as sharp as a terrier's.

No wait continues forever.

At half past midnight, the couple known as Mr. and Mrs.

Davenport ambled out. From where he stood, from the background photos that had been given to him, from the times he had stalked them already, he recognized them easily, even at this late hour.

He turned on the engine of his own car and waited for a moment. To start toward them too quickly would alert them and drive them back into the clubhouse. He needed to catch them halfway, maybe three quarters of the way to their auto.

Like a big cat lying in wait, he watched patiently. There was a slight stagger to their steps, which was rather perfect and predictable. If form held, they were probably quite drunk.

He marked the perfect point in the parking lot where he wanted them. They reached it. He released his break, rolled down both windows, and began to move. He kept his headlights on low. High beams would alert them also. A few seconds later, the male of the couple looked up, leery of a strange car moving in his general direction.

His wife moved in close to him. Then, in the fraction of a second before anything happened, the Arizona couple knew they were in serious danger.

The battered car sped toward them, the lights blinding them. It came to an abrupt, noisy halt parallel to them. They looked in with wide eyes and saw a black man at the wheel. He raised the wrench and pointed it at them, leaning so far toward the window that the nose of the gun was at the window frame.

Not a word came from the automobile. David started yelling loud, racist, accusatory, and filth-ridden epithets.

In a final reflex to protect himself, David crunched his arms in close to his ribs. His wife tried to duck. They heard little more than the first fusillade of shots as their bodies tore open in pain.

The first volley of bullets tore into their arms.

Their screams and their blood filled the night. The next volley of shots tore into their heads and necks. David dropped face-down onto the asphalt. Sarah Lee's body dropped next to David's. Their bodies were still moving slightly when the gunman, making sure that the repairs had been made completely, pushed the door open on the right side of his car and fired a double barrage of two final bullets into each of their heads and necks.

Then, working swiftly, the assassin ripped a sharp U-turn across the parking lot and escaped onto the dark road that led to the club. His opinion of local law enforcement was in no way enhanced when two police cars, sirens wailing, lights ablaze, sped past him five minutes later, headed in the direction of the club.

His escape was clean. He was in Missouri in a day, Pennsylvania in two days, and back in Flushing on the third. He took the fourth day off, went back into the city on the morning of the fifth, and picked up his art equipment. He was back in Washington Square sixty hours after the shooting. Later that same day, a man named Michael came by, bartered about a painting, and handed him an envelope full of cash.

Michael admired the painting as Carter rolled it and wrapped it.

"Nice job," he said.

Carter nodded and winked. He was, in fact, quite proud of it.

"You know," Michael added, "if anyone ever knew what you really do for a living, your paintings would cost more. Ever thought of that?"

"Yes," Carter replied. "And I prefer the anonymity."

"Don't we all?"

Michael gave him a pat on the arm that suggested they would work together again, maybe sometime soon. Carter nodded and, refreshed and happy to be home, went back to his art.

THIRTY-SIX

Alex stepped to Andy De Salvo's door and knocked. The door pushed open and she peered in. Andy looked up.

"You wanted to talk to me?" she asked.

"Hey, Alex, yes," he said. "Come in and sit down."

She came in and she sat.

"This trip to Panama," he said. "How are the preps going?"

"Pretty much set. I travel at the end of the week."

"Panamanian government involvement?"

"Police and soldiers. I've been guaranteed safe passage. So has Yardena Dosi. Joshua Silverman says her husband is going to travel with her."

"Do you know their path? Flights?"

"Rabat to Algiers, Algiers to Cuba, Cuba to Panama City."

De Salvo snorted. "Well, it's not a Carnival Cruise, is it? What about your own personal protection?"

"I'll be armed, of course. The US Embassy in Panama City is going to provide two plainclothes bodyguards. Most likely Marines. You know how it works."

"Too well," he said. He leaned back in his chair. His expression was pained. "Listen," he said. "You getting any vibes on it?"

"Like what?"

"Got a good feeling about the trip? Bad feeling? Sleeping well these days? Lying awake at night?"

"Honestly, I don't like this at all. I'm as jittery as a dozen scared cats," she said.

De Salvo leaned back in his chair. "You should be," he said. "Alex, look. We're getting some nasty feedback on the ground."

"What sort?"

There was a long pause as De Salvo fingered a pencil on his desk. "Rumors," he said. "There have been some rumors floating about the bars and underworld in the area. Seems some foreigner showed up a couple of weeks ago. French, according to our sources. He was asking questions, ready to throw around some major money on a political assassination."

"It's Central America," she said. "I'm sure the area abounds in bar rumors."

"No doubt it does," De Salvo said. "But what made this one a little different was that the victim was rumored to be foreign and female. The supposition was an American woman. And she wasn't in Panama yet but would be appearing for a meeting, then leaving again quickly, except she was going to leave in a box and not on her feet. Pardon my crude candor, but you can see where this is going."

"There was a longer pause before Alex responded. "Any names?" she asked.

"Of course not. None," he said. "Why would there be names? That would make things too easy, wouldn't it?"

"What else do we know? Or not know?"

"The person who is believed to have been making the inquiries spoke French."

"How do we know that?"

"He made a phone call to one of our doubles," he said. "Sounded him out, told a little about the job to be done, the assignment. Our asset says the French was pretty good. The Spanish was imperfect and had an accent, but the French was good." De Salvo paused. "The last name was Debray. Or Duburry. Never saw a spelling. And who knows what passport he's traveling on? You know what that says?"

Alex stared across the office at her boss. At the same time, she held a mental picture of yet another den of venality and murder in Central or South America, men from the criminal elements of society placing a price on her head.

"Do we know of anyone by that name?" Alex asked. "Or pseudonym?"

De Salvo opened his hands in exasperation. "*I* don't. *You* don't. I've asked our CIA people to check it, but so far it's a new one for everyone. I'm *assuming* it means nothing to you."

"Nothing," Alex said. She thought for a moment.

"Not one of your questionable buddies whom you might put up to such a thing?" She glared at him.

"No, of course not," he said.

"French, as in from France?" she asked. "Or from somewhere a little farther afield? North African, maybe? Algeria, Tunisia, Morocco?"

"Don't know," he said.

"Do we have dates?"

"The story surfaced two weeks ago. So figure in that time frame while we were devising new strategies against the Dosis."

"I assume you're suggesting that I'm the target?" she asked. "How do we know it's not Señora Dosi and some underworld sorehead looking to take her out?"

"We don't know it's you. But at the same time there was no

notion that Yardena would be traveling to Panama in the near future. Quite to the contrary. Until floating the idea of safe passage to her through the government, it would have been highly unlikely that she would set foot there. So we might rule that out."

"Whereas I . . ." Alex began.

"We were just starting to talk about you going down there for a face-to-face to finish off Párajo. Now, much as I hate to say it, if there's a leak in this office, or more logically thinking, in the CIA . . ."

"Then that's when initial overtures in arranging a hit might have been made."

"Exactly," De Salvo said. "And, just for further head-scratching, that was also right around the time that Yuri Federov's daughter was in New York."

"Got it," Alex said.

Alex blew out a long breath. Okay, again she was a target. What else was new? Once again, she hated to be intimidated. Why give in to the scum of the earth? The bold lessons of history were not written by those who hid.

Quickly, she ran through some scenarios. She could have all of the flight manifests of all airlines flying into Panama searched for two weeks surrounding that suggested date. But that would be tens of thousands of entries. Some airlines wouldn't cooperate and it would take scores of man hours, if not hundreds, even with the most advanced computer software, to find a name.

Further, it was quite logical that the "Frenchman" might have traveled on a different passport and assumed the French identity after arrival. So such a grand exercise was doomed to failure and frustration. A record was kept of hotel registrations also, but the same problems abounded. And suppose the individual stayed with accomplices? The search had only a chance in a million of yielding results, and even then it would take weeks. The proposed face-to-face with the dragon lady was in less than one week.

"Okay," she said. "You've warned me. Now what?"

"I'd suggest sending someone else in your place," he said. "I don't know how much security we can muster for your meeting with Mrs. Dosi. A handful of locals, some soldiers in civvies. I don't mean to summon up images of Kiev, but one good sharpshooter with a PRG launcher and you're dead, Alex."

"So you're taking me off the assignment?" Alex asked incredulously.

"I'd like to, yes."

"No way!" she snapped.

"Alex, I can't do it unless you agree to it. This is your case. But I strongly urge you not to—"

"I'm going to Panama," she insisted.

"I wish you wouldn't."

"Andy," she said. "The people in Washington have me in their crosshairs just as much as Yardena Dosi does. I ran some inquiries on that Congressman Sawyer who was hassling me. Turns out he's been getting lobbyist donations from five of the Dosis' shell companies for twelve years. So who knows if they'll force my resignation or if the DOJ will order you to fire me just to stroke some crooked Neanderthal congressman? This may be the max point of my career here. I want to sit down with that woman and look her in the eye. That's what this job is about."

NOEL HYND ★ 292

Andy sighed. "You're young and foolish, Alex," he said.

"Anything else?" she said.

"Nope."

"May I tell Eric I'm going to Panama—and why?"

"No."

"Andy . . . !" she answered, surprised.

But her boss was shaking his head. He was emphatic. "You can tell him you're assigned out of the country again, but not where you're going or when you'll be back. That's firm and unyielding. That's the new policy of this office. It's a major security breach. Nothing I can do about that."

"Andy, I promised him last time. The time I went to Honduras. I promised that he would know at least where I was going. How much of a breach in security is that? He's my significant other."

"I'm not concerned what he is," De Salvo said. "He could be your pet gerbil for all I care. If you made that promise, you shouldn't have. The Department of Justice is breathing down my neck to make sure I enforce those rules evenly in this office. You can't discuss something like this."

"Andy . . ."

"That's final."

There was a moment of icy eye contact. Then Alex felt an anger building within her. Rather than say anything else, or dig a deeper hole, she got to her feet and started to leave the room.

"So?" he asked when she reached the door.

"So, what?" she asked.

"Panama?" he asked. "Why not use an embassy safe house while you're there? And for that matter, we could get an armed double for you. A stand-in."

"The Dosis would smell a rat right away and they'd bail. The whole operation would crash."

"I just have this rotten feeling about you going to that place," he continued. "Párajo is more than any of us bargained for and—"

"Andy, you told me I could make my own decisions in this job, and I'm making them until you tell me that I can't, at which point I'll resign. How's that?"

"Maybe I should fire you, Alex. To save your life."

She remained in the doorway. "Here I am. Here's your chance. Fire me."

He gazed at her without speaking. Then he shook his head. "God bless you, Alex."

"I'm going to Panama," she said. "I'll be fine."

THIRTY-SEVEN

They sat together, Alex and Eric, on the long leather sofa in his apartment.

"I have to go on a trip," she said.

"That's nice. Where to?"

"It's not nice and I can't tell you," she said.

"Oh. One of those."

"One of those," she affirmed.

"What part of the world? North Pole? South Pole?"

"Neither. Closer to home."

"US?"

"No. I need a passport," she said.

"Ah, I see," he said. He settled onto the edge of the sofa and placed a hand on her hip.

"Do you want to date someone else?" she asked.

"No. Why do you ask me that?"

"Because I know you'll be upset. My going off again. You not knowing where. Or why."

He drew a long breath. "I only ask myself where it ends, Alex," he said.

"What do you mean?"

"I mean, where does all this lead to, Alex?" he asked. "What do you want from life? I know you enjoy your work, or you say you do. But what are you getting out of it? A sense of accomplishment? A sense of righteousness?"

She opened her mouth to object, or throw in an opinion, but he seemed piqued and was not having a response yet. "You're young. There's a lot you can do. But how much are you going to pay? Are you going to give your life to that job?"

Her first inclination was to argue. She opened her mouth to do so, but couldn't. "I don't know," was all she could say, flustered.

"You should have an answer for that question, Alex," he said. "There must be a reason you do what you do. But you can't explain it to me and I wonder if you can even explain it to yourself."

She shrugged. "What if I can't?" she asked.

"Then, and I'm just suggesting here," he said, "it's your life, not mine. Maybe you should take time off. Reexamine. See what you really want out of life." He paused. "Do you really want to go through the moment that I went through, the one where God has to tap you on the shoulder and remind you to take stock?" He let the question hang in the air for a moment. "Think about the time off," he said. "Think about coming and joining me in Europe for the film. Will you do that?"

"Time off?" she laughed. "With Yardena Dosi still out there?"

"Ah, so this is about those serpents again, is it?"

She said nothing. And by saying nothing, she answered.

"Even if you got them," Eric said, "I have a hunch. Even if you got them and landed them in prison for ninety-nine years each, there would be another Dosi."

She pondered it for a moment. "No," she said. "Maybe not."

NOEL HYND ★ 296

"How so?"

"I don't know. You know, I'm a person of faith. I pray, some people think it's funny, it's quaint, it's odd. Some people call prayer trying to communicate telepathically with someone who's not there. But I think someone is there. So that's my guide. When it's time for me to retire or leave this job, I'll know. God will tell me, I'll see the signs, I'll feel it's right. Okay?"

"Okay," he said. "But how do you know the signs aren't in front of you right now? And you don't see them?"

She shrugged. "I don't," she said.

"I'm not trying to make an issue of it. But see, the thing is, Alex, I care about you. I worry. You've been shot at once, hit once . . ."

"Twice," she said. "One time in Paris in a subway. Another time in Washington, on the street."

"And how many times have you been shot *at*?" he asked. "Include Kiev. Include the times in Paris. Include the time that you told me about where a bullet came through your window when you were living in the West Sixties."

"I don't know," she said.

"Let's say a dozen times," he said. "How long do you think it will be before the odds run out on you? Alex, you're a target every day. There's going to be another shot and if that one misses, one more. It's a form of Russian roulette you're playing. Eventually, your number is going to be up."

"I never told you this," she said, "but there are some things in progress. The Dosi thing. It might be over soon."

"Sure," Eric said, unconvinced. "How? With a death?"

"Eric, I'm tired of this conversation."

"I'm a little tired of worrying about you," he said.

"You're not obligated to."

"And you're not obligated to put yourself in the line of fire the way you do," he said angrily.

"I know," she said. "Look, I suppose if I were married and had children—"

She stopped in the middle of the sentence. "I'm sorry," she said. "I'm way off base going into something like that with you."

"Are you?"

"Yes."

"Why?"

"Because it's too hypothetical," she said.

"I like hypotheticals and I want to know how you think," he said. "So finish your thought. I want to know what you were going to say."

"If I were a wife, a woman with a family, I suppose I'd have to be more careful," she said. "Because I would have responsibility to other people."

"Husband? Family, eh?"

"Well, obviously."

He smiled and shook his head.

"Why are you laughing?" she asked.

"Underneath gun-totin' Alex, there's a potential soccer mom," he said.

"Maybe."

"There is," he said. "It's what I always suspected." A moment, then he added, "I like that."

"Can we get off this subject?" she asked.

"It's making you nervous?"

"Some."

"Okay," he said. "Then we'll change it. And we'll talk more on it when you get back from wherever you're going."

"Thank you," she said.

There was a long pause between them. It was as if they had successfully navigated another threshold in their relationship and were better for it as a couple.

She looked into his eyes and saw something that told her that she could trust him further and, for that matter, trust him with almost anything. She spoke before she fully realized what she was saying.

"I'm going to Panama City with heavy security," she said, breaking every rule in the FinCEN book. "I'm going there to negotiate an end to Operation Párajo. I'm going to be face-to-face with my adversary. If all goes well, the operation can start winding down."

He was thoughtful for several seconds, almost stunned. "Wow," was all he could say at first. "And if all doesn't go well?" he asked.

"I'm not even thinking in those directions," Alex said. "And you shouldn't either."

Another moment passed and he opened his arms. She leaned into them and he wrapped them around her. "I love you," he said. "You'd better take care of yourself."

In his arms, she nodded. "I love you, too," she said. "And there's nothing more I want to do than come back alive."

THIRTY-EIGHT

The next morning, a private boat navigated the traffic near the routes to the Panama Canal. It came from the seas to the south toward Colombia and Ecuador. It slipped into a private beach five miles south of Panama City. A lifeboat lowered from the yacht into a waiting launch. A small, lithe woman with dark hair stepped into the launch. She wore jeans and a windbreaker. In her duffel bag she carried various changes of clothing and a Glock.

The launch, manned by a crew of two who didn't say much, was a covered motorized vessel about eight meters long. It weaved its way into the busy, small-craft traffic lane in the choppy water and moved at a leisurely pace northward. One man drove the boat. A muscular young man in shorts and with a pistol in a holster sat across from her, stared at her, smoked, and smiled.

She smiled back.

The vessel then turned abruptly and headed toward a cove. The young man with the pistol asked the woman if she spoke Spanish.

"I'm fluent," she answered.

"There will be a truck waiting for you at a shipyard," the

young man said. He spoke with a heavy Cuban accent. "He will take you to the city."

"Gracias," the woman said.

The small voyage continued. The sun was strong, the day warm. The woman pulled off her windbreaker and leaned back to enjoy the sunlight. She wore a tight green T-shirt. The young gunman kept his eyes on her. The woman could feel the man's gaze, but didn't acknowledge it more than an occasional smile. She was used to such things.

They docked half an hour later. The woman jumped off the rocking vessel to the pier. She had great balance. She climbed into a small panel truck that had the name and address of a tire repair specialist. The interior also had the smell of rubber and oil. The driver was a pleasant man with a bald head. He listened to a radio that was taped to his dashboard and tuned to some local evangelical station. There was no air-conditioning. The woman didn't complain.

She kept the side window open to avoid asphyxiation. In half an hour, the vehicle hit the congestion of Panama City traffic southeast of the city. In another fifteen minutes, the van rattled through the streets of a renewed area on the waterfront, a barrio in which new high-end buildings were interspersed with old warehouses.

The woman gave a specific address, which was a busy corner in that neighborhood. It was an area beyond the warehouses that had small shops, cafés, and businesses. The driver found the corner after consulting with a battered map. He stopped the van at the requested corner.

The woman jumped out, carefully holding her duffel.

She was at the fringe of the Casco Viejo, the historic Spanish

Colonial sector. Not too far away, traffic buzzed on the Amador Causeway, which connected four islands in Panama Bay. The driver suggested several of the hotels in the neighborhood. It was obvious he had no idea what she was there to do, only that she was in the business of sidestepping official entry and customs.

"Thank you. I know where I'm going," she said.

"Will you be safe? A single woman doesn't walk everywhere safely," he warned.

"I do," she said.

He nodded. He got the message. Given Panama's recent history, most citizens knew when to not ask questions or initiate conversations from which one might learn too much. The passenger looked like a woman to be reckoned with. And the driver looked like a man who knew how to keep his mouth shut.

"I understand," he said. "*Vaya con Dios*," he said.

"Gracias," she said with infinite courtesy. "One other thing."

"Si, señora?"

She reached into her jeans pocket and pulled out a fifty-dollar bill. "I know who you are but you don't know who I am," she said in Spanish. She handed him the money. He accepted it. "You never saw me," she said. "This ride never happened."

His smile wavered into a nervous grimace. "Of course," he said.

She watched the truck pull away and quickly disappear. She had the impression that the driver was anxious to get out of there, which was fine with her.

The woman hooked her small canvas bag onto her upper body like any other ambitious young tourist and toured the neighborhood, though the heft of the bag and the weapon within it served as a constant reminder of her assignment. She found the hotel she wanted. She registered with one of her fake passports and cash. She had booked a small suite with two adjoining rooms. She always liked the extra room as a buffer in case anyone broke in. It would give her precious extra seconds to access her gun.

She went to her suite and studied her local maps.

She changed into cargo shorts, concealed her pistol in a shoulder bag, and went out late on a humid afternoon. She looked like a graduate student on holiday. She had been in this city before and knew her way around. She found and checked the location where her assigned work was to take place.

By coincidence, the assignment was to take place at a spot where she had been before. When in Panama previously, she had been with friends. They had all gone out and danced and partied the nights away. One awesome place was the Fiesta Casino just behind the Hotel el Panama. There were other new clubs along the same strip that rivaled those in New York and Miami. Apparently, the woman whom she was stalking liked the club and area or was being taken to them. So the entrance of the Fiesta Casino was of particular interest.

She prowled the neighborhood and, following the instructions that she had received from the man who had hired her, looked for rooftops that would give her access and a good shot of the entrance.

She selected three locations for further inquiry. She entered all three buildings with ease, once following an old man through the outer gate and once forcing a front lock. The final building had no security at all. The intruder took this as a good omen. She liked the rooftop location. It even had a small tool locker that would provide her extra concealment. She decided she would use this as her position for the assassination.

She explored most thoroughly the area around the casino, memorizing escape routes. She examined in detail a nearby building that was six stories and residential. There was a new elevator in it and a set of back stairs that no one used. She tested the stairs, ran into no one either time she used them, which was also good, and timed her exit at two miutes to escape the building.

Toward nine in the evening, she went back to the building to see how it looked in the evening. She returned to the roof. She was careful not to directly touch anything. She slipped a pair of latex gloves onto her hands. Surveying the skyline of the great city at sundown, she savored the heady feeling of being young and alive. She drew an appreciative breath.

Panama City surrounded her and thrilled her. She looked in each direction, could see the landmark old churches and towers and the postwar neighborhoods and ships in the distance passing through the canal.

More immediately, though, she explored something she had noted on her first visit: a partitioned-off section of the rooftop and tool locker on its northern edge. In it, there were some workmen's tools and equipment that had been left to rust on the floor. She looked to see if there was anything she could use. But she found nothing. The shed, however, would protect her from anyone watching the roof from a distance. Since there was a three-foot wall on the roof, and since this building was taller than anything nearby, her actions were concealed from the view of everyone else.

As she stood near the edge of the rooftop, she gazed

downward two hundred feet. She saw the entrance area of the casino, its canopy, and the places where cars would approach and stop to discharge passengers. She liked what she saw. And the cityscape left her breathless in anticipation. So many thoughts had gone through her head about the dangers of this assignment, who she suspected the target might be, and the retribution that might—or might not—follow. Yet now everything was moving smoothly.

In the late evening, she ate a light dinner at an outdoor café in the port area. Other couples laughed and danced around her. She braced herself with a couple of drinks and went back to her hotel. Okay. She had seen enough. She could go ahead with this.

She bolted the door to her suite and made a single phone call on her cell phone. It was to a man who wasn't native to these parts but who should have been in the area by now in preparation for business.

After two rings, a male voice answered with a noncommittal, "Yes?"

"This is La Loba," the young woman said. "I'm here."

"Perfect," came the answer from Vicente. "We'll meet tomorrow."

"*De acuerdo*," she answered. Agreed.

They clicked off simultaneously.

La Loba watched the news on one of the English-language channels on her television and went to bed. With her pistol on a chair by her bed, she slept well.

THIRTY-NINE

On her final day before departure to Panama, Alex had a working lunch with her boss. They reviewed everything, including safety procedures and disaster scenarios. Andy wished her well. He seemed tired. Unnaturally so.

Then in the afternoon there was a final briefing from a representative of the Department of Justice as to what to discuss with Señora Dosi and what not. Also in the late afternoon, a CIA representative briefed her on who her escorts would be, meeting her at the airport. The airport at Panama City was a major hub for Central America. As such, it was both large and potentially dangerous.

The procedure was similar to Honduras. She would be met by a US Marine guard, an officer in civilian attire, plus a "negotiating partner" who would join her at the meetings with Yardena Dosi. The partner would be military and armed. They would also bring a weapon for Alex. It was shaping up as that sort of event.

She left work at six p.m., hit the gym for a short workout, showered, went home, changed into some casual clothes, and met Eric after his performance.

Again, they dined late at Il Trovatore. They were in a small room in the back. There were two other couples and a table of six. Eric had been recognized, but no one was making a production of it. The late-night clientele at Il Trovatore was very Manhattan-sophisticated. They were used to spotting celebrities frequently.

"Are you angry at me?" Eric asked. "Making you spill the beans on your travel plans?"

"I'm not angry at all," she said, though she still sounded chilly.

"It's just a tough thing for me to get used to you going off under shadowy circumstances. I never know when I'm going to see you again. From some of the stories you tell me, I sometimes wonder *if* I'll see you again."

He sighed. He rolled his eyes. Reaching from across the table, Eric's hand landed on hers. She loved it when he casually touched her.

"Sorry," she said. "But it's what I do." She paused. "For now, anyway."

"It's not like I don't understand," he said. "I *do* understand. I'm getting used to it, wrapping my limited intellect around it."

"Your intellect is fine," she said. "It's one of the things I love about you."

"My mother taught school. That was a profession I could understand. Oh, don't worry. Sometimes I don't comprehend my own profession any better than yours."

"Then we're equal," she said.

"Soul mates, I guess. Isn't that what it's called?"

"It's one term for it."

"You still getting hassled by those zipper heads in Washington?" he asked. "About that money from the Russian?"

"I seem to have dropped off their radar screen for a while," she said. "Legal counsel says I'm within the law and I handled the gift properly, reporting it, declaring it for the IRS. If someone wants to make an issue," she shrugged, "surely they can. They can make a mountain out of any molehill."

"True enough," he said. The waiter served them. "By the way," Eric continued, "speaking of gifts. I have one for you that you don't have to report."

He reached into his pocket and pulled out a small rectangular jewelry box, red with a white lace ribbon. It was from a jeweler around the corner in Greenwich Village.

"Go ahead, open it," he said. "It won't bite you."

She untied the ribbon and opened the box.

It contained a small hand-carved golden cross, much like the one she wore around her neck. But it was worn and had a patina of age to it. It was on a delicate gold chain.

"Like it?" he asked.

"Sure," she said tentatively. "But it's just like—"

"—the one you have. That's the point. I don't expect you to replace the one you already have. So drop it in your purse. Or somewhere where you'll see it. It'll remind you that I'm thinking of you."

"Thank you," she said, her enthusiasm building.

"It has a history, too," he said. "It's an antique. I bought it from a trustworthy dealer who handles Broadway memorabilia. It belonged to Vivien Leigh when she appeared on Broadway in *Romeo and Juliet*. Nineteen forty, I think. I bought it a week ago. I was going to save it for Christmas or Easter, but, whatever."

Alex turned it over in her hand. It had a delicate but substantial feel to it.

"Wow," she said. "Thank you. I've never had anything exactly like this."

"I haven't either," he said, looking past the gold charm and looking her squarely in the eye. "So travel safely. Please? And no unnecessary risks, okay?"

"I promise," she said. "I'll wear this necklace on this trip, okay?"

"You don't have to. The other one, the one from your father, is so special."

"So is this one. Now," she said.

The next morning, Alex rose very early. In her neighborhood there was a small Methodist chapel that opened for morning prayer at six a.m. She prayed that God would watch over her.

She prayed so hard that her eyes almost hurt and began to tear. She prayed because once again she was deeply frightened and she wanted to come back from this trip alive and build a future with Eric. And she prayed because she deeply feared something ominous about this trip and she didn't want to feel she was down there in Panama all alone.

Then she felt better. She was calmer, steadier, and more at peace with herself and the world.

Whatever was God's plan for her, she told herself, she would travel that road. She fingered the small new cross for reassurance just as she would have touched the old one, just as Vivien Leigh may have done at similar moments.

On her cell phone, she received a call from Andy De Salvo. Intelligence had confirmed that Yardena Dosi and her husband were on the move. They had flown to Madrid and then continued on to Mexico City. From there, after an overnight stay, they had continued on to Panama.

"They're already there, Alex," Andy said. "For heaven's sake, be careful."

"I'll be careful," she said.

She was finally ready to travel.

FORTY

Two mornings later, La Loba found herself in a private session with Vicente. He presented her with a Remington 700, a specially made fifty-caliber sniper rifle.

"I've used one before," she said with no emotion.

"So I hear. Pakistan?"

She gave him a glare and a snort. "None of your business," she said.

"That's what I thought you'd say."

"Then why did you ask?"

He produced a small sports bag, no more than thirty inches in length.

"Obviously you can't walk through the city with it. You know how to break it down?"

She answered with a profanity.

"Good. Let's see you do it. I can't let you leave with it unless you take it down and reassemble it. Then you can take and pack it."

"Reasonable enough," she said.

La Loba's hands were deft and supple. She methodically broke down the pieces of the Remington and examined them, much the way another woman might examine a new car or a piece of jewelry, with pride and admiration. Vicente studied her as she worked and was impressed with her sense of the weapon. For good measure, she did the procedure twice.

Finally, she slapped the stock onto the weapon, clamped it, and turned the final screw.

"I'm impressed," he said.

"You should be." La Loba stood.

Vicente assessed the weapon. He checked it, examined its mechanism, and admired its smooth working order. He handed it back to La Loba for safekeeping.

"Here's your transport bag," he said. "It won't raise an eyebrow in the area where you'll be shooting."

He produced a structured case for a bass guitar. She smiled. It fit perfectly within.

"Okay?" he asked.

"Okay," she said.

He then explained the further details of the assignment—what the target vehicle would look like, where the escape cars would be, etc.

Vicente allowed himself a smile. He put forth a palm and extended it in a congratulatory gesture. La Loba slapped it.

"Thank you, sir," she said.

"Don't mention it."

"You'll go into your shooting position about an hour before the rest of the team. I gave you the address of the place. The Casino Panama. It's the establishment the victim will go to. You'll hit the car while the target is arriving at the club. You know the procedure. Your job is to hit the car. I'll have people on the ground to finish what you start."

"How close is the rooftop I'm shooting from?"

"About fifty meters."

"I won't miss," she said.

Vicente's eyes narrowed. "The hit is for Saturday night when there will be the most action and confusion at the casino. Use Friday to study your layouts and your sniping position. I'm going to give you a cell phone that works locally, plus one number: mine. Don't use it for anything else. Don't even think of exchanging numbers with other team members. I'll only call you if there's a major development or when she's on the way. I'll be the spotter. I know what hotel she will stay at. You're independent from the team members. They won't even know where you're shooting from."

"I like it that way," she said.

"I figured you might," Vicente said.

From his pocket, he found the cell phone that she was to carry. He gave her the phone's number and his. It was an android. She riffled through the controls. The equipment made sense to her. She pocketed it.

"What's Plan B?" La Loba asked. "What if the situation in Panama City blows up?"

"It won't," Vicente said. "Just fire your shots and go home."

"I got it," she said.

For the first time, Vicente embraced her. La Loba reciprocated.

FORTY-ONE

The next morning, Alex stood in the security line at JFK in New York, waiting to be checked in for her flight. Time for everyone to be searched.

As she had done so many countless times previously, Alex took off her shoes, belt, and jacket and put them in one bin. Her computer and Kindle e-reader came out of her carry-on and went into another bin. She dumped her wallet, change, keys, passport, and boarding pass into a third. Beyond that, it went smoothly. When she was at the gate waiting, she brought up a short-story collection in Spanish on her Kindle. *Historia Con Final Feliz* was the title. Why not? Everyone likes a happy ending, she thought to herself.

Might as well get into the mood. In another forty-five minutes, the flight boarded. It took off on time at a few minutes past ten a.m.

A few hours into the flight to Panama, as the aircraft passed above the Caribbean, the pilot noted that passengers on the left of the plane could see Cuba. Alex glanced out her window and, *verdad*, there it was, nestled in the blue sea about a hundred miles to the east. Been there, done that, she thought to herself. She had no desire to return until the island had taken a few more steps toward democracy and free expression.

Cuba disappeared. The jet continued its path southward to Panama. Alex slipped into headphones and napped for a short while. She missed Eric already. Horribly. A wave of sadness remained, but at least she felt she was moving forward, starting to get a grip on her life again. She wondered how Eric was doing, as well as her new pals at the gym. Note to self, she thought. Work my way back into better physical shape when I get back to New York.

She drifted into a light nap. She opened her eyes. It had seemed like only a few winks, but she had fallen asleep for the better part of the remaining two hours of the flight.

The American Airline 757 gave a violent shudder. Alex blinked and was awake, her heart jumping suddenly. She glanced around. They were on their descent into Panama City. The bumpiness continued and Alex drew a breath. The plane was banking now, moving through a layer of clouds, its left wing tipped toward earth, the right wing toward heaven. She peered out the window into an infinity of cottony white.

The aircraft descended below the cloud cover and the landscape came into view.

They flew just under a thick layer of low clouds toward the Panamanian capital.

The aircraft angled in from the sea. The aisle-seat passenger in Alex's row was a teenage girl who gave a nervous glance. She shook her head. "We okay?" she asked.

Alex smiled. "It's fine," she said.

She looked out the window. It was an amazing sight. In another five minutes they had flown across the isthmus and were at the Pacific Ocean, where Panama City was located. Out of Alex's window, she saw islands to the south of the city.

At first, they were dark and gray under an overcast sky. Then, as the big silver bird banked and prepared to land, she saw hundreds of barges waiting to enter the Canal, which cut a shimmering and impressive strip across the isthmus, lock by lock. As they continued to turn, Panama City appeared. There were tall modern buildings bursting upward from the flat coast. They came all the way up to the water, crammed all along the coast. It was startling to see so many high-rises in Central America. The cities of Honduras, for example, were so much smaller.

Then came the landing. As frequently happens, she didn't realize there was an airport nearby until they had practically hit the ground. It had all been forest and plants and jungle, and then just as they were about to land, the airstrip appeared. The plane arrived right on time in Panama City at twenty minutes past three p.m., local time.

Immigration and customs was blessedly smooth and short. She passed through easily. The terminal was warm and humid. Suddenly the clothes she had worn from New York felt unbearably heavy.

She scanned a crowd of people waiting for arriving passengers. There was a well-dressed man with a sign that had her name on it.

Alex approached him, speaking in Spanish. *"Buenas tardes. Soy Señorita LaDuca."*

"Mucho gusto," he answered.

They switched into English. It was like arrival in Honduras all over again, but with higher stakes. Alex tried to go with the flow.

"I'm Major José Montejo. United States Marines," he said. "I've been sent to pick you up. Let me take your bags."

"Thank you," she said.

Major Montejo took her to a new Escalade with air-conditioning that worked. A blessing. Although he would serve as bodyguard and driver later for Alex, today she had a separate bodyguard and driver.

The car turned off the elevated freeway onto the parallel street running under it. The driver executed a hair-raising U-turn in the middle of traffic and then turned right up a well-manicured driveway with palms in the center strip.

The Escalade came to a plaza with a white, low-lying building and stopped at the door. *"Hotel el Florita,"* the driver announced. *"Su hotel, señorita."*

Alex checked in. She found a package waiting for her in her room. She opened it and found a Beretta with twenty rounds of ammunition. She checked the weapon. She also found a digital camera and an extra memory card. She showered, ordered a light meal from room service, and realized she was exhausted. Toward ten in the evening, she collapsed into bed and slept.

The next day was mostly recovery. But Major Montejo had a small personal agenda. There was a club in the center of the Zona that he liked. Music and dancing. He asked Alex if she'd like to come along and see it. It was safe, he assured her. He'd have another guard drive and they would meet up with friends.

Alex demurred at first. Then she changed her mind. Sitting in solitary hotel rooms often left her stale, she knew. So the next morning, she told the major that she had changed her mind.

Yes, indeed. She'd join them for a night out. It was innocent enough. Nothing of any importance, she reasoned, could happen.

FORTY-TWO

One evening later, La Loba returned to the rooftop in the Casco Viejo and waited. Her Remington set up on its tripod, she stood near the edge of the roof, protected by the roof's façade. She gazed downward two hundred feet at the entrance area of the casino. She watched the canopy and the places where cars would approach and stop to discharge passengers.

Increasingly, this looked like an easy hit. She could use one, she thought to herself. The job in Pakistan had not been the easiest one to escape. Taliban everywhere. Good thing they never thought to look for a woman. Thanks to their sexist attitudes, she had worn a burqa and moved through their security easily.

Again, she liked what she saw. Everything was flowing smoothly. Then at 10:12 p.m., her cell phone vibrated. Her heart jumped a few beats. She answered.

"Loba," she said, no louder than a whisper.

"The target's on the way," said a voice. She recognized Vicente. "Two minutes."

"*Yo lo tengo,*" she answered. She had it.

She edged her way toward the top of the facáde and peered over. There was no breeze and no visual interference. She figured that the street-level gunmen must be in place by now, too. Otherwise, Vicente wouldn't have given the green light.

She wore latex gloves on both hands and a digital watch on her right wrist. She carefully threaded six bullets into the weapon in the proper order: armor piercing, incendiary, then four regular rounds.

The old building was perfectly placed for her purposes. There was an inefficient air conditioner rumbling in the window. Because of the imperfect fit, La Loba had been able to poke a hole into the gap between some bricks. The hole was just big enough for her to insert the nose of her rifle.

Loba watched from the window and admired the view. Down on the ground ten floors below, winding through the center of Panama City, a highway ran toward the building. Then it cut close by on the western side.

Two minutes later, La Loba saw what she had come to Panama for. There was a black Hummer rounding the corner and turning toward the casino, moving slowly in the cramped traffic of Saturday night.

Squinting, she fixed her gun-sight on the Hummer. She parked the red dot on the front windshield. The driver's face was right in the Remington's crosshairs as she followed the vehicle. Then she led the red dot onto the center of the hood. She had an excellent shot and wished she could take it here, but she knew this was a team hit and she needed to wait for the street shooters to be in their range.

Her finger was tight on the trigger.

With one eye, La Loba had a full profile of the Hummer. She tracked and waited.

The Hummer rolled to a halt. This is just too easy, La Loba thought to herself.

The laser dot rested on the hood of the car fifty meters away.

She brought the dot to the center of the hood. The car was at a complete standstill, but of course would try to move as soon as the driver realized they were under attack.

Loba knew her moment had arrived.

She pulled the trigger. She felt the recoil through her shoulder. She heard the sharp *puff!* of the rifle. She saw the hood of the Hummer shudder from the impact of the first round, and she saw the resulting explosion of metal under the hood.

First shot successful!

She deftly moved her sight to the front window and fired again, this time the incendiary round.

Through her site, she saw the front window of the Hummer explode into shards, followed quickly by flames leaping up within the vehicle. What followed flowed by instinct and experience, all within a few seconds. She threw three more shots into the center of the vehicle's passenger compartment.

She saw the impact but not much more. An inexperienced assassin would have stayed and watched the melee that followed. Not her. She left her rifle on the ground, turned, and fled as quickly as her feet would carry her.

On the street, chaos.

Few people realized that shots had been fired, but everyone was aware of an explosion and fire in a luxury vehicle. The muzzle of the Remington had been successfully contained and there was enough street noise to cover the impact of the shots—except for within the Hummer. A fire had started midway between the two rows of seats. The driver was slumped forward. The fourth shot had hit him in the side of the skull and had blown away part of his head, killing him instantly.

In the back, two figures, one a woman with part of her

clothing on fire, burst screaming from the vehicle, both blood-ied by the explosion of glass and metal within the Hummer.

At that same moment, Rafael and Dominic emerged from the congregation on the sidewalks. Rafael was on the sidewalk nearer the casino. Dominic quickly crossed the street.

The man in the back of the car staggered out in shock and confusion on the street side. He looked up, saw a gunman lifting an arm toward him and pointing something big and black— a .45 caliber Springfield—in his direction. In that instant, he knew he was a dead man.

Dominic emptied three rounds at the target, hitting him in the upper chest twice and once in the neck. Still, the man man-aged to react reflexively and tuck his arms in to protect himself. It was a useless, futile gesture and a final one as well. The victim was dead before he hit the ground.

Hitting the woman who emerged from the other side of the car was trickier. There was a crowd on the street, and Rafael was experienced enough to know that local authorities wouldn't mind the hit so much as long as no local people were killed. An underworld hit among adversaries was one thing. That was exciting. Dead innocent bystanders were bad for busi-ness, however.

So Rafael had to move in closer to get the mission accom-plished.

In those final seconds he saw that the material of the tar-geted woman's dress was on fire at the left shoulder. So was her hair. She was screaming and slapping at the flames. But at the same time, from a peripheral view perhaps, she knew she was a target and went for her own weapon in a final effort to defend herself.

Rafael opened fire. His first shot hit her in the gut and sent her sprawling backwards against the Hummer. She was still alive, screaming and looking at her executioner, as blood pumped from a ghastly wound.

The man who was shooting was putting an end with an exclamation point to the woman's brilliant career that had spanned continents. There was eye contact between them. But Rafael persisted without the slightest hesitation.

He fired three more shots then, from as close as six feet, in the space of two seconds. One hit directly into her face and obliterated her features. The others hit the neck and upper chest.

Then Rafael turned and ran, not even watching the woman's remains go completely slack and sink onto a street in a Central American capital, a city where she'd had her greatest triumphs. Dominic was already fleeing in the opposite direction.

The two guards at the front of the casino knew that their moment for the evening was at hand. They did what they had been paid a thousand dollars each to do: essentially nothing, other than stay out of the way and not interfere.

They withdrew to a position of cover. They herded as many clients of the club into the front lobby as possible as the chaos spread. It would be a full two minutes before any police arrived.

By that time, La Loba was down the stairs and out the back exit of the apartment building, her heart in her own throat but walking calmly toward the nearer of the two getaway cars that awaited her. By the time she jumped into the backseat of a waiting escape car two blocks away, Rafael and Dominic also had vanished from the venue of the assassination.

Behind them, they had left chaos, a shattered Hummer burning like a candle and two passersby with minor wounds. There was a dead driver and, on the street, a handsome man dead in a pool of his own blood, and a foreign woman facedown, as dead as the man who had shared the backseat with her.

FORTY-THREE

Two miles away in Panama City, Captain Barry Wilkins, a plainclothes American bodyguard at the hotel where Alex had been registered, received the news of the shooting on his cell phone. He bolted to his feet from his seat in the lobby. He did not wait for the elevator. He ran up the four flights of stairs to the floor where Alex and Major Montejo were registered. He went first to the major's door and banged on it.

The major, preparing for the evening out, came to the door in a hotel robe. He had been swimming and needed a shower.

"There's been a shooting," Wilkins blurted out. He then told everything he knew to his superior officer, who responded with profanity.

Montejo turned, grabbed the closest clothes that he could find, dismissed the younger officer to the lobby, turned, and rushed to a door farther down the hall. He banged on it.

"It's me. Major Montejo," he shouted. "Please open if you can hear me."

Twenty seconds later, Alex LaDuca opened the door. "Yes?" she asked. "What?"

"Yardena Dosi and her husband have both been shot," he said. "A sniper got them, followed by gunmen on the ground."

Alex opened her mouth to speak, but couldn't. She was too stunned.

"There are going to be repercussions," Montejo said. "My feeling is we should get out of here right away."

Alex said, "I'll pack."

"I'll alert everyone and get emergency guards from the embassy," he said, already punching numbers on his cell phone. "Everyone meets in the lobby in one hour."

"Got it," Alex said.

She closed the door, organized herself quickly, and dressed for a flight. She was downstairs in forty minutes. Twenty-five minutes after that, an armored vehicle from the embassy pulled up before the hotel. Alex and the seven members of her delegation climbed in.

They were at the airport within another hour. A private aircraft was waiting. They were out of Panama by midnight, as was the assassination team in a different direction. The Dosis, however, remained behind in the Panamanian capital.

FORTY-FOUR

Two nights later, Alex and Eric were back at Il Trovatore. Eric had phoned ahead to Mario and asked if the private room was available. It was, and Mario had held it for him.

They settled in. The fireplace was going. They began with much small talk and shoptalk, how Alex was still tracing down some missing pieces and questions of Párajo, not the least of which being who had done the hit on Yardena Dosi and her husband. Eric talked about what was new in the show, some potential changes on the cast aside from him, and a few funny stories of other shows running in the other Broadway theaters.

Yet, beneath it, Alex sensed something a little "off."

Something was different tonight and Alex couldn't place it. She wasn't sure if she was getting some ominous vibrations from Eric, and in truth, things hadn't seemed completely settled since her return. She wondered whether this last classified absence had wrecked their relationship. She prayed that it hadn't. But if it had, there was no reason not to address it.

"So?" she finally asked. "Why are we in the private room tonight, Eric?"

He sighed. "You sense something a little different tonight, do you?" he asked.

"Yes," she said. "So what is it?"

"I've been doing a lot of soul-searching, Alex. And I've finally made up my mind about something. And you know me; when I make up my mind, then I'm set on something. If there's something that needs to be done, I want to get it done."

"I respect that," she said.

"So we're here because I've been doing a lot of thinking," he continued. "A lot. About you. And me. The future. These trips you go on. Risking your life all the time. My being away on a film assignment." He sighed. "There are a lot of things that aren't right," he said.

"Uh-oh," she heard herself say.

"No," he said. "Hear me out. There's some stuff that needs to be said. I should have said these things earlier but I didn't. So it's on me. Tonight we get to everything. Things need to change. And they will. After tonight, things will be different."

"Eric, are you breaking up with me? Is that what this evening is all about?"

A long pause. He looked stern and taken up in the moment. "Certainly not!" he said.

"You're angry about something."

"I am. I'm angry that you risk your life like that," he said. "I don't like the way you do that. I know you have faith in God, you think things will turn out for the best, but . . . Alex, I worry!"

"Well, thank you," she said.

"If I were your husband," he said, "I don't know. I can't say I wouldn't allow it because what you want to do is up to you. I would never stand in front of what you wanted to do."

"You're not my husband," she said.

He looked her squarely in the eye. "Well, I'd like to be," he said softly. "I'm just nervous that you won't say yes."

He fished into his jacket pocket and came up with a small blue box with white ribbon around it. Ironically, it was from the very place that Sam worked in security. Alex stared at it.

"Eric? What's that?" she asked.

He laughed. "If you want to know what's in it, *open* it for heaven's sake."

"I don't believe this," she said, her pulse quickening. She undid the ribbon. She opened the box. A stunning diamond ring with a Tiffany setting winked back at her. It was all she could do not to gasp. It must have been three karats.

"Well?" he asked. "Alex, I love you. You know that. Will you marry me?"

For a long moment, she couldn't speak. Then, "Well, sure. I mean, yes. Of course."

He broke into the broadest smile she had ever seen in her life. And she was convinced that she was smiling just as wide. He stood and came around the table. She stood to meet him and they embraced.

"You didn't think I'd say no, did you?"

"Well, come on now! Try it on, try it on."

Her hand was jittery as she pulled the exquisite ring from the box. She nearly dropped it. "Holy smoke," she said, unnerved and incredulous but joyful. "I thought you were going to try to break up with me."

"Are you kidding? Who would I hang with for the rest of my life?"

She snuggled in close to him. But her hands were still so shaky that she continued to have trouble with the ring.

"Here," he finally said. "You don't mind if a man takes charge now and then, do you?"

"Not if it's you. *Never* if it's you."

He placed the ring on her finger and slid it beyond the knuckle. It came to rest perfectly.

"It's a perfect fit," she said. "How did you get the size right?"

"Lucky guess," he said. He winked. "My sister is your size and weight. She went to the jeweler's with me and was your stand-in while you were off ducking bullets in Pango Pango."

"It was Panama," she corrected.

"Let's hope it won't be again."

She looked up from the ring, turned, and allowed him to take her fully into his arms. They embraced long and passionately, and she then pulled back.

"Eric," she said.

"Eh?"

"I love you."

They kissed again.

Then, "I leave *South Pacific* June sixteenth," he said. "This time it's final. For real. Final answer. The producer finally has a solid replacement for me. That Sunday is my last performance. So. What would you think of getting married the following Saturday?"

"I'd love it," Alex said.

"Then it's a plan."

"It's a *great* plan," she echoed.

FORTY-FIVE

The days that followed began as joyous ones for Alex. She was home in the United States, secure and appreciative of her surroundings. The ring on her finger, the anticipation of marriage, and the spreading of the euphoric news pitched her into what she happily hoped would be a splendid new era in her life.

At work, she had shared the good news with her boss, Andy, who was ecstatic for her and regaled her with stories of his own romance with his wife Helen. He told Alex their romance continued to this day. They had had their troubles over the years, minor ones, none that couldn't be surmounted, but they had been "blessed," as Andy put it, to have had a "marital love affair," his words again, of thirty-eight years. Alex and Eric were still discussing whether to have their wedding ceremony in New York or California; both had links to each place, but details would surely follow and Andy and his wife would surely be invited.

Beyond that, her workload eased a bit. She arranged two weeks off from the office in late June following the nuptials. Both Alex and her fiancé had an affinity for Paris, and they had already decided to spend at least one week there. Eric knew all the top places, meaning some of the most expensive places, and had cachet and entrée everywhere. Whatever else their quirks, the French loved their American film stars and assuredly he counted as one. So he was going to handle that end of things.

As for the two million dollars from Yuri Federov, the sniping from Washington had subsided. Alex had no way of knowing if the break in hostilities was temporary or permanent. Who knew with politicians? She did know that some of the people who had been yelling for her scalp had gone on to grandstand on other issues. So maybe she had a reprieve or maybe she had a permanent pass. She vowed to remain patient. Time would tell.

Then there was Operation Párajo. Much mopping up remained, but she started to delegate some of that to others at FinCEN. The major players had been brought down outside the United States by forces no one understood. One of the many rival money-laundering cartels was suspected, but it was unclear which. Most of the minor members of the Dosi operation who remained free were on the run. Local police agencies in Central and South America were dealing with them. Even if they saved themselves through bribes, she knew they were pretty much out of business. For all intents and purposes, the Dosi operation had been crushed.

The big question persisted, though. Who had administered the coup de grace to the rogue financiers? Years ago, Alex had discussed some major cases with a retired law enforcement man from New Jersey. They spoke of major cases that did not have clean endings. He had talked extensively of the Lindbergh kidnapping. Alex had sought a larger understanding of the crime, which, to many, had never been adequately resolved.

"Well, Alex," the friend said, "one thing you have to remember is that the Lindbergh case was making it hot for the entire underworld in New Jersey. Bootleg trucks rolled at night and a lot of them were being stopped while the police were looking for the missing child. The local mob wanted the heat turned down; they wanted the situation resolved even more than anyone else."

She tried to apply that lesson to the Dosi killings, if there was a lesson to be learned. Who wanted the Dosis taken down permanently? Sure, she hadn't ordered the hit. Nor had anyone she worked with at FinCEN. To a fault, they didn't operate that way. CIA? She doubted it. Local police in Panama? Local government? Local rivals, looking to rebuild the organization in a new style, but unable to as long as the matriarch was still around?

Possibly. Probably.

And what about this "Debray"? Wild-goose chase, most likely. A rumored word that would lead nowhere, she reasoned. But still, in odd moments, she traced down some records and files that the CIA had made available.

So late on a bitterly cold Wednesday afternoon in New York, Alex sat at her desk going through airport records, examining flights and incoming passenger lists to Panama City for the general dates during which this shadowy Debray was thought to have arrived.

She scanned videos from the airports but found no connection. She had a sense of failure on this, that she would never be able to find what she was looking for. A little wave of boredom and tedium began to overtake her. Maybe she should just chuck this. Some questions were, after all, best left unanswered, even unaddressed.

She stared at her two computers. The painful past began to haunt her. She remembered how she had first been seduced into all the computer research at the FinCEN offices in Washington, how she had trawled into the past of a shadowy brute named Yuri Federov, little knowing how much he would affect her life.

The ice of Kiev and the monstrous death of her first fiancé, Robert, seemed a world away, yet still a painful and bitter memory. It still haunted her. Even more now that she was about to marry someone else. Guilt? Survivor's guilt? Was it getting worse? She wondered.

"Whoa," she whispered to herself. "Get a grip. Don't turn into a head case now."

Well, she was talking to herself. Wasn't there an old wives' tale that suggested that talking to yourself was the first sign of incipient madness?

Her mind rambled further as she prowled passenger manifests in Panama.

Old wives' tale.

Ha! She laughed at that one. She was thirty-one years old. Okay? Was that an old wife or a young wife? Or was it one of those Pirandello things where it was neither, but it was what a woman made of it. She smiled again to herself. Well, she was going to be a *new* wife; that was sure, as long as something horrible didn't happen again. So she set her mind to be the best wife she could possibly be for such a wonderful man.

More guilt brushed up against her spirits.

How long had it been since Kiev? There had been times in the last years when she could have given the specific answer. It's been four months. It's been two years, a month, and three weeks.

No more. Now it was just a boulder in the past. Something that wouldn't move, something to move carefully around when she thought of it.

Leaning forward, she attacked the keyboard with more gusto. She leaned back from her screen. What was she looking at? She was tired. She barely knew what she was doing, she realized.

Involuntarily, she plunged herself back into the darkest chambers of her memory and found herself sorting through the events of the bleak February in Kiev. She was in some of the worst chambers of her memory, when suicide scenarios tiptoed across her psyche every day.

Then some words echoed. They came to her as boldly as if spoken by a tangible spirit who was there in the room with her.

"If I did die suddenly," Robert had said not long before his death, "I would want you to pick up and go on. I would want you to have a life, a family, a soul mate, happiness."

It was almost as if his spirit was in the room with her, invisible, a ghost, a visitor from heaven, projecting such thoughts.

She glanced back to the monitor. She was about to shut down this program for the day when another voice spoke to her from a place she didn't understand.

"Stay with your search, Alex. You'll have your answers soon."

Now she laughed. The voice had an accent. Russian. She had transposed Federov's voice into her own stubborn search instincts. Yeah, sure enough: she understood what was going on. She had taken enough psych courses in college to get it: Párajo was about over, and she was elated because a wonderful man was going to marry her. She was feeling a little loopy.

Well, okay. She was entitled.

She looked at the computer screen, the topic heading on the

program she was searching, and grimaced. She had made a serious mistake. She was wasting her time here.

"Go home, girl," she said to herself.

"No, don't," said either an angel or a devil standing on her
shoulder. Or was it instinct, the keen sense that follows every
professional to the grave if he or she works in the field long
enough?

"Look carefully."

"At what? The wrong application?" she asked.

She frowned at what was in front of her. The prevailing wisdom was that "A. Debray" had flown in from Europe, so she was
supposed to be checking the passenger manifests for Air France,
TACA, Iberia, Lufthansa, and the other carriers. Instead, without realizing it, she had booted up the wrong records and was
looking at the arrival lists for some of the American airlines.

That's when she encountered a flash of light, a revelation.

She blinked. She spotted the name. Antonin Debray, it was,
not just "A. Debray" anymore; she had the first half of his handle
unless this was a coincidence. Coincidences in situations like
this, of course, were akin to the reincarnation of Elvis, something she didn't believe in.

And this Monsieur Debray was arriving from . . . of all
places . . . John F. Kennedy Airport in New York City.

That put another painful charley horse in the long arm
of coincidence. She was in hot pursuit now, unraveling kalei-
doscopic images into a vision more prosaic so she could see
them.

She noted the time, date, and flight and brought up the
embarkation tapes for Kennedy. She watched as passenger after
passenger moved through the boarding gate.

Then her eyes froze. She hit pause on the screen and magnified the image. She stared and had her answer.

Then, at that very moment, her IM flag lit up on her computer screen. It was her boss.

ADeSALVO: Alex, could you please come in here right away?!

"Now what?" she mumbled to herself.

She got to her feet, went to her door, and walked down the hall. De Salvo's office door was as it usually was, half-open, half-closed, his normal view upon the world. She arrived, gave a casual knock, and stepped in.

"Yes?" she asked.

Andy was at his desk. From the get-go, he didn't look good. His expression was quizzical, his face pinkish. He was slow to look up, but from where she stood, it appeared that he was looking at his photo album of Portugal.

"Alex," he said, "you'll take care of this office, right?" he asked. "In case anything odd happens?"

"Andy?" she asked, looking for what he meant. "Sure," she said. "If you're out, you mean?"

"Yeah. Out." He laughed. But it wasn't a laugh of amusement. Already she was sensing something seriously amiss.

"Just asking," he responded slowly. "Angel that you are," he said. "Or maybe you shouldn't look after this office. Who knows? Who cares?"

He put down the album. His gesture, his handling of it, was awkward. The book lay askew across the desktop in front of him. "Alex, I don't feel good," he said. "I phoned my wife. I phoned a cab. I'm going home early." He paused. "I might be out for a while."

Tentatively, she took three more steps into the office. "Andy, you don't sound good," she said. "Maybe I should get the building doctor."

"No, no, no," he answered. He made a little laughing sound. "I'm fine," he said. "But I don't want to cause a stir. Maybe you can walk with me to the elevator?"

"Sure. Now?"

"Right now, yes," he said. "I think that would be good."

"Of course. Let me get your coat for you. We'll go downstairs."

He started to get up, but struggled with the arms of his chair. To her eyes, he had no strength and his balance was off. He slipped clumsily back down into his chair. And from where she stood, she could now see the line of perspiration across his brow and his face.

His voice was off kilter, too. "Alex, you're a dear. You're a beautiful person, inside and out. So I want you to know something: I love you like a daughter. I really do. God bless you and keep you." He paused awkwardly. "Alex. There's a bad pain in my arm. And my chest . . . Maybe you *should* call the doctor."

And suddenly for Alex, it all crashed into place. *Oh, Lord. Oh, Lord*, she said to herself, not as a profanity, surely, but as a prayer, as if a request for help and guidance.

"Andy, just stay there! Stay calm, breathe easily."

"Sure thing, Alex." He was making no sense. "Be good, also. You take care of yourself, too, okay?"

She whirled and rushed to the door. She yelled, "Stacey! Robert! Mario! Emergency!"

She turned. Andy tried to stand, but instead he slumped back into his chair, landing hard this time.

"I've got this most horrible pain," he said. "I want to go to Portugal. I don't deserve this."

He clutched his chest near the breastbone. Then he slouched further in his chair. His eyes rolled and he gasped.

Alex rushed around the desk and came around to Andy's side. He reached for her in desperation but his body continued to slide. His arms trembled. She could already hear the commotion in the hallway behind her. Stacey arrived at the door first.

Alex held her boss's heavy upper torso in her arms. Her boss writhed in her arms. She turned as she guided him to a comfortable prone position on the floor. Several other figures arrived at the door and crowded into the room. Robert came speedily around to the other side, pushed the chair far away, and helped her. Alex turned toward them as she undid her boss's necktie and ripped away the top buttons of his shirt.

"Heart attack!" she yelled to Stacey and the others. "Call 911! Get the defibrillators from down the hall!"

His eyes flickered again. He still had a pulse, and Alex could feel it pounding, but Andy's shirt was soaked now, his eyes were spinning, and his throat made horrible gurgling, gasping sounds. His chest continued to rise and fall. Then, with a shudder, it stopped.

"Oh, Andy, no!" she said. "Hold on! No! Don't go. Don't leave us."

He was, she knew, in respiratory arrest, which meant he was probably in cardiac arrest. She didn't waste time searching for a pulse, because she knew she wouldn't find one.

She placed the palm of her right hand on Andy's chest just over the lower part of the breastbone. She pressed her hand in a pumping motion, once, twice, three times, supported by her other hand.

"Andy, no! Don't do this," she whispered. She could hear the commotion beyond the office door. Footsteps, people shouting, some screaming, yelling distantly down the other corridors.

She tried to get his heart beating again. She worked furiously, her hands pumped furiously. Nothing was working. She felt the tears flood into her own eyes. Now she worked on instinct, things she had learned long ago but hadn't used in what seemed like a millennium.

Oh, God! Please guide me! she thought to herself.

She tilted Andy's head back. She lifted his chin. She pinched his nostrils shut with two fingers to prevent leakage of air. She drew a deep breath and tried to stay calm. She leaned to him, placed her own mouth over his, and blew slowly for three seconds, trying to adequately inflate the stricken man's lungs and chest.

His chest rose. It fell.

She repeated. It rose. It fell. She repeated again. But no independent breathing followed. She continued. More voices in the room. Hurried men rushing closer. She continued for several minutes, working the chest. Mario, one of the new counsels, knelt beside her.

"I used to be a lifeguard at Jones Beach," he said. "I'll do the CPR if you do the breathing," he said.

"Okay."

He pressed Andy's chest. He pressed it hard. Alex continued the mouth-to-mouth. The artificial respiration and the CPR continued in tandem. Nothing worked. Alex heard the rumble of heavy footsteps and the sound of excited voices in the room as a crowd of people gave way. She heard the rattle of approaching equipment.

Someone yelled, "Alex! The med techs are here!"

Alex eased away, her face twisted in a tortured expression as she gazed at the lifeless, ashen face of her boss, her arms folded in front of her as she remained at the side of the fallen man. The technicians moved into her position valiantly with defibrillators. They applied them to De Salvo's chest.

"Ready!" one said to the other.

"Ready!" the other said.

They applied a first shock and the body leaped.

"Come on, Andy," Alex whispered. "Come on, come on. Breathe for us. Don't do this. Oh, please, God, please . . . Don't die. Don't die on us."

They shocked him with the defibrillator again. And then a third time. Then a fourth. Alex heard an urgent voice from the door. "Give us space, people. Give us space." More medical technicians rushed into the office from downstairs. Now they had a gurney. Alex looked to them, then looked back to Andy De Salvo. They shocked him a fifth and sixth time. Still nothing.

The resuscitation efforts continued as the techs lifted him onto a gurney. Now the air was filled with the static and clatter of a two-way radio. Two uniformed New York City police officers entered the room.

"You got an ambulance arriving in one minute," one of them said.

"Express elevator is on the floor. We're holding it. Ready to descend."

"Let's get him to the hospital," one of the techs said. "NYU Downtown. That's the closest."

They lifted Andrew De Salvo's body onto the stretcher and put up the wheels. "Someone who works here should come with us," one of the cops said.

"I'll go," Alex said.

"You can ride in the van," one of the techs said. "Van" meant ambulance. They were going to NYU Downtown Hospital, less than five minutes away.

Alex raced for her coat, wallet, and cell phone. She caught up with them down the corridor. It was all a blur. Her coworkers touched her and said things as she flew by. Nothing registered. She would barely remember.

The ride down fifty-two flights was like plummeting down a laundry chute. It was express and sailed downward at speeds she didn't know were possible in an elevator. Yet it seemed to take forever.

Then they were on the first parking level and the ambulance was backed up to the elevator access, lights flashing. The technicians wheeled the gurney as fast as they could and then slid it into the van. Alex hopped in and took a seat. They tried the defibrillators again. More failure. She gently reached for Andy's body and touched a hand, then held it. She looked to his face, which was turned toward her. She could not hold her tears.

"No . . . no . . . no," she kept saying.

One of the techies looked to Alex and shook his head, even as he tried to draw forth a miracle. "It's not good," he said.

Alex mouthed a shaken response. "I know," her lips said, even though her heart had trouble believing it.

The efforts continued. The emergency team in the van tried to monitor his heartbeat, but already Alex knew. There wasn't one. The boss was gone.

Alex remained at the hospital until an official pronouncement was made. Gradually, a dozen or more employees from

FinCEN assembled in the emergency waiting area. But there was no tension, just immense grief and sorrow. A young doctor named Gersh came out at 5:32 in the afternoon with a hospital chaplain. Between them, they offered a short Roman Catholic prayer, in keeping with Andy's faith, and said all the expected things; that the tech team in the office and the doctors and nurses in the hospital had done everything possible, that all efforts had been made, but the deceased had suffered a massive heart attack and had died almost instantly.

There had probably been very little pain, Dr. Gersh said, and the attack had been so massive that once it had begun, very little could have been done. Andy's final moments flickered before Alex again, that knowing look in his eye, that request to go home early, to see the wife whom he loved so dearly, the way he looked at her, his gentle, caring words to her at the end, and the helplessness that overtook him when his moment came.

She was so wrapped up in this that she almost tuned out what the doctors and chaplain were saying. Then she tuned back in.

"Has anyone called his family?" someone asked.

Everyone looked around. No one had.

"The hospital can make the call," the chaplain offered. "Would anyone happen to have the number?"

There was a thick silence. Then Alex nodded her head. "I have a number," she said softly. "But Helen should hear it from someone she knows." She thought further. "But she shouldn't be alone. I have his son's number." She looked around. "Give me some privacy," she asked gently. "I'll make the call."

They gave her space and privacy. She listened to the phone

ring in a suburban home many miles away. Then she heard the voice of Andy's son as he answered the phone. He was in his twenties but sounded just like his father.

Alex's voice broke as she began to speak.

FORTY-SIX

Three days later, on a cold morning in Westchester County, Alex stood by the grave of Andrew De Salvo near the pall-bearers. Family and friends would lay Andrew De Salvo to rest this day in an aging cemetery in Larchmont. As Alex stood in the cemetery, a sharp wind off the Hudson River slashed through her. Eric stood by her side, his gloved hand holding and comforting hers.

Alex's eyes were pools of sorrow. They were moist and hidden behind dark glasses. When she raised her eyes again, the minister was still talking at the graveside. Alex's gaze settled upon the pine coffin.

As the service continued, Alex held in her mind her final visions of the man she had worked for and had come to admire so greatly. He had protected her, he had taught her. He had been her mentor and, toward the end of his life, which had come far too quickly, he had attempted to warn her. Be ethical, be upstanding, and respect your faith and your fellow human beings. But remember that you have a life to lead, too, and you're entitled to your own goals and happiness.

Andrew De Salvo. 1948–2013. A good man. Now there was a basic truth.

As the service continued, Alex's mind drifted. On the day

that Andy had died, Alex had returned to the office that evening. She walked into her boss's office, just to look, ostensibly to make sure no secure documents were exposed. None were.

The office seemed ghostly, however, abnormally cold. It was almost as if Andy De Salvo's spirit were still hovering in a holding pattern, presumably between this world and heaven. A mood had overtaken her and she had sat down at his desk. She had never done that before and wondered if she would ever want to do it again, officially or unofficially. It was when her eyes came to rest on Andy's photo album of Portugal that she had broken down and cried uncontrollably. She had felt like a little girl again, lonely and unable to be comforted when her father had passed away. She felt so helpless.

She had been sad for Andy. Sad for the thought that he was gone. Sad for the times when she felt that she hadn't been as polite as she could have been, sad for the few times they had argued or gotten on each other's nerves. Sad, because that's what happens when a person leaves your life.

Guilt, remorse, second thoughts, a window in your heart that will never close.

The door to the office eased open.

Wet-eyed, Alex was startled. Her head shot up.

It was Mrs. Valdez, María, one of the overnight cleaning staff. She had been busily making her rounds of one of her three jobs. Mrs. Valdez, sweet natured, five and a half feet tall and pudgy, was equally surprised to find someone in the office. It was well past ten p.m.

"Oh! Excuse me!" Mrs. Valdez said. "I didn't mean to disturb."

"No hay problema, María," Alex said. Alex knew most of the staff and chatted with them in Spanish when she had the occasion.

"We had a tragedy here today," Alex said. "You know what, yes?"

Mrs. Valdez looked stricken and deeply saddened. "Yes, I know," she said. "I heard. *El jefe*, he seemed like a nice man."

"He was a *very* good man," Alex said. "He will be missed."

"We do what we can here," the cleaning lady said. "We live, we laugh, we love, we work, we die. We make plans; God smiles. We go when He calls us," she said.

"We do, indeed," Alex agreed. Alex admired the woman's earnest faith and devotion.

Simultaneously, Alex stole a glance at her watch. She would be able to join Eric after his show. "You can straighten up in here if you wish," Alex said. "I should go home."

"*Buenas noches, Señorita,*" the cleaning lady said with a smile.

"*Buenas noches,*" Alex answered. "*Que Dios los bendiga.*"

"*Dios ya me ha bendecido de muchas maneras, Señorita Alejandra,*" she said. "*Estoy aquí en Estados Unidos, por ejemplo.*"

Alex nodded and let the lady go about her work. Alex used her cell phone to call her car service. Ten minutes later, she was downstairs in the lobby, waiting. Her timing was excellent, though. After less than sixty seconds, a yellow car on call pulled in front of her building.

She stepped from behind the glass doors and out into the cold New York night, quickly scanning the sidewalks as she walked, always aware of the Glock under her coat. The driver was a pleasant man in his fifties, in a Sikh turban, a jacket, and a tie. Melting-pot New York, an aspect of the city that she loved. The pace of the nighttime streets refreshed her and pulled her out of her deeply grim mood.

She had called Eric earlier in the day, but he was involved

in a meeting with his producer. She didn't want to hit him with a tragedy right before he went on, though she also respected the fact that he was a strong man and could handle it.

So she hadn't seen him or spoken to him yet on this day. She had, however, left a text message that she would join him after the show.

She gave the driver "Forty-Fifth and Broadway" as a destination. He didn't ask why she was heading for Broadway after showtime rather than before, but cabbies didn't ask such questions, nor did they usually care.

A few moments later, the taxi dropped her off. She enjoyed the brief walk to the stage door of the theater, where a crowd was already gathering. She waved to one of the guards. He recognized her. She had a standing backstage pass, a "friends-and-family-thing" that always allowed her access.

Moments after that, she was with Eric. As soon as he saw her, he knew something was wrong. He could read the expression on her face that well and that quickly. She told him about the day, all of what had happened. He said nothing, but she could read the shared sadness and empathy in his eyes. Eric took her supportively and firmly into his arms and held her in a long embrace. It was the first time she had almost felt good in hours.

"Yes, Señorita Valdez," she said, remembering what María had said. "God has now blessed me, too. One door closes and another opens. You just have to look for it."

Now, on this the day of Andy's funeral, standing in a black cashmere overcoat, her gloved hand in Eric's, Alex was conscious of her gaze as it involuntarily drifted back to the pine casket. The wind off Long Island Sound increased. Alex could barely hear. The ferocity of the wind made the occasion even colder and even more unpleasant. There was a very brief snow flurry. The sun hid behind the gray clouds for a moment. It was as if, from somewhere, God was suggesting that henceforth the world would be a little diminished. Alex moved in closer to the man she loved until his hand left hers and wrapped around her in comfort.

A few minutes later, the wind subsided and the sun returned. Simultaneously, the pine coffin was on its final journey. De Salvo's remains were lowered into a small dirt chamber. The service was over, the congregation of mourners began to exchange good wishes and comfort, and then they dispersed. There was a reception planned, but Eric had a matinee and she was more comfortable going with her future husband than elsewhere. She did seek out Helen De Salvo, however, who looked shattered. Alex said all the appropriate things and Eric joined in. For the first time, Alex met the rest of De Salvo's family, another son and a daughter, who had moved away, plus a grandchild.

Alex introduced Eric as her fiancé and watched the stunned expression in some eyes when they realized that "my fiancé, Eric" was the Broadway star of the same first name.

Then Alex and Eric made their way toward Maurice, Eric's driver, who waited with the limousine. In the parking lot, a small group of fans—mostly women, but with an occasional male—spotted Eric, who had spotted them first.

"They're everywhere," he said quietly to Alex. "Keep moving quickly."

They yelled to him and approached, seeking a close-up look and maybe autographs. Eric normally would have obliged. This time he shook his head.

"No. Sorry," he called back. "Any day except today."

"Why not?"

"This was a funeral," he said. "Inappropriate. I'm sorry."

His fans, moments ago so expectant, looked at him with disappointment. There were about a dozen of them. They had waited for him, it appeared, even in this dismal cold weather. They surrounded him as he held Alex under an arm and they kept moving. Alex wondered how so many could have assembled so quickly, but she had seen such manifestations before. It only took one fan with a Tweet or a Facebook post to bring out a small mob.

Maurice, always alert to trouble, started quickly toward them. Maurice intercepted the small crowd about twenty feet from the car. Eric did a quick scan. Nine or ten women, two men.

They handed Eric *Playbills*, movie posters, and pictures and magazine covers. He reversed himself and began patiently to sign them.

"I'm okay, Maurice," he said. "Start the car. Go ahead, get in," he said to Alex."

"You sure you're okay?" Alex asked.

"I'm fine. Go on ahead. We'll be out of here in one minute."

Appeased, the crowd slowly thinned. The satisfied autograph seekers reverentially stepped back, each after having been satisfied. Alex slid into the backseat of the car and watched from a few feet away. Suddenly, an uneasy feeling overtook her.

She felt a presence. Something strange. Something not quite right. Professional paranoia kicking in again? she wondered. Or something else? Instinct: her hand went to her pistol and settled there. She watched.

"Eric Robertson?" a male voice asked. The voice rasped slightly. There was a belligerent undertone. "*The* Eric Robertson?"

Eric's eyes rose and he was startled. Amid all the teenagers and easily satisfied females was a middle-aged man. At first he looked as if he were aging and homeless. Eric was taken aback. He could tell instantly: this was not an autograph seeker or a fan. He felt as if he were about to be accosted. But why?

"You think you're a big shot, huh?" the man said. "Hollywood hot shot. Big deal."

"Have a nice day," Eric said, moving toward the car.

"Don't blow me off! I want to talk!" The other fans stood helplessly and gawked. The man cursed profanely and violently at Eric.

Alex didn't like this. She drew her weapon, just in case. She kept the Glock low and out of sight. She looked at the man's hands. Empty so far. Maurice was suddenly on high alert. He gunned the car's engine. But he opened his door and was poised to jump out.

Eric moved away from him toward the car. The man gave Alex the creeps. He wore a rumpled brown coat and looked like he lived in it. Eric kept moving. With a better view, Alex now thought the man looked like a homeless nut. The man then reached to grab Eric, while reaching into his pocket.

"Eric, look out!" Alex called.

Maurice was out of the driver's seat. The man swung a fist at Eric, who blocked the blow and shoved the man backward. Maurice came out, hit him hard with a shoulder, and knocked him over. Eric ducked into the backseat of the limousine. Maurice returned swiftly to the car. He made sure Eric was in safely and closed the door. Just as quickly, Maurice ducked into the front seat and closed his own door.

But the assailant staggered up onto his feet again. Alex could hear him cursing profanely and, looking past Eric, saw the man draw something, a dark object, from his pocket. He rushed toward the car but Maurice hit the accelerator hard in reverse to turn the car to leave.

The man held the object, continued to charge the car, and when he couldn't reach the car, hurled the object. It smashed with tremendous impact against the window on Eric's side. Alex saw Eric recoil and heard herself scream. The window held. The impact left a dark liquid and shards of brownish-green glass. After the fact, the object looked as if it had been a pint bottle of whiskey.

Maurice glanced into the rearview as if looking for instructions.

"Just go, Maurice," Eric said calmly. "We're good."

"Good?" Alex gasped after a moment. She replaced her Glock in its holster. "What was *that* all about?"

"Some nutcase. Happens all the time," Eric said.

Eric flexed his hands and fingers and shook his head.

"You hurt?" she asked.

"I'm fine."

"Contact?"

"He got a little piece of me. No big deal."

"What a world when your fans just about maim you," Alex said.

"He wasn't a fan." Eric shrugged. "You take the bad with the good. It's a big rotten beautiful complicated world."

Alex leaned back into the leather seat. She gathered herself. Too much of an echo from Kiev, she realized. Sometimes she wished she could stop the world and get off and go to a safer place, not that she knew of one.

Eric allowed himself the thinnest of smiles. "I guess we're

going to need a car wash," Eric said, looking out his window. Alex leaned against him in the back of the limousine. His hand, now warming, came to rest on her knee.

Their vehicle hit the Saw Mill River Parkway a few minutes later. Eric glanced at his watch. He was due at the theater in forty-five minutes.

"How are we doing on time?" Alex asked.

"We're fine," he said. "We're just fine."

He hugged her. She appreciated his optimism, but wasn't so sure she agreed.

FORTY-SEVEN

In the days that followed, there was some brief discussion between Alex and Eric over whether to have the wedding ceremony in California or New York. Eric had many friends in the movie colony. Alex still had friends from where she had grown up in Southern California and attended college and post-graduate at UCLA. But in the end, they decided on getting married in the East. Easier for everyone.

Eric had a close friend named Steven Gold, a director of movies with two Oscars to his credit, who had a three-acre estate in Montauk, at the plush far end of Long Island. Eric had been in one of his films and they had remained friendly. Steven, whom Alex had met once backstage at the Gershwin Theatre, volunteered the use of his estate as a venue for the wedding. Eric asked Alex if that worked for her; she was thrilled, and just a tiny bit star-struck at the same time.

So the plans for the wedding proceeded. Notice was short, but that made it easier to keep press and paparazzi at bay. Alex arranged time off from FinCEN, while at the same time not knowing if she was going back to the job at all. In a way, all that was suddenly secondary. She and Eric created a bridal registry at some of the smart stores in New York, Alex bought a dress for the occasion, and Eric asked an old friend named Gary Price from his undergraduate days to officiate. Price, a free-spirited young man from a wealthy family, had gone into the Protestant clergy and was currently assigned to Saint Thomas on the East Side of Manhattan. So the wedding equation fell quickly and easily into place.

Eric's final curtains as Lieutenant Joe Cable arrived with packed houses and much fanfare. The producers announced his replacement, a handsome young star who had made his name as a tough guy in a cop series on one of the broadcast television networks. He now wanted to put his more sensitive side on display, demonstrate his fine tenor voice, and show that he could handle adoring Broadway audiences at the same time. It was a great fit. Tickets surged and the show remained on solid commercial footing, which made Eric feel better about leaving. Like most productions that he had worked on, the spectacle had been made better by his presence.

"To tell you the truth," Eric said to Alex one evening a few days before the wedding, "I'll miss being Lieutenant Cable eight times a week. To me that show represents what's best about America: strength, wisdom, decency, tolerance, victory over the forces of oppression, our exceptional nature, and our freedom. Know what I mean?"

"I know exactly," Alex said. "As corny as Kansas in August, high as Old Glory on the Fourth of July." She smiled. As usual, on the important things, they saw eye to eye.

"I've chosen the best life partner I could ever imagine," he said. "But I knew that already."

"We love the same things, in addition to each other."

The day of their wedding arrived. Even the weather cooperated. It was a jewel of a day on eastern Long Island, the sky bright blue and cloudless, the temperature mild, and the breezes balmy. Eric jokingly accused his producer pal Steven of having it scripted.

"Not a chance in the world," Gold answered. Gold always had a charming world-weary cynicism, even when he was in the best of moods, as he was on his friend's wedding day. "And even if I *had* hired someone to script it, the writer wouldn't have turned in the assignment on time. You know what those guys are like. They're worse than the actors."

There was a beachfront at Steven Gold's estate, and he was happy to host the ceremony. Reverend Gary from Saint Thomas on Fifth Avenue performed the ceremony. There were about a hundred and fifty guests in attendance, about a third of them from the American film and Broadway theater community. But there were many friends and family as well, two of Alex's aunts from California, some peers from FinCEN, plus the shadowy Sam Deal who wouldn't have missed an occasion like this for the world, even without the free food and drink. Then there was Alex's old friend Ben from Washington, who turned up with his own latest squeeze, an elfin third-year NYU law student named Trudy. Among the last to arrive were Don Thomas, Alex's old friend from D.C., and Laura Chapman, Alex's peer from Washington along with her longtime partner, Rick McCarron, who was also Alex's most trusted CIA contact. Alex felt blessed to be surrounded by so many of these people she loved.

By a few minutes before noon, almost all the expected guests had arrived at Gold's estate. Alex kept an eye open for Gian Antonio Rizzo, who had promised he would try to be there. Alex had one bit of unresolved business to discuss with Rizzo, so she was anxious to see him. She also had a hunch he might be a no-show. As of two minutes before noon, there was still no Rizzo. Alex sighed. But the show was set to go on.

The guests who were there crowded the chairs and mani-cured back lawn of the estate. Two temporary bars were open and busy. A handful of children, the boys in white shirts and dark shorts or slacks, the little girls in summer dresses, scurried about and tried not to get stepped on. Beyond the lawn, down at the beachfront, there was a pier. A modest cabin cruiser, mod-est for this stretch of Gatsby-esque Long Island, was moored beyond the site. A six-piece band played on a back patio. Tables were prepared for a vast buffet of food after the ceremony. By this time, many of the guests were playfully referring to their host as "the Great Goldsby."

Yet even as the hour approached, Alex considered the day with disbelief. Who ever could have believed what path had been in store for her when she left Wells Fargo a few years earlier and came to work in Washington? The cases, the endless nights of work, the cold, bitter tragedy on the streets of Kiev, her near suicide, a move to New York, an assassin firing through her win-dow in a high-rise, and another one narrowly missing her on a Manhattan street.

Then purely by kismet, or fate, or faith, or the beneficent hand of God, all of these horrible things that had so bedeviled Alex for the last few years, all of these crazy events and cir-cumstances, had led her to a cooperative apartment on West Twentieth Street, one floor below the man with whom she would fall in love.

Who knew? Who ever could have known what God had in

NOEL HYND ★ 356

store for her? In the darkest hours of the past few years, who could have seen a path that led here? From somewhere within her bubbled up a verse from Corinthians that she had learned as a young girl, one she had always liked. "We walk by faith, not by sight." Many times over the last few years, Alex had felt as if she were walking with her eyes closed. Now, of course, still in tune with her faith, the more comfortable this walk had become, and the more confident she was of her destination. Ultimately, that was what her faith was all about—the "the assurance of things hoped for," promised in Hebrews.

At noon, her fiancé came by and took her hand. "Ceremony's going to start," he said. "Not going to flee now, are you?" he asked with a wink.

"Not a chance. And by the way, you're not supposed to see the bride before the wedding."

"Tough luck," he said. "We break rules all the time." He gave her a kiss on the forehead. "That's your last kiss as a single woman," Eric said. "Next one you get, you'll be a bride."

A few minutes later, surrounded by friends and family, Eric and Alex stood in a shaded area of the sandy beach contiguous to Steven Gold's estate. They held hands, flanked by their closest friends, Eric's parents watching in wonder. Alex bit her lip when sad thoughts crept into her head, visions of those whom she loved and who couldn't be there, her father, her mother, and then there was a final vision of Robert, her fiancé whom she had lost in Kiev, a handsome, good-natured, strong man who had always told her that if anything happened to him, he would never want her to be alone, so find a good man, be true to each other, and lead a good Christian life.

To all these people, she said silently to herself, I miss you.

And I still pray for your souls. Then she looked up and listened to Reverend Gary as he led them through a brief ceremony. Eric's brother was the best man and produced the box with the wedding ring.

"Don't drop it in the sand," Eric whispered to his brother, eliciting muffled laughter from those close enough to hear. Laura Chapman produced a ring for Alex to give to Eric and handed it to her.

Eric and Alex slid the rings loosely onto each other's finger. The minister moved the ceremony to conclusion and pronounced them man and wife.

"You may kiss the bride," the reverend said to Eric.

But he was one step ahead. He took Alex in his strong arms and kissed her. Then he lifted her off her feet and kissed her again as the onlookers broke into a round of applause.

The festivities continued as the party moved back up to Steven Gold's mansion after the service on the beach. Guests found their own buffet lunch and seated themselves with friends and peers, the FinCEN people intermingling with Alex's friends and relatives. Most of the show people kept together at first, but then the two groups also intermingled. A couple of Eric's friends were handsome leading men in their own right, and some of the people working in the so-called traditional jobs occasionally pestered them for autographs and photos, which were easily and politely forthcoming. Champagne flowed freely, even a celebratory glass here and there for those who normally didn't indulge.

The dancing continued. The cake, scheduled for two p.m. by the caterers, waited at a safe distance so the more rambunctious of the dancers wouldn't knock it over.

After lunch, but before the cake, Alex and Eric made their

rounds of the tables to meet and greet the guests. They were about three-quarters of the way finished when, out of the corner of her eye, Alex looked across the room and noticed a dapper man in a beautiful dark suit glide in and mingle among the guests closest to the door. She smiled. She would have the moment she wanted today, after all.

The final arrival was in his sixties and exuded charm, as always. She released Eric's hand. "Excuse me for a minute," she said to Eric and Eric's sister. But she also turned to Eric. "When I signal, come over and meet an old friend of mine," she said. "But I need to talk to him privately first, okay?" Eric took her hand again.

"Not without a kiss," he said. She laughed and kissed him on the cheek. "Okay," he said. "You have permission to talk to another man for five minutes. Go."

Playfully, she touched his arm as she left. But she turned more serious when she crossed the room and approached her old friend. The man saw her coming, smiled, and opened his arms to welcome her. He embraced her.

"Hello, Gian Antonio," she said.

"Alex, my dearest," he said. "As beautiful as you always are, you've never been so beautiful as on your wedding day. He switched into Italian. "*Le mie congratulazioni.*" My congratulations.

"*Grazie!*" she said. Thank you. She remained in Italian and so did Rizzo. "I'm glad you could be here."

"I wouldn't have missed it," he said. "I'm enjoying retirement, as you know. Travel with my Mimi. I help her get set up in her businesses, and see the world with my tired old eyes."

Alex laughed. "You're incorrigible," she said. "In more ways than I can count."

"Oh!" he said. "I come bearing gifts, wise man that I am." He searched his pockets, almost making a show of his mock forgetfulness. "Word reaches me through the grapevine that you will be visiting Europe for your honeymoon."

"Paris," she said. "Ten glorious days."

"And you'll be staying where?"

"The Hotel Meurice. Expensive for my tastes, but Eric insisted. And he's paying. So call it a guilty pleasure. A guilty, *expensive* pleasure."

"Then you'd be a fool to decline the offer," he said. "And those are the best kind, the expensive ones. Not everyone in the world is so blessed as to be able to enjoy them. So we thank God for our blessings, don't we?"

"I try to every day."

"A dear friend of mine is a chef at Foquet's in Paris," he said after a pause, and still fishing through his pockets. "A sumptuous meal awaits you there. It's on me, my gift to you, *mia carissima*. Private room, wine from his private cellar. You will love it. Look here."

He produced from his pocket an envelope. She opened it. It was a handwritten note from the chef himself, in French. Alex was to make a reservation at least a day in advance—normal time was four months—and present the note on arrival.

"Now I have something else for you, too," Rizzo said. "Something you must have misplaced along the way. Somehow it was in my possession."

From the breast pocket within his jacket, he withdrew a sleek silver pen. Alex recognized it immediately. It was hers, lost some time ago.

"Where did *that* come from?" she asked.

Rizzo shrugged. "My apologies. Somehow it drifted among my possessions."

She took it back. "I guess it's been all over the world," she said. He gave her a quizzical look. "Thank you."

"My pleasure."

An awkward moment. Then, "Well," he said. "A traveling man gets thirsty. I should find a drink."

"The drink can wait for a moment, Gian Antonio. I want you to meet my husband."

"I would be honored."

"But first I also want you to be honest with me for a moment."

"Alex?" he asked, professing no knowledge where she was leading the conversation.

"Antonin Debray," she said.

"Who?"

"Come on, Gian Antonio," she said. "At least tell me why."

"Alejandra, I have no idea—"

"Gian Antonio, I'm in a similar line of work as you are, remember? I know a few tricks myself. The CIA gave me a name. Antonin Debray. French passport. I ran that against airport security videos. I'm not angry. I have half the story. Please give me enough of the rest and I'll never ask again."

His expression changed. His eyes took a harder cast.

"Consider it the third part of your wedding gift," he said. "I give you peace of mind so you can live happily with your husband and not look over your shoulder for the rest of your life."

"So you arranged the hit in Panama?"

A long pause, then, "Yes, I did."

"I recognized you in the airport security videos. You traveled as Debray and you set it all up."

"I did. And I will not apologize."

"I didn't ask you to apologize. I just asked you to explain it. We had a discussion in New York. I rejected the notion of having Yardena Dosi murdered."

"Yes, you did. But I didn't."

Alex was not comfortable with this, but now, in this place, hearing the full story start to emerge from her friend, she was not completely uncomfortable with it, either.

"As long as that Dosi woman was alive, she was going to come after you, Alex," Rizzo said. "I lost agents to her and her organization along the way, too, people of mine, good people. There was one who was killed in North Africa and another who was murdered in Mexico. You think you can sign an armistice with a person like that?"

"The agreement wasn't my idea. It came from higher up."

"Sure, but you were the soldier in the line of fire. She would have come after you or come after your husband, if not a week from now, a month from now, or a year. I could not have that. I worked an accord through Rome and Washington. They said if I could get her, do it. Take her out. Take the black queen off the chessboard so that the white queen might claim victory and live her life in peace. So yes, this was my gift to the world but in particular my gift to you. Her death. The person in the world who most hated you, wished you the most harm, was most likely to harm you or your husband, or God willing in the future, your good Christian children, is destroyed. May Señora Dosi's evil soul burn in the deepest depths of hell, and her husband with her. She was a vile, venal excuse for a human being, and he was not much better. The world is now a better place."

Hearing this from Rizzo was almost too much to take in

at one time. Alex stood there in her wedding dress before one of her dearest friends and listened in disbelief as he confirmed the details of how he had engineered the murder of Yardena Dosi.

For a moment, she didn't speak. Then finally, "I'm glad I don't have your conscience, Gian Antonio. You're a practicing Roman Catholic, aren't you?"

"I feel I did the right thing," he said, switching back to English. "Have you read Thomas Aquinas?"

"Many times."

"Whether an act is good or evil depends on the end," Rizzo said. "That's what I believe. If I'm wrong . . ." He shrugged. "So my soul will burn in hell. Or maybe not. I think God will forgive me. I've made His world a better place." He paused again. "Your husband isn't the only man who loves you, Alex. I like to think my gift enables you and your husband to have a long and happy life together. If you feel I betrayed you in some way, forgive me. I deeply feel I acted in your best interests."

He paused. "In Italy, we had the real Antonin Debray under surveillance for years. A professional assassin living in Paris. When Señora Dosi's people contacted him, we speculated that it was you she wanted to kill. We were right. So we took matters into our own hands in Paris. I replaced him and traveled under his name to South America. The world is a better place for it."

Alex blew out a long breath. "Gian Antonio, I . . ."

Then her voice caught and she couldn't speak. For several seconds, one part of Alex broke into open revolt against the rest of her. She still held some anger against Gian Antonio, and yet she couldn't hold it anymore. He had put his life and soul on the line for her. She deeply hated the act of homicide, especially one that touched upon her. And yet she also knew he was right. The world was a cruel and unforgiving place, imperfect in every way. He had made it safer for her. He had created a more hospitable universe for her and Eric. And with the gangs being blamed for the payback in Panama, the Dosi regime was in ruins. Aside from some mopping up, Párajo was both concluded and a smashing success.

"Yes?" Rizzo asked.

Instead of speaking, she leaned into him and embraced him. She felt a sob in her throat and fought it back. "Where does it end?" she asked. "The killing, the corruptions. Every day becoming a sleazier version of the day before, dragging everyone down with it."

"It's an imperfect world," he said, comforting her. "We both know that. We do the best we can."

"God bless you, Gian Antonio," she said. "And thank you," she was surprised to hear herself say.

A moment later, Alex felt a tap on her shoulder. "Hey, hey," Eric said amiably. "Old friends are one thing, but the bride is mine. Today and every day to come."

Rizzo yielded and Alex stepped away. She quickly brushed a tear from her eye. "Eric," she said. "This is my friend Gian Antonio Rizzo. From Rome. We've worked together."

"I've heard your name many times," Eric said, offering a hand, which Rizzo accepted. "It's a pleasure to meet you."

"Likewise."

"Will you be in New York long?" Eric asked. "I'd love to get to know you better."

"Those who know me well don't like me so much," Rizzo

said. "Unfortunately, no, I won't be staying. But I know you'll be in Paris, maybe over the summer. That's just an hour away from Rome by plane. I'll fly up and we can meet."

"I'd like that," Eric said, wrapping an arm around Alex's waist.

"I would, too," she said.

"Then it's a promise."

Another voice intruded. "Mrs. Robertson?"

Alex didn't acknowledge.

"Excuse me? Mrs. Robertson?"

"Honey," Eric said. "That's you he's talking to."

"Oh! I'm going to have to get used to that," she said.

"Please get used to it. I love hearing it," Eric said. He kissed her.

The owner of the voice was Henry, the photographer. "Perhaps," he said, "I could get a shot or two of you with your friend, from Rome, is it?"

"From Rome," Rizzo said.

"Do us the honor of being in a photo," Eric said to Rizzo.

Alex stepped into place between them. The two men extended arms around her shoulders and smiles swept across their faces. Henry stepped back slightly, focused easily, and snapped the camera three times, recording the moment forever and freezing it in time.

As Gold passed by, Eric reached for his arm.

"Steve, this was great. I owe you a favor big-time."

"You owe me a film, you no-good gypsy," he answered affectionately. "Ah, but what do you care about me? I'm chopped liver as far as you're concerned. You just married the most desirable woman in the world. I'll see you two after your honeymoon, if there's anything left of either of you."

Eric playfully whacked his friend's arm and they embraced. Alex gave Steve a hug.

"Thanks, Steven," she said.

"Don't mention it. Just take good care of him. I want him to look at some scripts later in the year."

FORTY-EIGHT

The transition of power at FinCEN would take several weeks by anyone's standards.

The Monday after Andrew De Salvo's funeral, a representative of the Department of Justice named Matthew Mayberry had arrived in New York and assumed the throne behind the desk in Andy's office. It took him less than two hours to phone Alex at home—she had asked for and received three weeks of paid leave—and ask her to come in and, perhaps, "talk."

She did. Mr. Mayberry was a pleasant enough soul, and while he had his ideas and ambitions, he was quick to admit that he had no idea whatsoever what was going on in the place.

He alluded to the fact that the attorney general had a candidate to replace Andy, but it would be done only on a temporary basis. He asked Alex point-blank if she wanted Andy's job. She told him point-blank and with all certainty that she didn't know. She would have to think about it.

"Fair enough," he answered. "You just got married, didn't you?"

"I did."

"I suppose I shouldn't say this," Mayberry said. "But I'm a fan of your husband's. I think he's great."

"I do, too. That's why I want to spend some time."

"Don't blame you," he said.

With the tension eased, Alex continued, "Look, Matt, here's the bottom line. You bring in your temporary guy from the Justice Department. I'll work with him over the next week, bring him up to speed on everything. Párajo was the biggest operation we had going and there are probably going to be some choices made on what's next. I'll be back in three weeks. I might be up for taking the job on a permanent basis and might not be. I don't know. I have to think. I'll let you know in thirty days, okay? Chances are I'm going to want to spend more time with my husband." She paused. "He has a film coming up in Europe. I'd like to be on the set for most of that time. Plus he wants me there."

"Once again, I don't blame you. I understand," he said.

"Is that half-wit Texas congressman still on my case?" she asked.

"Why are you bringing up that?"

"Because it's annoying, that's why. Are you in contact with his office?"

"I can be," Matthew said.

"Then *do* be, how's that?" she said. "Tell him that I know full well where his questions were coming from and that the Dosis had channeled campaign contributions to him through four of their shell companies. I know the voters of his district are dumb enough to keep electing him, but I've got enough to send to the Justice Department on him right now to earn him seven indictments. You tell him that, won't you? I have it on a GBS that I hide under my pillow every night right next to the handgun. If I hear so much as a whimper out of him again, I talk to the DOJ about convening a grand jury."

"I'll tell him. He'll be thrilled."

"Then that's it from my end."

"Busting his chops, huh?"

"Yup."

"Way to go. He's a jerk."

They both laughed.

"Oh. I have another message for you, however," Matthew continued. "Friendly, I think. And off the record certainly."

"I'm listening."

"You know a fellow named McCarron in the CIA. Friend of yours, right?"

"Oh, sure. He came to my wedding. That makes him a friend, although he was one previously."

"He tells me that a Mr. and Mrs. Davenport were murdered in Arizona a few weeks ago."

"So?"

"That doesn't mean anything to you?"

"No."

"It looked like a hit from a nation in the Caribbean. Retribution of some sort. They were living under the name of Davenport, but I think they were actually named Frederickson."

"Ah!" she said. "Got it."

"Should we be sad?"

"Not really." She paused. "God will judge them, I suspect."

"You've learned your lessons here, haven't you, Alex?"

"Thanks. Yes. I think so."

The following week, Alex and her husband sat in the first-class cabin of an American Airlines jet from New York as it made its descent into Charles De Gaulle International Airport in Paris. Her hand was in Eric's and she hoped it would remain there for years to come. She hoped they would be able to live the healthy, respectful lives they both wanted, channeling out the cheapening distractions of daily life. Together, she hoped, they could lift up their eyes to the hills, grow old together, and become richer, not in the fiduciary way, but in a spiritual and loving way.

She knew she would try. She knew he would, too.

She also knew that even after all she had gone through, she had found her way through the storm and into a clearing, into a noble path in life. It had been there all along. She had only needed to look far enough and in the right places to find it.

The Russian Trilogy

Conspiracy in Kiev

Noel Hynd

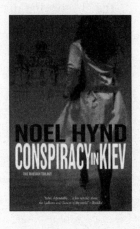

A shrewd investigator and an expert marksman, Special Agent Alexandra LaDuca can handle any case the FBI gives her. Or can she?

While on loan from the Treasury Department, Alex is tapped to accompany a Secret Service team during a presidential visit to Ukraine. Her assignment: to keep personal watch over Yuri Federov, the most charming and most notorious gangster in the region.

But there are more parts to this dangerous mission than anyone suspects, and connecting the dots takes Alex across three continents and through some life-altering discoveries about herself, her work, her faith, and her future.

Conspiracy in Kiev — from the first double cross to the stunning final pages — is the kind of solid, fast-paced espionage thriller only Noel Hynd can write. For those who have never read Noel Hynd, this first book in The Russian Trilogy is the perfect place to start.

Available in stores and online!

Midnight in Madrid

Noel Hynd

When a mysterious relic is stolen from a Madrid museum, people are dying to discover its secrets. Literally.

U.S. Treasury agent Alexandra LaDuca returns from *Conspiracy in Kiev* to track down the stolen artwork, a small carving called *The Pietà of Malta*. It seems a simple assignment, but nothing about this job is simple, as the mysteries and legends surrounding the relic become increasingly complex with claims of supernatural power.

As aggressive, relentless, and stubborn as ever, Alex crisscrosses Europe through a web of intrigue, danger, and betrayal, joined by a polished, mysterious new partner. With echoes of classic detective and suspense fiction from *The Maltese Falcon* to *The Da Vinci Code*, *Midnight in Madrid* takes the reader on a nonstop spellbinding chase through a modern world of terrorists, art thieves, and cold-blooded killers.

Countdown in Cairo

Noel Hynd

Why won't the dead stay dead?

Federal agent Alexandra LaDuca travels to Egypt to investigate the sighting of a former mentor, a CIA agent everyone thought was dead. She is thrown into the deadliest game of double cross of her career as the events that began in Kiev and continued in Madrid find their culmination in the volatile Middle East.

Her assignment is to locate a man she once knew. But to find the answers, Alex needs to move quickly into the underworld of the Egyptian capital, a nether society of crooks, killers, spies, and Islamic fundamentalists. And she must work alone, surviving by her wits, her training, and a compact new Beretta.

If you've been waiting for Alex LaDuca's next adventure, this fast-paced thriller is it. If you've never met Alex, *Countdown in Cairo* offers a first-rate introduction. You will be holding your breath from its explosive beginning to the very last twist.

Available in stores and online!

The Cuban Trilogy

Hostage in Havana

Noel Hynd

From bestselling author Noel Hynd comes this new series, The Cuban Trilogy, bursting with intrigue and set against the backdrop of Havana, an explosive capital city of faded charm, locked in the past and torn by political intrigue.

U.S. Treasury Agent Alexandra LaDuca leaves her Manhattan home on an illegal mission to Cuba that could cost her everything. At stake? Her life . . . and the solution to a decades-old mystery, the recovery of a large amount of cash, and the return of an expatriate American fugitive to the United States.

After slipping into the country on a small boat, Alex makes her way to Havana. Accompanying her is the attractive but dangerous Paul Guarneri, a Cuban-born exile who lives in the gray areas of the law. Together, they plunge into intrigue and danger in a climate of political repression and organized crime. Without the support of the United States, Alex must navigate Cuban police, saboteurs, pro-Castro security forces, and a formidable network of those loyal to the American underworld.

Bullets fly as allies become traitors and enemies become unexpected friends. Alex, recovering from the tragic loss of her fiancé a year before, reexamines faith and new love while taking readers on a fast-paced adventure. If you enjoy thrillers such as those by John le Carré, David Baldacci, and Joel Rosenberg, you'll love this series.

Available in stores and online!

The Russian
Three Complete Novels

Noel Hynd, Bestselling Author
of Cemetery of Angels

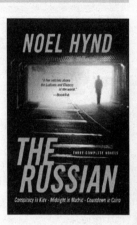

A thrilling compilation of three complete novels in bestselling author Noel Hynd's Russian Trilogy.

Conspiracy in Kiev

Working with the U.S. Treasury, federal agent Alexandra LaDuca travels to Ukraine to track a Russian-Ukrainian mobster named Yuri Federov during a visit by the American president. Personally and professionally, Alex's life will be changed forever by the explosive events that transpire in the Ukrainian capital.

Midnight in Marid

U.S. Treasury agent Alexandra LaDuca returns from *Conspiracy in Kiev* to track down stolen artwork, a small carving called *The Pietà of Malta*. It seems to be a simple assignment, but nothing about this job is simple, as the mysteries and legends surrounding the relic become increasingly complex with claims of supernatural power.

Countdown in Cairo

Alexandra LaDuca is smart, tough, and cool under fire. But when she travels to Cairo to investigate a former mentor who was believed to be dead, Alex is caught in a bizarre game of double cross, and her life is more perilously on the line than ever.

You'll be holding your breath from the explosive beginning to the very last twist!

Available in stores and online!

ACKNOWLEDGMENTS

Having visited Honduras and Central America several times in the last decade, the author is grateful for background, conversation, and research from many sources, most of whom would be better off remaining nameless here. I appreciate also being able to draw on various journalistic accounts of drug trafficking, military operations, and money laundering in the Caribbean, Honduras, and Panama. Here I credit many articles in the *New York Times* and the *Washington Post*. I have drawn on several reported accounts as background and basis for the pure fiction contained in this novel.

Similarly, I thank the United States Department of Justice, the *Columbia Encyclopedia*, the *Encyclopedia Britannica*, and even the often-maligned Wikipedia for many of the facts contained herein. I should note also that my Financial Crimes Enforcement Unit is a fictional take on the real agency of a similar name, much in the same way that Kojak was a take on a real New York Police Department.

I confess to being lousy at weapons and have probably made more mistakes in print on that subject than any other. Thus, many thanks to my new friend Bruce McCarroll of Nevada who has helped me along and guided me. Careful readers will note that I've kept to similar phraseology, sniping logistics, and weaponry to keep from getting into trouble again and, well, shooting myself in the foot in print.

As usual, I'm grateful to my good friend Thomas Ochiltree for his endless insights on international politics and diplomacy. At Zondervan, Sue Brower's patience has been saintly and I also thank Andy Meisenheimer and Bob Hudson for their many efforts on the six books in these two trilogies. (If you're wondering, Alex LaDuca will return.) Thanks also to Jodi Hughes at Thomas Nelson for politely cracking the production whip to get this book finished. And always, I'm ever grateful to my wife Patricia for her help, advice, and support in more ways than I can ever calculate.

The author welcomes comments and correspondence from readers either through the Zondervan website or at NH1212f@ yahoo.com.